Out of Palestine

Out *of* Palestine

THE MAKING OF MODERN ISRAEL

Hadara Lazar

ATLAS & CO. *New York*

Copyright © 2011 by Hadara Lazar
English translation © Hadara Lazar

Published by arrangement with the Institute for the Translation
of Hebrew Literature and translated by Marsha Pomerantz
Images in the photo insert appear courtesy of the author.

Interior design and typesetting by Sara E. Stemen

All rights reserved. No portion of this publication may be reproduced or transmitted in any form or by any means, electronic or mechanical, including photocopy, recording, scanning, or any information or storage retrieval system, without permission in writing from the publisher, except in the case of brief quotations embodied in critical articles and reviews.

Atlas & Co. *Publishers*
15 West 26th Street, 2nd floor
New York, NY 10010
www.atlasandco.com

Distributed to the trade by W. W. Norton & Company

Printed in the United States

Atlas & Company books may be purchased for educational, business, or sales promotional use. For information, please write to info@atlasandco.com.

Library of Congress Cataloging-in-Publication Data is available upon request.

ISBN: 978-1-935633-28-0
Ebook ISBN: 978-1-935633-39-6

15 14 13 12 11   1 2 3 4 5 6

For my parents

Contents

Introduction 1

CHAPTER ONE "You are half a Palestinian" 9

CHAPTER TWO "That gorgeous man who was Haj Amin" 33

CHAPTER THREE "I'll have some fun with the parrot" 47

CHAPTER FOUR "Everyone does his best to be a gentleman" 65

CHAPTER FIVE "I suppose you met him in Jerusalem" 79

CHAPTER SIX "We were never airborne in Palestine" 97

CHAPTER SEVEN "The nuisance value" 117

CHAPTER EIGHT "There are two Englands" 137

CHAPTER NINE	"A twenty-inch stick, a knife, and empty hands"	157
CHAPTER TEN	"A sporting chance"	183
CHAPTER ELEVEN	"We lived very slowly"	207
CHAPTER TWELVE	"We simply vanished"	230

Epilogue   261

Participants   269

Chronology   279

Acknowledgments   289

Introduction

Every year on November 11 at eleven o'clock, a memorial service for soldiers of the British Army who fell in the two world wars is held, and all over England small paper poppies to put in one's lapel are sold. Close to that date and at approximately the same hour, identical rites are held in British military cemeteries all over the world, from France to Burma. A few years ago, I drove on November 11 to the British military cemetery in Ramleh, an old Arab town, now a mainly Jewish town, not far from Tel Aviv.

At the entrance, people sat on plastic chairs with parasols open against the heat and the sun. In front of them there was a spread of green grass with row upon row of tombstones. The military reverend of the Royal Air Force stood facing the crowd, saying a prayer, and behind him was a large stone structure that looked like an altar, covered with a huge Union Jack, its blue and red vivid in the bright light. Everything was according to protocol.

The prayers went on. Short speeches were delivered. The honor guard presented arms. One by one, the representatives of the countries whose soldiers were buried here were called to put wreathes on the altar. The list was long. Some of them were not even states at that time or were called by other names. But most of them were representatives of countries like Australia or India, which sent soldiers to serve in the armies of the British Empire. These soldiers arrived here at the end of the First World War when they conquered the country and eventually brought about the rule of the British Mandate on Palestine, and they came again as part of the British Army during the Second World War, toward the end of the Mandate. The altar was being covered by wreaths, when suddenly the call of a muezzin was heard.

Beyond the eucalyptus trees, among the industrial buildings, rose the minaret from which came the voice calling all believers to prayer; it carried slowly in the hot heavy air. It was alien to the cemetery, where everything had stood still since May 1948. But even in this place, a place out of time, one couldn't disregard what was happening all around: the terror attacks, the Israel Defense Forces actions in the occupied territories, the two Arab intifadas, and all the wars that had been started since the British departure. And I thought that many of the people I had talked with while writing *Out of Palestine* would have refused to meet me today, and many of them have already died and are not here to see how the dream of peace has grown distant—a dream that was never as optimistic as the dreams at the beginning of the Mandate but, all the same, was intended to change the world.

For the time of the Mandate opened with a feeling of a major change in the old order and of a new beginning. General Allenby, who entered the Old City of Jerusalem on foot, brought with him great promises both to Jews and to Arabs, to Pan-Arabism and to Zionism. Suddenly everything was possible or seemed possible to the inhabitants of the country. For thirty years, life here changed its historical pace. The Mandate rule provided safe borders, a safety net, and great hopes. The immense expectations brought about by the Mandate transformed the lives both of people who had lived there for generations and of those newly arrived. All were offered a new mode of existence.

To the indigenous Arabs it was clear that this was a preparatory period for full self-rule. For the Jews as well it was a time of preparation for their "national home," according to the Balfour Declaration, given on November 2, 1917—for this was the original role of the Mandate. The British found themselves carriers of a dream. In spite of all political considerations and imperial logic, Palestine never became just another one of the colonies conquered at the end of the Ottoman Empire.

It was because of the Jewish national home and the Arab autonomy that a special rule was established in Palestine, a rule suitable for an interim period, in which the British were due to prepare the inhabitants for independence. The communities enjoyed a wide autonomy, but were not expected to make political decisions and therefore were not officially responsible for the political reality they had created: the Arab Revolt and the massive acquisition of land by the Jews. The Mandate authority was responsible for all this, and its subjects were able to continue to act without paying the price for their actions. Jews and Arabs were able to go on living side by side because the authorities prevented any real confrontations and postponed difficult decisions. Out of their imperial experience the British tried to conserve the status quo, the historical continuity, while at the same time creating enormous changes in industry, in road building, in communication, in education. These changes were accompanied not only by a massive Jewish immigration but by a large Arab immigration from village into town and from nearby countries into Palestine. The

Mandate authorities tried to control these changes, to see to it that they not turn destructive.

It was a period of great expectations. The Mandate rule created a well-made framework that could be compared to the well-wrought frame of an old picture. But the picture itself was not old. It was dynamic, modern, full of contradictions. The Mandate tried to preserve a coexistence of two alien communities, living apart and disregarding each other. Between them existed animosity and fear.

Within the framework created by the Mandate, Jews and Arabs lived according to their own rhythms. The Arabs made slow, very slow preparations for self-rule: they, of course, were the natives, the land was theirs, and the British were only there to help them, preparing them to take control. Circumstances, mainly the activities of the Jews, pushed them to respond, but all this took place in a traditional, stable world, retaining the old order and absorbing the frequent changes without really adapting to them.

But the Jews were in a hurry, as revolutionaries usually are. For it was a revolution of a special kind of immigrants: the usual difficulties—the uprooting, the alienation—were supplanted by a feeling of freedom from exile and from everything that had been left behind. Their was a burgeoning sense of identity with their own land, protected by British rule. The Mandate allowed them to create a society, but not a state. In spite of all difficulties and disasters they managed it, so to speak, as if in a swimming pool and not on the open seas. It was a messianic time as well. "I say: the Messiah has not yet come and I don't wait for him," answered Ben Gurion in 1949 to those who claimed that the Messiah had come with the founding of Israel: "The Messiah is needed in order never to come, for the Days of the Messiah are more important than the Messiah himself."

The Jews and the Arabs had great dreams, but the carriers of those dreams, the British, woke up first. As the years passed and the reality became more difficult to ignore and the solution seemed further away, the British abandoned their special role as the carriers of the dreams and reverted to being rulers in the old empire's tradition. Though enlightened as much as possible, impartial as much as possible, instigating checks and balances—harsh sometimes with the Arabs and sometimes with the Jews—so as not to upset the delicate balance, the fragile peace was threatened all the time. They did not promise anything anymore but just maintained a status quo, while both Jews and Arabs wanted only to disrupt it.

Up to the last moment the British acted as if guided by a certain principle: when there is no future they should preserve the present, until the moment when they themselves would disappear and the great change would come, and within the void and the anarchy left behind them everything would break up: the coexistence, the status quo; and only one dream of a single homogenous existence—the Jewish one—would materialize. But over the years it became clear that there could be no realization of one dream only.

It was a fragile coexistence in a land claimed by two peoples, and yet it seemed that a military solution was not necessarily the only one. There were still means to prevent all-consuming violence, to tame the local madness. I wanted to deal with that period in my own way. This is a book about Jews, Englishmen, and Arabs who lived in a historic time and neither wanted to nor could escape its significance.

This is not a history book. I have met with about a hundred people—Jews, Arabs, and English—who lived or spent time in Palestine during the Forties, and talked with them about this period. The essence of this book is what those people remembered after four decades about the last years of the British in Palestine.

I arrived at this quest by chance, when I discovered an old issue of *Time* magazine, including a report from Jerusalem on May 14, 1948. On the morning of that day the high commissioner, General Alan Cunningham, informally inspected a last guard of honor and immediately afterward left Government House on the Mount of Evil Counsel—according to Byzantine tradition, this is where High Priest Chaifas and his colleagues decided to arrest Jesus. Several hours after the high commissioner had sailed from Haifa harbor, a Jewish state was established.

A small plane flew the high commissioner to Haifa. The flight marked both an end and a beginning: a small plane carrying a British general, still high commissioner, over a land that he was about to abandon. And the time that preceded that flight, a time that has been central to the Israeli myth, became for me real yet undefined in a country whose past always infiltrates its present. I wanted to start my own search into that time.

I wished to know what people remembered about what had happened, to find some connections between their words and the myth of those days, and to describe how their memories changed with time. I wished to meet the English who got up and left; the Arabs who lived so close to me as a child yet were frightening; and I wanted to meet the Jews, too, whom I know firsthand, as a native eager to hear their memories.

I had no intention of dealing with the period in any methodical way. The chapters are built according to what interested me: some of them around a certain subject or a certain meeting, some of them about an earlier period or a later one—all dictated by the subject, the cast of characters, and the nature of the quest.

Almost everything in this book is a direct quote. I took the liberty of omitting but never adding to their words. What people remembered when they spoke to me was important. This is a work of testimony, then, a work of remembrance—not of history.

CHAPTER ONE

"You are half a Palestinian"

After the United Nations partition of Palestine and the subsequent outbreak of war between Arabs and Jews, the great Arab exodus began. Seven hundred and fifty thousand Palestinian Arabs left or were driven out. About four hundred Arab villages were totally depopulated; by mid-1949 most of them were either completely or partially in ruins and uninhabitable. The majority of refugees were settled in camps that exist to this day, on the West Bank, in the Gaza Strip, Jordan, Lebanon, and Syria. Some of the refugees dispersed to various Arab countries; a minority went to other countries around the world. Over the ensuing generations, a large diaspora has been created. Many have never seen the country from which they originated, and many still live in the shadow of 1948, which was, they thought, a temporary exodus, but which turned into an exile. Most of the people who appear in this chapter live in Europe.

Fuad Shehadeh was one of the first Arabs I met for this book. He is an advocate, from a Christian family that lived in Jerusalem during the Mandate years. He moved with his family to Ramallah in 1949, and it was in his office there, on the main street, that he received me—a gracious, lively man who had recently lost his eyesight. When I asked him about life in Jerusalem before the

British left in 1948, his conversation turned to memories of the last years of the Mandate. Before long, a change came over his face. He was no longer remembering, but describing wonderful times in a Jerusalem whose beauty was beyond compare:

"We could feel the culture that prevailed in Jerusalem. The evenings were such a joy. At the YMCA, the sports and the swimming, drinks at the King David, and our hard work as students." And he went on in a monotonous, heightened tone. The rhetorical flow bewailed what had been, transposing ordinary places and ordinary matters into the best of all possible worlds, and his lament surprised me. I haven't yet discovered how common it was among Palestinians who had left their homes during the 1948 war.

"You must see Naser al-Din al-Nashashibi, a writer, journalist, and intellectual," Shehadeh advised me when I told him I would like to meet other Arabs who had left the country in 1948 and never returned. Those who left their names behind on streets or neighborhoods or buildings—such as Dajani Hospital in Jaffa—and those whose names are mentioned in the history books, such as the Husseinis and the Halidis.

When I asked him where I might find Nashashibi, he told me that he lived in Geneva and had a house in London. "He's one of those who dash over to London for the weekend," he explained. He mentioned an address in Knightsbridge. But when I asked for the phone number, Shehadeh said he couldn't remember, that I should look it up in the directory. I could not find Nashashibi's phone number in the London directory. When I called information, I was told it was an unlisted number. The letter I wrote him went unanswered. It's difficult with Arabs, I was told after I'd failed to find the phone numbers of other Arabs whose names I'd been given in Israel. They're wary of you, they're wary of one another, and with good reason.

I learned, meanwhile, that Nashashibi had been the editor of the Egyptian paper *Al-Gomhuria* in the 1950s and '60s and, naturally enough, had served as Nasser's spokesman: "We will never agree to negotiations, to bargaining or an armistice," Nashashibi wrote in 1961, "nor to any declaration that if Israel gives in to the Arabs on the matter of borders or allows the refugees to return, we will begin negotiations with Israel and make peace. No. Never."

In 1962, in his book *Return Ticket*, he writes about Jews he saw from the walls of Jerusalem's Old City: "You bunch of rowdies, dregs of the world . . . dogs, thieves, go back where you came from." So when I finally was able to phone him in Geneva, I was surprised by his friendly tone. He said he would be happy to meet me during his next visit to London. I phoned on the appointed day; he asked me to come to a hotel in Knightsbridge, and to phone him from there, and he would come to fetch me from his flat.

It was early evening when I reached the luxurious hotel in Knightsbridge, and I wondered again why he had arranged to meet me in a hotel. Did he not want to give me an address that I already had in my hand? Was someone here in the lobby checking me out? There were many Arabs in the lobby, though it was already November, a time of year when Middle Easterners are not much seen in London. Nashashibi arrived a few moments later. A short man in his sixties. Light brown hair, light skin, something Turkish in his face. A brisk man with a broad smile on his lips and vigilance in his eyes who shook my hand thoroughly.

Two buildings away from the hotel we turned in at an apartment house. The address was not the one I'd been given. There were a series of security precautions at the entrance. The door of the flat was opened by a good-looking black woman, Nashashibi's secretary. Nashashibi led me into his study, seated me in a leather armchair, and went over to his traditional English desk, large and gleaming, sat down in a chair that was considerably higher than my armchair, took out pen and paper, and opened his investigation: the precise spelling of my name, my address and phone number in London, my address and phone number in Israel, the names of people I had met with. The questions were short and rapid-fire, leaving me no time to think. "Okay," he said at last, "ask," and looked at me with expressionless eyes. I, sitting primed on the low armchair, asked the first question that came into my head. Where had he studied?

"I graduated from Beirut University in 1943," he answered. "Political science and public administration. The university is where Arab leaders were educated; it is a minaret of education. I joined the university because I felt I must join the leadership that was endowed to my family. We—I say it with all modesty—are the Nashashibis of Palestine, we are leaders in our country, and we gave our country not only political leaders but also theologians and scholars and high government officials."

Thus he lectured about his family, in a low, pleasant voice, with a slight Arabic accent, until the phone rang. It was not a local call, and went on quite a while, in English, a few sentences in French. Meetings in Switzerland were arranged. Names of film stars were mentioned. Behind him on the wall was a portrait of himself as a young man, in the traditional dress of a Turkish notable. The conventions of the painting were Eastern. I wanted very much to look around. It was the first house of an Arab exile that I had been in, but I was afraid to turn my head toward the adjoining drawing room. I was still under the effect of his interrogation. Did he really need to know all those details about me? In the bookcase next to me were many books in Arabic: dispersed among them were photos of Nashashibi with Nasser, with Nixon, with American senators and well-known journalists.

"My grandfather was a deputy in the Turkish parliament," he continued. "My uncle was a deputy in the Turkish parliament, always representing Jerusalem. My uncle was the mayor of Jerusalem and the head of the National Defense Party, and I thought I would continue to carry the torch. I was called by Musa Alami [an eminent Palestinian advocate and stateman] to join the Arab Office."

He told me about a book on Musa Alami that he was about to publish, and I said, "You were known as a moderate in Jerusalem," but he wouldn't let me finish my question. "If you define moderation as he who understands the dimension of his problems, and the abilities and the potential of his rival or his enemy, or he who believes in discussion more than force and bloodshed." He was delivering a prepared speech, but he added: "We were in favor of the 'Yes, all right, take and ask for more. Accept what you have been offered, and the future will enable you to ask for more.'" His soft voice stressed the word *more*.

The phone rang again. Nashashibi spoke with an American-style heartiness, until he switched to Arabic, and then his tone became less forced. This conversation, too, was lengthy; he was completely involved in it. I turned around to survey the drawing room, which was dim and not spacious. One table lamp was lit in a distant corner, casting soft light on a sofa and on a low table.

A number of objects were displayed on the table, including silver and crystal tableware. Above the sofa hung a large oil painting in a heavy old frame, a small lamp fixed above it. With its dark, densely built walled city and the bare hills around it, it seemed to be Jerusalem. I did not get up to check. I felt I had to watch my step. When the phone conversation came to an end, I asked Nashashibi where in Jerusalem he had lived.

"In our quarter," he answered, with some surprise, as if I'd questioned the obvious. "It was always called the Nashashibi quarter. Mount Scopus, they call it now. On old maps of Jerusalem, you'll find the Nashashibi quarter, where all the Nashashibis live: Ragheb Bey, his brother, Fahmi, and his sisters and his daughters." As he went through a long list of Nashashibis who had inhabited the quarter, I had the feeling that for my sake he was situating himself in a timeless past. Did they speak that way among themselves that way, I wondered, or was it said only for my benefit?

I did not ask him why he had not stayed in the quarter after 1948, since that part of the city remained in Arab hands. Instead I asked him whether they had seen Jews socially during the Mandate years, and he said of course. They would get together at the King David or at parties at the home of the high commissioner or the district commissioner, and after noting that "it was one city, one country, you see," he went on to tell of the famous Jewish doctors who came to their home: "People like the Zondecks, the gynecologist, the surgeon, the internist—the three were our good friends. They used to come to tea."

He pointed out that Jewish doctors treated them, and mentioned well-known personalities from the Arab world who would come to Hadassah Hospital to see these renowned specialists.

"I liked those doctors, I liked Agronsky; later he called himself Agron. I always read the *Palestine Post* and I still read the *Jerusalem Post*. The Hebrew University was one of the first in the Middle East, famous. The Jewish artists, the doctors, the theologians, attracted us. We found in them a sense of love and a sense of peace." I was waiting for him to say, and he did, "All this has changed completely."

I asked Nashashibi how the English had influenced the Arabs in those days. "Due to the Palestine problem," he began, "in the heart of every Arab was a black spot for the British." Here he mentioned the Balfour Declaration of 1917, which allowed the Jews to establish a national home in Palestine, and the conflicting British promises for Arab rule in the territory, and the alleged deceptions of the British—with whom they had been on such good terms, he admitted. They had entertained the British, and many young Arabs had done their best to speak English with the proper accent: "You should not be astonished that we were not very fond of the British in spite of what they gave to us. In spite of our admiration and their great effort, we never liked them."

He went on about the British, whom he said wanted no part of either the Jews or the Arabs, but rather a route to India and a crusade of their own which, like the others, had failed. Apparently Nashashibi was thinking about the fact that now, too, Jerusalem was not in the hands of the faithful, because after a slight pause he added: "I went to see the Sultan of Brunei. He is five thousand miles away from Jerusalem, and he told me, 'When the Arabs fail to get back Al-Aqsa, we will interfere.' Now I say this as advice to you: Better you understand the Arab Muslims, because the non-Arab Muslims are very difficult to understand."

As he spoke in the soft, mellow voice, his manner pleasant, some familiar phrases went through my head—the conventional wisdom of those who claim to "know the Arabs": their endurance; their patient waiting for the right moment—trite phrases that now took on new force. I felt my unease turn into something menacing. I have no explanation. Nashashibi was friendly enough from the other side of his desk. His articles in *Al-Gomhuria* and the book *Return Ticket* had been written many years before; still, the room with its books and its pictures and the man sitting there on his lofty chair closed in on me. The room seemed claustrophobic. I thanked him for the talk and said I would call to arrange another meeting, and he said: "What else did you want to ask?"

I asked him an innocuous question about the differences between Christian and Muslim Arabs. He launched into an explanation about how there were no real differences when the phone rang again. The conversation was now in English, a friendly tone. "That was one of yours," he said, "a friend of mine from Geneva." He mentioned a Jewish name, and then returned to the theme of the Muslims and the Christians, and their supposed unity. He named a few Christians, including Henry Cattan, now living in Paris, who was one of the leading lawyers of those days and a mufti man (Grand Mufti Haj Amin el-Husseini was the most prominent Palestinian leader, extremely militant and anti-British). I said I was going to call Cattan, and asked whether I could mention Nashashibi's name. Nashashibi got up, came over to the armchair, and looked at me with great amusement:

"My dear, let me not be an obstacle in your way. You don't mention a Nashashibi to a mufti man," he said. I apologized, a little bewildered. I simply couldn't believe that the old rivalry still prevailed forty years later. Since he seemed amused, I though it a good moment to take my leave. As he walked me to the door, I asked him whether he might put me in touch with other Palestinian Arabs living in London. Nashashibi said he would think about it; he didn't want to send me to someone who would refuse me. I asked whether he knew how I could find Auni Dajani, a scion of one of the oldest families in Jerusalem, who had also been an attorney in Jerusalem and was now living in London. He said he knew him, but unfortunately could not give me an address or phone number.

Someone else found Auni Dajani for me. He is a successful London businessman. His wife, Selma Dajani, is also a member by blood of that large family. Her father, Fuad Dajani, founded the Dajani Hospital in Jaffa. I twice visited their luxurious Knightsbridge home and found them friendly and hospitable, but cautious in what they said. Auni Dajani had practiced law in Jaffa and Jerusalem and taught at a law school in Jerusalem alongside Jewish lecturers. When I asked about Jewish friends, he replied: "I can't remember names now. You are taking me by surprise." He brought out photos of all the Dajanis who used to gather once a year at the original family home on Mount Zion. The more evasive he was about the Forties, the more expansive he became about the family's eight-hundred-year history. The Dajanis, patrons of Mount Zion, were called the "Daoudis," Auni Dajani explained. From one year to the next, the photos showed fewer fezzes and traditional effendis' outfits and more European suits. The last photo was taken about a year before 1948. It showed some hundred Dajanis, including old people and children, as though they had assembled for a final group portrait against the background of old stone arches.

"I hope to write a book about Jerusalem," Auni Dajani said, "When we went there a few years ago, we took the children with us. My daughter was born in Jerusalem but not my sons, and it was important for them to go. They consider themselves Palestinians." Here he asked whether I might inquire for him, through people in Israel, where the family's founder, Sheikh Bader, is buried. The hill where he was interred still bears his name, but Auni Dajani had not been able to find the grave when he was in Jerusalem. When I asked him whether there were other Palestinians in London that I should meet, he said he would think about it.

The more I tried to reach the elusive Arabs, the more engaged I became in my search. I tried different ways, some rather unorthodox, of seeking out Arabs. I reached Leila Mantoura, the daughter of Tawfiq Canaan, a well-known physician in Mandatory Jerusalem, after finding her gallery for Oriental objets d'art. The secretary of the gallery asked me a few questions, saying that Mantoura would contact me. I was afraid that was a way of evading me, but Mantoura did in fact call. After I explained the matter at hand, we arranged an appointment in the gallery, on Kensington Church Street, the street of antique dealers. When I arrived, a young, apparently Arab woman sent me up to the second floor, where I was greeted by a tall woman of about sixty, dressed in a loose sweater and trousers. Slender, with sharp features, light hair and eyes, an entirely non-Mediterranean appearance, she had clearly been beautiful once—indeed, still was.

She seated me in the dim recesses of the room and I asked her to tell me about her father, who had been a Protestant and ultra-nationalist, a literary man, and the first folklorist in the country.

"My father was the first Arab doctor," she began. "He graduated in 1904, I think, and so the Arabs didn't trust him very much. The first job my father ever had, you won't believe it, was in Shaare Zedek, the Orthodox hospital of the Jews. From the beginning of the century he established a deep relationship with the doctors and the patients there. Those friendships went on for a long time. I was the youngest of four children, but I remember Dr. Mandelbaum and I remember Dr. Ticho. My father worked in ultra-Orthodox Mea Shearim. We lived in Musrara, which was next to it. Now it is only a broken-down street."

Here she stopped. "But why are you coming to us?" she asked. "Go to the refugees who remained in the camps and not to those who managed to get out." She had immediately pigeonholed me—as if it were not I who had come to see her, but a representative of those who had caused the camps to be created. I told her I wanted to meet those who were far away from the country. I was wary of using the usual terms. Who knows how she saw herself— as a refugee, an exile? According to what I'd been told, she had gone the route twice—once when she left Jerusalem as refugee, and again when she left Beirut for London, again to start from scratch. Mantoura lit a cigarette and continued:

"To show you how involved my father was with the Jewish community, when he decided he had enough money to get married, he went to a Jewish lady called Miss Landau, who was a very famous lady, and said to her: 'Look, Miss Landau, you are a good friend. I want a wife,' and she said, 'Now let me see which good girls of your age and education are available.' And she made a short list of eight young girls in Jerusalem, some of them Europeans, some of them Arabs, and she invited them all with their parents to meet my father. But he had his eye on my mother. She was German, born in Jaffa.

"I was born in 1927," she went on. "There had already been massacres, there had already been misunderstandings, and the Jewish Agency [the 'shadow government' of the Jewish community] was working full blast. So my relationship with the Jews was on a completely personal level. My relationship was either with the younger generation of my father's old friends, or old friends of mine like the Schwartzes who lived on our street. I became friends with Ruth Schwartz-Dayan [the future wife of Moshe Dayan]. Friendship lasts, and when she was working for Maskit [an Israeli folklore store] we had endless arguments, and I would say to her, 'Okay, the falafel has become Israeli, the hummus has become Israeli, and now also the embroidery!' " I wanted to say that they had caught on because they were Arab. That that was their attraction—a tasty local food, a beautiful embroidery—but I decided against it because Mantoura was speaking steadily now, her voice rich, her face conveying such an intense feeling, and I had the impression that the slightest distraction would stop her:

"I grew up knowing there would be a problem, because that was being discussed all the time at home, but I had no hatred. I hated the British because they imprisoned my father and my mother and my aunt when war broke out. I personally wanted the Germans to win. It was not because of Palestine. The friendships we had with Jewish people did not end, however. I spoke German and understood quite a lot of Yiddish and loved music. I went quite often to Rehavia, which was called in the Thirties Neue Berlin; Rehavia was all German Jews, and you would not hear much Hebrew. They were discussing Schiller and Goethe and Beethoven and Mozart. It was a transformation of German Jews en masse, and I used to sit there and listen to them, sometimes with other Arab friends and sometimes with Jewish friends. We used to go and spend Passover with them, and at Christmas they used to come and spend the feast with us."

"Did the fact that German Jews were persecuted in Germany affect you?" "Members of my family in Germany were put in concentration camps and died there," she protested, "but we only learned about it in 1943.

"During my school years tension was already very high," continued Mantoura. "My father and mother asked me not to shop at the Jews'. We always used to get our clothes from German Jews in Jerusalem called the Kleins, and in the Forties we stopped going to the Kleins. You had to pay on the Jewish buses one mill [the lowest unit of currency] more for the Hagana and two mill more for something else, and that caused a lot of resentment.

"By that time I was already anti-Jewish in an apolitical and emotional sense. The Jews were already considering themselves better than the Arabs, very much like Israel now. We had to carry identity cards in the Forties, and we were stopped by British police and sometimes by Jews. I remember going to Zion Square because my old school was behind it, and I would visit, and I would be stopped. I don't know whether they were Hagana or the Irgun Zevai Leumi, but they wanted to check my identity, and my identity papers were obviously Arab. I didn't look like an Arab. They were insulting and they would act superior; that was already beginning in 1943 and 1944."

I didn't protest that the events she described must have taken place later. It was the way she wanted to tell it, or how she remembered things. But I thought about how she must have appeared at the time to boys who had stopped her. A tall, fair-skinned girl, well dressed, who had come to visit her old school.

"In 1946 I finished college in journalism and history," continued Mantoura. "My father didn't want me to work. I studied to increase my knowledge, to learn languages to become a diplomat's wife. At that time I went to the trials [of Jewish members of the extremely militant underground, caught during terrorist attacks against the British]. Two guys were being tried, and I got a special pass to go in.

"It was a military tribunal, and I was watching it, and afterward I became so sick that I didn't go back. I couldn't understand the two on trial. I could not understand their dedication and the obstinacy. That's when I really got scared." Was it this fanaticism alone that disturbed her, I wondered. Or perhaps in this strange and total devotion—two young guys getting up and singing the national anthem, "Hatikvah," when their death sentence was pronounced—she had had premonitions?

I asked whether she had ever returned to Jerusalem:

"My father had the best folklore collection in the country, and his library is in the Hebrew University. I went there in 1974 and saw the books—'Property of Dr. Tawfiq Canaan,' and underneath, 'The Hebrew University,' and this hurts very much. We lost property. I worked as a charwoman. This hurts much more than losing a house." Then she fell silent. A moment later she said she had to leave soon. I asked whether we might meet again. She said she didn't know, and lit another cigarette. I rose and thanked her for the meeting. When we went down to the gallery and I admired the beautiful things on display there—old copper bowls, Roman glass vases—and she thanked me politely, suddenly distant. Our moment had come to an end.

Afterward, at home, when I listened to Mantoura's words, something bothered me. Her words, straightforward and fluent, lacked something I couldn't define. There was an honesty in them, but the honesty was flawed. But it wasn't just in what she said. In my questions, too, was an excess of caution. I was at the beginning of my search. I was facing for the first time the enmity that persists to this day.

I decided to look up Henry Cattan, and easily found his number in Paris. When I called, an old man answered, in a voice full of suspicion, and perhaps fear, and asked me to write him in greater detail. "Tell him what you are planning to write," Mantoura had advised me. "Tell him that we've met. Write him the truth."

Then one day a faint voice, hoarse with age, called me, speaking careful English with a foreign accent. It was Cattan. He had come to London for a visit, and we arranged an appointment in Mayfair, at the flat of some relatives. When I arrived there at 11 a.m., the door was opened by a short, old-fashioned gentleman in his seventies, who greeted me very graciously and listened attentively to my long explanation of the nature of the book.

We sat on brocade sofas in a room that seemed temporary, a kind of residential hotel. I had the impression that he was looking at me with great curiosity. I was the first Israeli he had met, except by coincidence, since he had left the country. I was relieved when he began to recount the history of his family, one of the most ancient in Jerusalem:

"We still have a house in the Old City. I have the deed in which one of my ancestors, called Jerius Cattan, declared it to be Waqf [a sacred Muslim form of ownership of land] for his male children and descendants 450 years ago. We are original inhabitants in Palestine. The earliest Christian community." As proof of his claim he mentioned the Holy Fire ceremony held at the Church of the Holy Sepulchre before Easter, in which the most ancient families march with twelve banners. Members of his family are entitled to hold two of them.

He spoke willingly, weighing every word and every detail. He described Antimus Park, which today is the center of town: "There were private villas that belonged to the Orthodox Patriarchate. One villa, I remember, was occupied by Prince Emmanuel. There was the house of our neighbors, and they were Jews. I remember that on Friday evening they came to ask my father to put out the light. In spite of the fact that there was gloom over the country after the Balfour Declaration, during the Mandate there was coexistence between Arabs and Jews." He talked about court cases that had had to do with Jews. He mentioned the names of witnesses who had appeared in trials. In the middle of a long story about Jewish policemen who had committed perjury, he smiled: "Excuse me for telling you these stories, but I remember them."

He mentioned the names of the English who had frequented his home in spite of political differences, and I asked whether he was sorry that the English had left in such a hurry. "No, I was not," he answered, "except that the British left a mess. They left the country in a complete chaos. The whole country was not protected by them anymore, and instead of handing over respective areas to Arabs and Jews, they did not. This partly helped the exodus of Palestinian Arabs.

"When I came back from the United Nations—I appeared for the Palestinians in the 1947 sessions—I saw the mufti in Cairo," he explained. "I was representing the Arab Higher Committee, and he was the president. I told him, 'Haj Amin, the British are going to withdraw. They can't remain here after this decision.' I knew the situation in Palestine, that people could not survive in the chaos that would be created once the British withdrew. He told me, 'You are mistaken. The British will walk out by the door and come back by the window.' That's what he said." He glanced out the window. Sheer curtains were drawn, and a loud drilling noise was coming from the street. I asked whether he had said good-bye to his British friends before they left. He replied that he hadn't been in Jerusalem then. But he described at length how Iraqi soldiers had dug themselves in near his home and were fighting intensely with the Jews. One day, when an armored car opened fire on him and his children, he decided it was enough.

"I told my wife, 'The children have not been going to school for six months, the private teacher cannot come,' and it was best to move. We decided to take them to Beirut and come back. We left our house with our servants, with our animals, dogs and cats and everything." Here the quiet, somewhat detached voice, the careful English that had become fluent, stopped. He could not talk about it anymore.

Some time after that, Eleanor Cattan came into the room. She is French, and we talked a bit about Paris and about the Champs-Elysées, the area where they live, and about the fact that so much had changed there in recent years. Henry Cattan recalled that he'd run into a Jewish lawyer on the Champs-Elysées. He mentioned his name, the fact that he was a good lawyer, that they talked for a while. I sensed that face to face with me, something had suddenly surfaced from a very long absence, and it was hard for Cattan to recall those events of forty years ago.

Eleanor Cattan asked whether I had lived in Palestine. I answered that I was born in Haifa. And Henry Cattan said: "She was born in Haifa. She comes from there, and that's why I say—you are half a Palestinian," and he smiled at me with the graciousness of a host, in full charge of his emotions, not letting on that meeting me was a little like meeting the place he had not returned to and apparently would not return to—a place existing and vanished at the same time.

"Almost all Palestinians who left in 1948 still feel, in a very deep and personal way, the shock of the events of that year, when their world suddenly disappeared," said Albert Hourani, who had worked in the Arab Office in Jerusalem during the Forties; he was now a fellow at St Antony's College, Oxford. I had asked him, over afternoon tea at his London club, the Oxford and Cambridge, on Pall Mall, why it was so difficult for Arabs to talk to me. "However much they blame themselves or their leaders or the British," he explained, "they cannot help thinking that Israel has been built on the ruins of their society. So they cannot help thinking of you as an Israeli, who is going to write for an Israeli audience, in a language they probably do not know; all kinds of complicated questions come to their minds: 'What is it safe to tell her?' 'How is she going to write about us?' 'What use will those who read her book make of what we have told her?' and so on. In these circumstances, there cannot be really free and spontaneous conversation, at least not unless you are able to see those people many, many times and go beyond these doubts and questions."

I was prepared to give up further attempts to speak with Arabs in exile. But the matter of the right of the Arab refugees of the 1948 war to return to their homes in Palestine was perplexing, particularly because they never spoke about it outright. I went back to see Nashashibi with a list of questions regarding the right of return.

This time he allowed me to come straight to his home. Again we were in his study, and again I was on the low leather armchair, but this time it was daylight: through the window I could see tree-lined sidewalks of Sloane Street. I began by asking what it was like to write in Arabic while living in England. He talked about the richness of the language and about the Koran, which he read every day. From there he turned to religion, pointing out that in Europe he would not know the time of moonrise, when the daily fast during the Ramadan ends, that because of the long summer days in Europe, the fast is considerably prolonged.

"Is that a painting of Jerusalem?" I asked, pointing to the old picture hanging above the sofa. "Certainly," said Nashashibi. "Who painted it?" "I'll tell you in a moment," he said, going up to it. "It was painted by Lawson Wood in the middle of the nineteenth century. English. I have another one in Geneva. It is Dutch." As I came over to look at the painting, he went on: "I am a Jerusalem man. We had our cafés, we had the King David. I bought my books from a bookshop on Jaffa Road. Steimatzky—is it still there? But the part of Jerusalem that I liked is the old part. I don't mean the Old City, but Jerusalem as it was until 1948. When it was really Jerusalem, when we entered from the north, just before you come to Mount Scopus from Ramallah. You could see the towers, the Russian towers, the German towers, the Muslim towers, the Jewish Wall, Al-Aqsa Mosque, the high commissioner's house. We were happy there because we could see everything in one glance."

As I was looking at the Old City and the bare Judaean Hills, Nashashibi leaned over the table and handed me a pair of odd-looking wooden binoculars. "Do you know what this is?" he asked. Jews bought them when they came to visit the Holy Land in the nineteenth century, he explained. He slipped a plate into the stereoscope and handed it to me: a three-dimensional sepia picture of ancient Jerusalem. "I bought it in a store run by religious Jews," he explained with a broad smile. "That's what they took with them when they returned to the diaspora."

I asked whether he had other plates, and he replied that he had a whole collection and changed the picture. And as I observed the cities holy to the Jews, an old thought recurred with new force: that these plates have a power not existing in the places themselves. The sites themselves must stand the test of reality, but remembrance and longing have no such test to pass, and the passage of time makes no claims on them: they belong to the era of "One day it will be different"—and also of "It can't go on like this."

"I bought that picture six or seven years ago," he told me when I handed the stereoscope back to him. "I outbid Teddy Kollek [the famous mayor of Jerusalem]. I insisted on buying it. He made me pay much more for it." Smiling with pleasure, he peered at it and said: "If I find a painting of the King David Hotel, I'll hang it in the salon. I don't know whether a day passed in which I was away from the King David. If I didn't go to lunch I went in the evening.

When we went, especially during the war, you could see the elite of the ruling junta of the Middle East, both Arab and non-Arab. In the hall of the King David I saw the shah of Iran, General Catroux, de Gaulle, the queen of Egypt, the king of Egypt, the generals from Beirut, French and English, King Zog of Albania." He began a highly detailed description of New Year's Eve at the hotel, the event of the year, noting that the high commissioner would come, and the chief secretary and lots of Arabs in addition to the British. But rather few Jews. "Mr. Ben-Gurion didn't like dancing," he joked—and Mr. Ben-Gurion had been indeed occupied with other matters in some obscure office in Rehavia.

"It was my favorite place, the best hotel in the Middle East, it was paradise. It was very clean, very snobbish, and my headquarters. I had my hair cut there, my drinks there. I met my friends there, foreign friends, visitors too. I would go to the bar from time to time, but preferred to have my tomato juice at one o'clock in the lobby, and watch the people and have some olives next to it. If you wanted to telephone you would come there. In those days there was a first-class telephone service. 'Get me London,' and in two minutes they would get you London. There was a telephone operator called Mathilda. She was so active and energetic. I still remember Mathilda after forty years."

Just then his secretary came in, followed by a friend, a guest from Lebanon. After introducing me, he said, "Shall we continue?" I asked about the last months of the Mandate, and the answer was very long and filled with propaganda, apparently for the sake of the friend. Then, out of politeness, I asked another question, simpler, or so I thought. I asked whether he had said good-bye to the British before their departure, and he began, almost in a whisper:

"You want me to say good-bye to the people..." and he didn't finish the sentence, as if to make it even more obvious that he had meant "the people who betrayed us." "I was a lord in my country, I was a master of my country. I live in London, in Geneva, or wherever, but that doesn't mean I forget my country. Palestine is in my heart, and Jerusalem is in my heart. I taught my children to love their country, and it is up to them and up to their grandchildren." He rested a moment, perhaps a rhetorical pause: "I am sure you would not respect me if I told you that I had forgotten about Palestine. Go to Jerusalem to Teddy Kollek's place, you'll discover the building was erected during the time of Sir Arthur Wauchope and his Excellency the mayor of Jerusalem Ragheb Bey Nashashibi. You can see the plaque, it is still on the Barclays Bank building."

A few lines from his book *Return Ticket* came to mind, lines someone had quoted to me in loose translation from the Arabic: "We will yet return, my son. I will take your hand and we will walk barefoot through the citrus groves of Jaffa." He was a Jerusalem man, I thought to myself, and from what he'd said he did not especially like Jaffa and would not wander through its citrus groves, particularly not barefoot. Yet he chose to write that way. This was a will to return that drew no distinction between Jerusalem the eternal city and Jaffa the port city that has long since lost its citrus groves, though Israel's export oranges still bear Jaffa's name: everything about it is symbolic, everything is immune to change, as if all time that really mattered came to a halt on May 14, 1948.

Around the same time I received an answer from a Jerusalem friend about the grave of Sheikh Bader—the ancestor of Auni Dajani. I called Dajani and told him that the Knesset and the

Hilton now stand on the site, and veteran Jerusalemites still call the eastern slope of the hill Sheikh Bader. Some of the houses are inhabited and some are in ruins. There's an old Jewish cemetery there that is no longer in use, but the location of Sheikh Bader's grave is unknown. Dajani thanked me, saying he would continue his search in Jerusalem, and added that I ought to see his cousin Khalil Daoudi, who worked in the Mandatory Administration and now lived in a suburb of Brighton. There was a whole colony of Palestinians there, and perhaps I would meet a few more.

One Sunday morning I took the train to Brighton, and from there a cab that brought me to a large, fairly new suburban Victorian home. A gaunt, elderly man opened the door and led me to the living room. "Sit here," he said dryly, and began speaking Arabic with a woman who answered him from the other side of the door. Then he sat down facing me. "Do you have some identifying document?" asked Daoudi. When I answered that I did not, he asked me to write my name. I wrote. "Print it in block letters," he said in an authoritative tone. After complying with his request, I listed the names of people I had met with, but he soon stopped me and asked where I live in Israel. "That's a nice place, Herzliya," he said, the hint of a childlike smile on his face. "There are citrus orchards there." It seemed a pity to tell him that most of the orchards were no longer there. "How did you get to me?" he asked. "Dajani spoke with you," I answered. "So why do you ask all these questions?

"Will you have coffee?" he said after a silence, and went out of the room. On the other side of the closed door I heard him exchange words with the invisible woman. Behind me was a well-tended garden. A yellow bush was in flower. Daoudi brought us

Turkish coffee, and I asked where he had lived in Jerusalem. He replied that he had lived in Upper Baka, but that he was born in Nebi Daoud, in the Old City, and he brought me a pamphlet that had been published by the family. This was the house that Dajani had mentioned, he explained, and just as I was studying the photos he said: "I don't want to go on with this." A moment later he said: "I'm sorry, I'm sorry that you came all this way to see me." I asked whether he could order a taxi for me, and he said, raising his voice: "I want to go back there without a permit from Shamir or from Peres. I want to go back to that house."

I put down the pamphlet, and he went to order me a cab.

CHAPTER TWO

"That gorgeous man who was Haj Amin"

The Sephardi Jews were driven out of Spain and Portugal in 1492, and arrived in Palestine via the Mediterranean countries. Ladino was the mother tongue of most of them. From the beginning of the sixteenth century they settled in the four "holy" cities—Jerusalem, Hebron, Tiberias, and Safed—mostly for religious reasons.

Up until the second half of the nineteenth century the Jewish population in Palestine was mostly Sephardi. At the beginning of the British Mandate the Sephardi families still constituted a large part of the Jewish population. As massive immigration came in from Eastern and Central Europe, they quickly turned into a minority.

It was a period," said Rachel Eliachar, "when my children were beginning to grow up, and we wanted them to study languages, and they would not do it. We spoke French and English at home, we spoke Arabic. And they said: 'We won't speak Arabic—they're our enemies. The English—they're our enemies.' "

"Times were different," she added a moment later in her full, lilting voice, her tone intimating that that was how it was, and perhaps the change wasn't for the better but one had to accept it; there was little point in them looking back to the days when children of good Sephardi and Arab families spoke various languages and maintained friendly, neighborly relations, with their fathers doing business together, according to the local custom.

If they really were people of the Levant—natives to the area—it wasn't apparent in the home of Rachel and Menashe Eliachar. They lived in a stone house like other stone houses on Alharizi Street in Jerusalem's Rehavia quarter. Alharizi Street is a narrow street, quiet, with no sidewalks. Tall trees stand like defenders of the thick-walled houses in which Jewish refugees from Germany had found shelter. The room in which we sat was not unlike the living room of any other respectable Jerusalem family: spacious, opening onto another large room. The heavy furniture seemed in its element, as did the dark carpets. Facing me was a high sideboard with glass doors, the objects on display resting in the dimness. Nothing was designed to draw the eye. Everything well preserved, as it had been for decades. Middle Eastern objects—a lamp, a jug, a copper table—were scattered here and there.

"Mainly our friends were upper-class Muslims," Rachel Eliachar told me when I asked her about ties with local Arab families. She replied with mild surprise when I asked what language they spoke: "Arabic. Those families were old friends." "Did you feel close to the Arabs?" "Yes," she said. "This was our milieu. We were born here. We were involved here."

"We had a wonderful villa at the centre of town," said Eliachar. "Among trees and rocks and fruit trees and orchards. In those days, society was feudal. There were good wealthy families who had relations with Arabs and foreign consuls and gentiles. Among the lower classes there was very terrible poverty. It's wonderful how today everyone has opportunities," she concluded with a smile, rising to the nearby table, where the hot water, the dishes, the cakes, the cookies, had been prepared in advance. Eliachar was impeccably well-groomed, her back impressively straight. Would I have known from her appearance that her origins were Sephardi? I think so. Even in her blue eyes, there was something veiled.

"Menashe," she called out with a French intonation, "I'm bringing tea." She moved quickly across the dim room, through to the room that opened out of it, and there, I noticed only then, at the far end, in a high armchair, sat Menashe Eliachar. His face was turned toward the balcony and the pines beyond, golden in the afternoon light.

"Ragheb Bey Nashashibi, the mayor, was a good friend of ours," she said after serving tea. "He would come to us and we went to him, or we'd meet at the King David, which in those days was a luxurious hotel in the sense that you didn't find the ordinary people there. Only certain people could afford to go to for a cup of tea. Today anyone can enter. But at that time it was really extraordinary. They flew things from Groppi's [a famous café in Cairo]. For instance, strawberries. I ate strawberries for the first time at Miss Landau's." Rachel Eliachar explained that Miss Landau—a famous lady, according to Leila Mantoura—was the headmistress of the Evelina de Rothschild School. She had studied at the school and they had become great friends.

"Miss Landau held lavish receptions for the entire British community of high-ranking Jerusalem," she said. "She was a bit anti-Zionist, always fighting with Menachem Ussishkin, the Zionist leader. I remember once she sent him an invitation in English, and he returned it to her, saying, 'I don't understand English, write it in Hebrew.' And she said, 'If you don't understand English, you're not invited.'"

"Next to our house was the church of Talita Kumi," she recalled, "and over there was the Jerusalem Girls' College, which opened up when the British arrived. And they said, 'Why don't you learn English instead of French?' We all spoke French at home, because under the Turks, French was the language one spoke in society. A woman came just to teach us French. When my two brothers and sister spoke with Father and Mother, they used the *vous*, and with Grandfather and Grandmother, *senior*. 'Senior Papa,' 'Senior Mama,' we would say. When the British arrived, by my time, I was already using the *tu* and learning in English." She spoke of Arab Christian pupils she had been friendly with: "They had homes in Talbieh, the elegant Arab neighborhood in Jerusalem. Then came the War of Independence, and, well, we all went our separate ways, until 1967. Then some friends came again and we went to see them. It's just a few years now that they haven't been coming." After a moment she added, growing lively, "But how many Arabs came to our place in 1967 to ask for help from my husband. One of them, a Muslim grocer named Wittar, had even before come to my husband's father, who had had the biggest food company with Arab partners. When he came in 1967, my husband gave him documents; in 1968 he received permission to buy from Tnuva [a food conglomerate owned by the trade unions] and to import.

"He would visit every Passover, and sent a huge platter with all kinds of delicacies. Honey with bees in it, crates of fruit and vegetables. Until he died. Since, only his daughters have been bringing things. His sons won't have anything to do with us. Just like my son, who says, 'What should I have to do with them? I couldn't care less.' It's a terrible shame. The day before yesterday the daughters were here for tea. Why did they come? I called to greet them for Ramadan. They wished me a happy Passover. We do this for continuity. My husband believes in it. That's all that's left, the last drop of all that friendship."

"Sometimes when I walk down the street," she added after a pause, "I say, 'Pinch me, is this Jerusalem?' " "Aren't you sorry sometimes that everything has changed so?" I asked. Eliachar cast a quick, searching glance. "I'm very proud of what we've done in this country," she said in the manner of her generation, which still sees the Jewish state as a miracle. "It's wonderful to see people who were nothing suddenly with cars and homes. It's wonderful."

"What was Jerusalem in the Forties?" I asked. She said they were very carefree years. "At the King David we met with Ragheb Bey. They were great friends; my husband's father was also deputy mayor. We visited Tiberias every winter, and when my husband wanted to come for the weekend, Nashashibi would always call and say, 'Menashe, we're driving up with the limousine, we'll take you to Tiberias.' "

"In 1947 were you still seeing Arab friends?" "In 1947," she repeated, her precisely drawn eyebrows lifting slightly, "that was a rather difficult period. Ragheb wasn't here, and his wife had already left, and they'd killed Fahri, and all the others were plain scared. My husband saw what was coming. 'Let us take the children on a nice tour to Europe, I don't know what is going to happen. The situation is not so good.' I think we were abroad about two months. By the time we returned the situation was as he said—not so good.

"It was a period of chauvinism in the young," she added. "It gave us a state. If not for that chauvinism, maybe the state just wouldn't have happened. Heaven help me if I bought from Arabs.

My husband always wanted us to buy from the Arabs, he wanted that friendliness. But the children: no. One day I bought beautiful apples from Lebanon, and I came home to discover my children had cut them into pieces and put them in saltwater. I understood the way they felt. I didn't say a word, I threw them out."

Into the momentary silence rose the chirping of birds, which gathered force as evening fell. There was no other noise. Menashe Eliachar still sat, facing away. I asked whether I could speak with him, and Rachel Eliachar said perhaps another time.

Some months later I came back to see him. It was morning. The spacious rooms seemed emptier, huddled in their own twilight. He sat facing me, straight in his chair, lean, frail yet imperious, a man accustomed to being heard. Menashe Eliachar was an "elder of the community," one of the Jerusalem Sephardim had told me. He had been president of the Chamber of Commerce and had continued the business of his father:

"The mayor was a partner of my father's. They brought in wheat and barley during the First World War, from Jordan to Jerusalem," he said, in a cracked voice, enunciating slowly. "The day the British captured Jerusalem, I went to see our house, which we'd fled. I ran into some sort of delegation, and the mayor took me along, and that's how I helped to hand the keys of the city to the British. They reappointed Selim Effendi el-Husseini mayor and made Father deputy mayor.

"Before we were great friends with the Husseini family," he continued. "My mother's father, Yosef Navon Bey, had the concession to build the Jerusalem-Jaffa railroad. He didn't want Jewish money, so the mufti's uncle invested in shares." When I asked him to tell me more, he said, "We were friends, our parents were, but the distance was great despite that. It was more a matter of being together in the office.

"I always felt that we should be able to come to an understanding with the Arabs," he said slowly. "I was among the founders of the Kedma Mizraha society [for Jewish-Arab coexistence]. The idea of Arab-Jewish cooperation began during most difficult times, during the troubles of 1936, when the son of the late David Yellin was murdered. A few days later, the son of the headmaster of the Schneller School was murdered. We saw that it would end horribly, and we met at Mikveh Yisrael with prominent Jews who supported cooperation. A group of us went to Jewish community leaders in Egypt. We told them that fire was spreading and that it would reach them too, and we asked them to arrange meetings for us with Arab ministers." "You thought that the Arabs would be willing to cooperate?" "We were certain that if we were forthcoming and systematic, we would be able to get through to them, and we would find some to join us."

When I asked whether he had in fact found such people, he replied: "People like Ragheb Bey Nashashibi, who was a dear friend of my father's. When my father died, he would visit me every holiday. I would visit him every holiday. He invited me to every public event. He had a huge house in Sheikh Jarrah and invited Ben-Gurion, Ussishkin, the Zionist leaders, but he would come to me afterward and ask, 'What kind of people do you have? One of them is speaking with me and another comes over, and he leaves me in the middle of the conversation to go and talk to him.' The Zionist leaders didn't understand their mentality, their greeting *as-salamu alaykum*—peace be on you."

Eliachar spoke quietly: "My grandfather on my mother's side was the sage Hacham Bashi, the head rabbi, the Rishon LeZion.

During Turkish times he was the king of the Jews, and the Arabs bowed when walked with him in David Street. At the time there were greengrocers on both sides and they would leap up to come and touch Grandfather's robe, which was to say, 'I am devoted to you with my head, my heart, and all my strength.' "

"Your friendship with the Arab families continued until the end of the Mandate?" I asked. He replied: "When Ragheb Bey left the municipality, he came to my office every day to drink coffee and used to advise me what to do and what not to do to prevent the mufti from gaining influence." But after a moment he added: "You couldn't trust them. At the time of El Alamein, when we thought that the Germans would be here any minute, we went out, Jawad el-Husseini, a member of the Husseini clan, who studied with me at the Alliance school, and a famous lawyer from the Nashashibi clan. They would say, 'We'll take those houses, that girl. Another few days, just wait, and we'll take the girl.' "

After a few swallows of tea from the cup that Rachel Eliachar had brought before she went out, he continued: "Jawad el-Husseini came to the office every week. He had a house in Jericho and we went down there as well." He was talking about after 1967. "Up to a year ago, three people from the Husseini family were still coming to visit me," he noted. When I asked where they were now, he said, "They all died."

The telephone rang, and Eliachar paid no attention. After a while he described how, in the Forties, he had tried to obtain immigration certificates for Jews who were being persecuted. On one occasion, he was refused by the official in the Immigration Office, an English Jew. "I went to Tawfik el-Husseini, the mufti's cousin, a friend of the family who had taken part with me when we handed over the keys to the British. He was with my brother during the First World War. Husseini took me to the man in charge of certificates at the time, and I explained and said I would be responsible for the man. 'In that case,' he said, 'I will make an exception and give you the permit on the recommendation of Tawfik el-Husseini.' As I was leaving, Najadi el-Nashashibi, Ragheb's cousin, noticed me. I told him what I had come for, and he said, 'Mr. Eliachar, if Nashashibi is available why do you go to Husseini? And then Najadi offered his help.' "

He seemed to be conveying that in this region there had been several ways of life, and that with the establishment of the State of Israel they had all disappeared. The state had destroyed the natural ability of people like himself to live in peace when there was no peace around them. Nevertheless, he had found his own way to participate in the Zionist enterprise. "The lands that we bought in my father's name, the thousand-*dunam* tract [a *dunam* is equivalent to a quarter acre] that is now the government center, the Israel Museum, and Hebrew University, was bought with the help of Abdul Fatah Darwish. He remained devoted to the business of redeeming land for the Jews even after one of his sons was murdered by the mufti's gangs."

"Did you think the Jews wanted to reach an understanding with the Arabs?" I asked him. At that moment, Rachel Eliachar walked in, poured us a second cup of tea, and sat down with us. "That question is a very difficult one," he replied. "Most were indifferent, the question of understanding the Arabs didn't exist, and the minority didn't know to treat the Arab question."

"How did the Arabs see the Ashkenazim?" I asked. "They didn't like the religious Jews, the *kapotes*," he said. "They would call out 'Ashkenazi *bach-bach*, go stick your head in an oven.' " He didn't talk about non-religious Ashkenazim. I asked whether they found Arabs who had been willing to reach an understanding. "Without a doubt," he replied, "on the Arab side there were those who thought there was a possibility, if we didn't go around shouting about it, and I'll give you an example: a few days after the Zionist delegation headed by Professor Weizmann arrived, a lavish reception was held. General Allenby was there, and all the different sects, and the chief rabbis. I knew languages and was in Maccabi and was chosen to be the liaison. We sat in the garden before tea, all the important people, and along came the mufti's delegation. Not Mufti Haj Amin, who hated Jews, but his uncle, Kamal el-Husseini, and Musa Kazim, who was later mayor and caused the troubles of 1929. And they were taken to seats near the entrance, very far from the center. I ran to the organizer of the affair and told him, 'That is no place for them, they don't want to sit there. You must seat them in a more honorable location. They're about to leave.' And he said, 'Let them leave.' Then I went to one of the Zionist leaders and told him the same thing, 'They're about to go, what can we do?' And his reply was the same, and they left. With us it was just that: 'We have the Balfour Declaration, and they are not our problem. The Arabs are the problem of the British.' "

Eliachar felt that in the first years after the British arrived, something irreversible had begun to happen. "If from the first moment we had included the Arabs—to talk to them, to understand their language and learn their customs, to enable them to feel that they can live in the same country in friendship—events might have developed differently. At the beginning it was possible.

I don't say that we wouldn't have later arrived at a Jewish-Arab conflict; in the end they would have understood that the Jews were coming to take."

"Did you talk with Arabs about that?" "I did," he said. "The first thing they mentioned was the contempt the Ashkenazi Jews had for Arabs. It was true."

"And how did those Ashkenazi Jews from Eastern Europe seem to you?" I asked. Rachel Eliachar spoke after a short silence. "We were the ones who received all those immigrants. First the pioneers. They were in a pitiful state; they were starving and glad to be received anywhere. We didn't take people in readily. Our families were afraid of the Bolsheviks. I wasn't allowed to go to the Jewish school because the teachers came from Poland and Russia."

I recalled the words of Yehoshua Palmon, a Hagana and Palmach man, and member of the old Ashkenazi community: "I went to the same school as the Sephardi children, and they were the aristocracy and I was the plebe. It didn't bother me, but if they hadn't given the Ashkenazi Jews only a fingertip [in a handshake], but rather had understood that they were brothers, sharing a common fate, maybe the Ashkenazim would have acted differently. The Sephardim stepped aside without sharing the knowledge they had accumulated."

Rachel continued, "My husband's family lived on Agrippas Street at that time, and Ben-Zvi and Rubashov [Zionist leaders who later became presidents of the state of Israel] took my husband to play when he was young, on Saturday morning, tossing him back and forth between them. One day his grandmother said to him, 'Don't play with them, they're not Jews. They don't keep the Sabbath.' We had to know where we were, who we were."

It was clear that "who we were" was a polite term. They knew very well who they were; they take their family ancestry very seriously. Once I mentioned a family that seemed like any other old Sephardi family and was told that they were nice people, but they had come from Salonika only at the beginning of this century. I was told in other conversations that many good families of Jaffa and Jerusalem had arrived only in the nineteenth century, were involved in commerce, while the truly old families were those in Safed or Jerusalem as early as the sixteenth century.

"Didn't they look odd to you, the Ashkenazim?" I asked. Menashe did not answer. Perhaps the talk had tired him. In the silence his face looked severe, withdrawn. A thin face, thin nose, eagle-like. A gentleman in the fullness of years, resting in his chair. "They seemed odd to us," Rachel confirmed, "but we adjusted to them quickly." It occurred to me that the phrase—"we adjusted to them"—this phrasing had an importance of its own. Those who are part of a place and are then required to follow the lead of immigrants do not do so by confrontation, and perhaps not as quickly as she was suggesting. They have their own ways, and certainly would not discuss the matter with me, the daughter of those immigrants. Despite the Israeli appearance they had assumed, the significant things have remained the property of a small circle, a circle that is shrinking, perhaps, but still maintained.

"All the waves of immigration that we had during the time of the British—we helped them all," she added. "Our house was filled with them—the Romanians, the Germans, the Italians. We learned from everyone who came. I think that easterners can adjust to any culture. We were like the weather cock, we adjusted. Take the Romanians. The beautiful women who used to show up here for cocktails. What outfits, what jewelry. That was really something. We also had everything, but with us you don't get to see it all at once.

"Most of the Romanians unfortunately ran off after the war and settled in Paris," she said. "It wasn't for them, this place. We also grew up in a house that was completely French. When he came from the Caucasus, from Tiflis, my grandfather built a house in the Old City, a huge house with four floors that wasn't destroyed, thank God, but that isn't ours anymore because the government took it. And at the time Grandfather needed furniture, the French consul was just returning to France and was selling his entire household. And my grandfather, may he rest in peace, went there and said, 'I don't want to look, I'll just buy it all.' The piano came from there, and the curtains and the furniture and the crystal and the Sevres and the Limoges.

"A big, beautiful Arab house," she said in that voice of hers that did not tire of life, as if telling me not about what had vanished from the world but about what was still part of life: "The entrance alone was larger than all these rooms together, and the living room had two doors. Arabs came to visit when I was a little girl, and I remember the mufti, Haj Amin el-Husseini, may he burn in hell, when he was young and absolutely gorgeous, reddish-blond with blue eyes, absolutely gorgeous. When the Husseinis came, Mother couldn't show her face, and the maids couldn't either. We had no male help in the house, so we, girls, had to serve. There's lots of ceremony with Arabs, with Muslims. We had to serve a large tray, arranged with glasses of water, and a glass with teaspoons, pretty glasses, Murano with gold, and a glass of gold-plated teaspoons and two big beautiful containers of quince jam and orange marmalade, offerings from our own kitchen. We never served cake. Everyone would take a teaspoon and taste the jam and put it in his glass of water and drink, you see? We had to go from one to the other, but they wouldn't take anything right away. That wasn't proper, taking something to eat right away. We'd say, '*Tfadal*, please,' and then the guest would say no, someone else was more honorable. We would go over to the more honorable one. And he would say, 'That one, *tfadal*,' and we went to him. We were at the end of our tether. Then we brought the Turkish coffee. Turkish coffee has to be brought at a certain time, not too early and not too late; after the Turkish coffee the guest had to leave, that's the way it is in their homes. Father, may he rest in peace, sat in a certain place, and I stood at one door of the living room and my sister at the other door, and when Father made a small gesture with his hand, that was the sign—bring in the coffee. The cook in the kitchen was by then boiling water, and we would serve. From one to the other, from one to the other we would go with the tray of coffee. And we were so glad to see that gorgeous man who was Haj Amin."

CHAPTER THREE

"I'll have some fun with the parrot"

The concept that the future frontiers of the Jewish state would be drawn according to physical settlement enticed the Jews to settle in Arab strongholds such as the Galilee, the Negev desert, and the Hills of Judea. To the Jews, the purchase of land acquired a national, political, and social significance, and of course elicited a strong reaction from the Arabs. The so-called White Paper issued by the British in May 1939 was designed to prevent the development of Jewish settlement in Palestine. However, notwithstanding those restrictions, the Jewish National Fund—Keren Kayemet LeIsrael—a worldwide charitable fund, allocated the bulk of its budget to massive land purchase. Yehoshua Palmon, whose memories take up a good part of this chapter, was among the most active in the purchase of land during those years. His family was among the old generation of settlers in Palestine who had arrived in the late nineteenth century, and Palmon was among those who had grown up among the Arabs, knew them well and cordially, and spoke Arabic as a second language. Nevertheless, they used their intimacy with the Arabs and their ways to further the Zionist dream.

"We can talk only if you don't knock what has been done here," said Yehoshua Palmon in a tone suggesting that he would just as soon not talk. He had always been involved in Arab affairs and was put in charge of Arab affairs in the prime minister's office. I was expecting to meet a man who had spent all his life working for intelligence and security, one of those who give you the feeling that this activity, usually best kept under cover, is not only the center of their world but the very cornerstone of existence. Palmon is one of them, but not altogether. "I'm a product of the old Yishuv [the Jews who settled in Palestine at the end of the nineteenth and beginning of the twentieth century]," he said, letting me know that he was also loyal to the tradition of the early settlers who lived among the Arabs.

"Native son" was the term used for people like him, born to Ashkenazi parents who had themselves been born in the country or had come at the end of the past century and had grown up here as a small community surrounded by Arabs, and were thus on hand to receive the British and the new Zionists. They had close ties with the Arabs, and quite a few were involved in the defense of the Jewish Yishuv and in the purchase of land. Palmon, who was himself one of the most prominent figures, called them "the land and Keren Kayemet people."

He was extremely polite. "Madame," he called me from time to time, a rather odd address from someone not disposed to formality. A man of about seventy, older than most members of the Palmach [commando units of the Hagana], of another generation and another school. It was clear that he was not a joiner and never had been. He was a short, thin man, a shock of metal-gray hair over his forehead. There was something boyish in his severe, withdrawn expression. After asking me a few brief questions, straight to the point, all to ensure that I would not misuse what he said, he listened attentively to my explanation of the project I had undertaken. "This is the second blossoming of the orchards this year. The frost stopped the first one," he remarked as we sat by the open doors of a room that was neither large nor elegant and looked more like a rural home than a villa in a Tel Aviv suburb. There were no other houses in sight, only citrus orchards. Beyond the powerful fragrance of blossoms and the dark green treetops came the heavy, close hum of traffic.

"I was born here" is the way he introduced himself. "My father was born in Jerusalem. He was among the first six people to move to Tel Aviv, and I was born in Tel Aviv." And he fell silent. "So you're a real Tel Avivian," I remarked to prompt him. "I don't know if I'm a real Tel Avivian," he responded thoughtfully, perhaps out of an old habit of weighing every word. "There's tiny Tel Aviv, there's little Tel Aviv, there's medium-size Tel Aviv, and there's Tel Aviv as it is today, and I've always had the feeling that I was born in some other Tel Aviv. It was something else. Not saying better or worse, although for me it was nicer."

And with a light, dry laugh, he paused, waiting for me to speak, and I, feeling somewhat awkward, asked, "How did you become involved with the Arab issue?" He gave me a look that said, "How could I not?" but responded with forbearance: "The country was Arab at the time. There weren't many Jews, and anyone who wasn't clearly inclined to live in a ghetto of four or five religious people and two families was involved with Arabs. Besides, when I was a boy in tiny Tel Aviv, there were Arabs all around, and they were interesting to me. The owners of the vineyards, the farmers. That whole area of the commercial center—it used to be a huge tract of vegetables, plot after plot, and also the eastern part that is now Neveh Sha'anan and HaMasger Street were all orchards, and all that attracted me."

"Why?" I asked after a moment. "First of all," he began, "my whole environment was enveloped in a love of labor—doing something, making something. I was especially fascinated by the vegetable growers and the orchard owners—watching the way the vegetables grow. I would stand on the side and watch, until we began to understand one another, and I started to help. This was a big influence on me; I also began to take an interest in Arabs as something different, and not necessarily 'goyim,' the people you keep away from. I saw in them some very beautiful things.

"There were two books at the time—*Love of Zion* and *Samaria's Guilt*, a good story of the Bible—and I looked at the way the Arabs worked, the way they grew vegetables, and it reminded me more of the Bible than the Orthodox Jews and their *kapotot* [a traditional Jewish black satin coat] and *mezuzot* [a written prayer nailed on Jewish entrance doors] did.

"I had a cousin, a blacksmith in Ekron," he went on, still thoughtfully, but his tone had changed, his reluctance now gone. "He was among the first to use machines that harvested wheat and barley. The mechanical part was pretty limited, they were drawn by donkeys. But in those days they broke off the wheat and barley by hand, or with a scythe. During my vacations—I was a high school student in 1928 and '29—I would travel with him to the Arab villages to help. We rode there on donkeys and we slept over for a few days, until we finished. It was in the mountains, the home of the landowner was in the mountains. And suddenly you ran into these biblical names and biblical customs, and the biblical appearance of the Arabs, it was so much more powerful, more authentic. It drew me, and I had this need to see more and to spend more time there. I knew the country very well. It eventually turned out that I'd done some very good survey work for the Hagana during the riots of 1936–39, and during the War of Independence."

"Perhaps you can tell me a little more about it," I said. From beyond his slightly darkened glasses, his glance rested on me. I wanted to hear how someone like him viewed the Arabs, what his meetings with them were like. Palmon did not answer at once. Again he reverted to what seemed like suspicion of speech itself—his own and others. "What of them did you get to know?" I tried from another angle. "I only got to know the country," he said. "I learned the customs, the relationships. We always say 'the Arabs.' There's no such term as 'the Arabs.' There are tremendous differences among them and ancient hatreds and all that, and that's what I got to know. During the Second World War I was the first to 'Arabize,' as they call it today; I was the commander. At the time I was in charge of the Arabized, those who 'make themselves Arab' for purposes of espionage and sabotage. I was there, in the villages. I slept and ate there, I heard how they talk. There were also boys of my age who didn't sit with the elders, so I played at talking like the elders.

"But later," he went on, "I didn't stay in one place for more than one night. I and another friend would go out together. We crisscrossed every inch of Samaria. We'd take an Arab bus, almost every Shabbat, go to a certain place, get out and walk. We'd concentrate on this or that group of villages, or the most interesting aspect, the most typical. We made a point of sleeping there, too."

I asked whether they were well received. "Of course. Sure, they could have killed us. They could have killed Arabs, too. The country was wild then. But if you did your homework, if you knew how to say hello correctly, if you knew how to greet people at harvest, or how to approach a house when no one was outside, and you did what you had to avoid women, then you were *mina ofina*, 'one of us.' In any case, not a stranger. So why on earth should they kill you? That homework was important, and I was thorough. So they put me up—it wasn't always someone's home. We used to stay in the village guesthouse, a sooty room with a few people sharing. One brought wood, another coffee, another sugar, and we would sit there in the evenings and talk. Guests like us were in demand because we'd seen the world, had come from somewhere. So if you talked well, told a good story, listened to their agricultural, economic problems, you would be very well received.

"I got to know Judea, Samaria, the coastal plain, and the whole country from Zikhron Ya'akov to Sinai. I had a feeling that I was coming home." His was no picturesque image. He went into the hostile areas, with a simple and mystical sense of homecoming.

"My family home was very nice," he felt the need to say. "But these people gave the impression of authentic Jews. Not in the religious sense, but they had inherited the tradition of our fathers, the tradition of the Bible and the Gemara, more than we had." "Would you say you felt more at ease with them?" I asked. "Definitely," he replied. "I felt at ease the moment I realized I was a Jew and they weren't Jews." And when I asked to what extent the element of foreignness was a factor, he replied: "That's also something you learn from the Arabs. When you come to an Arab, the easiest way to be accepted and respected is if you're a neighbor. You're not a member of the family, you're a stranger. The moment you want to be one of them, it entails obligations you aren't prepared for and don't want. It puts you under obligation and it does the same to them. I learned soon enough that the Arabs have all sorts of codes of behavior, and the most convenient and flexible of them all is the code governing neighbors.

"I got involved with the Arabs on our tower-and-stockade settlement campaign," he went on. "I would go with someone from the new settlement who had been named *mukhtar* [head of the village], and I'd say to the Arabs: 'We're neighbors, we have the obligations of neighbors. We have water, we can't withhold it from you. If there's food you need, we can't keep it from you, at least you can borrow some. We have a doctor, we don't want to keep him from you.' You could also say: 'You're obligated by the code of neighbors,' and that obligated them more than if you had talked about humanity or religion or honesty or things like that."

"And did it work?" I asked. "Even today it could work," he said, "because when we came, unlike the people who settle today, we gave them a definition they understood and accepted. But if we want integration, that means turning them into nobody, and therefore turning ourselves into nobody." He burst out laughing, and I joined in.

"Usually the land was bought from city people," he said. "Absentee landlords?" I asked. "No, from Arab leaders like Musa Alami." "Alami agreed to sell?" I asked in amazement. "On condition that no one would know," he replied. "Haj Amin el-Husseini, too. He often needed money because he wanted to hold on to his followers and buy new ones. Even the mufti had to pay to organize a terror group. There wasn't one who didn't sell land. They all needed the money for the struggle with their Arab rivals. But we were reliable, and they knew we wouldn't open our mouths and make trouble."

"Who made the contact with those leaders?" I asked him. "There was a middleman, an Arab," Palmon answered, with that mixture of patience and irritation one uses with people who ask too many questions. "There was no contact we couldn't make in those days. If I wanted to meet someone, there were lots of places to find them. But you had to know how to make contact with a person like that. You had to know what would appeal to him, what he was looking for. If you went there and told him about your inalienable right to the Land of Israel and that they were only guests here, there was no contact. You don't have to say the opposite, but you don't have to say exactly that." In these last vague words, said with composure, there was something clear and unequivocal: you don't have to say it's either us or them.

Hiram Danin, whose grandfather had been among the founders of the first new neighborhoods outside Jerusalem's old city, had lived among the Arabs in Beersheba when he worked in land settlement for the Mandatory government.

Later he joined the Jewish National Fund. When I visited his home in Jerusalem, he told me, "We still maintain secrecy. The first principle was absolute secrecy. The whole principle was—according to Yehoshua Hankin, head of land purchasing—'You have to know the Arabs but to act like a Jew. If you promise something, you have to come through.' I had true friendship with the Arabs, I came to know them, to know their customs. I also knew you didn't have to accept every story of theirs exactly the way they told it, but I always remembered what Hankin told me: 'The trouble when you deal with them is you can get drawn into their behavior, and if we behave the way they do, we might lose their trust.' They have a lot of respect for someone who keeps his promise and doesn't lie. They'd trust more Jews who didn't speak Arabic well. 'That's a Muscovite, he came from Russia,' they would say: 'If he promises something, he does it.' Along comes a Sephardi Jew, who treats them according to their customs, 'He's a liar like us.' "

That was the line the British followed in the colonies, I thought to myself: carefully maintaining the distinction between themselves and the natives. It was a distinction that said the British were more reliable, more efficient, or simply better. When I asked him whether he was a "Muscovite," Danin replied: "They respected me, because they knew that my word was my word. They have a highly developed intuition about people. When people dealt with them honestly, even the biggest cheats made an effort to restrain themselves. But you couldn't put too much faith in them; it was best to have someone else around to keep track. Trust is one thing, but you also have to keep your eyes open.

"It was very complex," he said. "From time to time, everyone would get together and coordinate how to deal with the problems." In the Forties, he explained, the JNF people made contact with Arab middlemen, and the intelligence people of the Hagana gave the JNF information on the dangers and threats, and the best of the lawyers looked for ways to transfer the Arab property, which sometimes wasn't even registered in the name of the seller.

"What was the method?" I wanted to know. And Palmon explained: "We would tell the Arab, 'We're not the ones who will buy from you. Transfer it to the name of an Arab that we will give you.' He would transfer the property into the name of the Arab. How did we manage it so that the second Arab could turn the land over to us legally? We'd say to him: 'My good man, sign here that you took a loan from us. We'll take you to court to get the loan back; you won't return it, you'll be declared bankrupt, and then we have the right to take whatever property is registered in your name, wherever. That's something the White Paper forgot about.' It forgot that loophole, and through that loophole we bought a lot of land."

"Among the Arabs were educated and talented people, and you could not escape the fact that they felt we were foreigners who wanted to displace them," remarked Dr. Avraham Biran, as we sat in his office at Hebrew Union College in Jerusalem. He had been a district officer of the Mandatatory Administration in the Jezreel Valley and later on in Jerusalem. An archaeologist, he had returned to his own field in the Fifties, and might be freer to speak than those who were still involved in land purchase:

"In the settlements in the Jezreel Valley and in the Beit She'an Valley there were problems," he admitted. "The JNF bought a little land in the area of Nazareth, around Ma'alul, near Nahalal, and there were big problems with land tenants, so the British district commissioner had to be the judge, not the Jews or the Arabs." He described a purchase: "That was where they'd bought from the Bedouin Zanati family; the sheikh was glad he had sold. He didn't see anything wrong. He had lots of land; what he sold wasn't cultivated, it had to be drained. In the end he took the money and moved to Transjordan. He had land on both sides of the Jordan. I was there in my capacity as Jewish governor, and they took pictures of us. We look very young, and the sheikh very handsome."

His mood turned sober for a moment. "A man like myself has a history," he said. "When I was a child in Rosh Pina, the fellah from Jaouni worked the land, and he received two-fifths of the harvest as payment. We had good relations with the Arab villagers. In a way we lived together. My philosophy, I guess, was that there's room for both. I didn't see displacement. Statistics showed that Arab settlements next to Jewish settlements prospered. In any case I thought we were doing well—settling desolate places, draining the swamps, moving a land tenant or two into dry areas."

"Moving a land tenant or two into dry areas" raised many questions in my mind. I went to see Palmon again.

"This bit-by-bit acquisition," I said. "Someone like you who knew the situation firsthand, did you look beyond the *dunam*-by-*dunam*?" "I knew that to an Arab, land is not an economic concept," he replied, "it's a political concept, it's territory, it's a blow to his sovereignty." "Did you ever think about where all this was leading?" I asked. "Look," he answered, "where all this was leading had to do with the other side as well."

"Do you think that at the time, during this vast land purchase, Yishuv leadership understood that they were pushing the Arabs off their land?" I asked. "What could they have done?" he protested. "They weren't pushing. The Arabs were being pushed. That's a big difference. Arabs sold land in the vicinity of Jewish settlements. They could live better, and things were easier for them. Our idea was—would they still have the means to keep themselves going, with an eye to the future, or not? Today we see that they still do. Eighty thousand Arabs of Judea and Samaria are working with little Israel."

I was inclined to stop questioning. What was the point if he, too, took the usual shortcut of people of the old school, who were believed to know what the Arabs were really like, and whose opinion was taken into account because no one else knew, and perhaps no one else wanted to know? I pressed on nevertheless. Even if he did arrive at the conventional thinking, the route he'd taken was not easy, and perhaps not conventional either.

I asked whether there had already been an element of "know your enemy" regarding the Arabs. "No," he replied. "Before 1946, who thought about a state? Here was a country ruled by England, a pretty good country, a place where you could live decently. I began to think it was impossible only when I saw the British's criminal treatment of our immigrants. Before then there was no need for a state. What for? To raise a flag? There was security, there was order, there was the rule of law. For that I don't need a Knesset.

"On the whole our local people pretty much got in the way," he remarked. "They didn't really understand the game. They didn't understand that playing with the British and the Arabs is like playing with ricochets—not to shoot at the target, because by shooting at the target, we couldn't accomplish anything. If you want contact with the Arabs you don't want opposition from them. You pay a political price and you have to be careful not to push them to the edge. That was a rule of thumb that continued even after the state was established. Jewish policy in the country has been suffering from cerebral palsy since 1967. I don't see anyone from the present government with any inkling of the laws of billiards.

"After the UN decision in 1947, things changed a bit," he continued. "If you were a Jew you didn't go to Tulkarm [an Arab town], you had to work in other ways." "Are you willing to talk about it?" "What's there to talk about?" he asked with some impatience. "First you traveled at odd times. For many months I would travel at such times that someone with common sense would say, 'You're crazy.

You come here at night?' I was building on earlier successes. I knew that if only I had a chance to say a word or two, hostility could turn into curiosity and some talk, and I could get out of it." "For instance?" I said. "For instance," he said, "you're in Jenin. You get off the bus and you see that you've aroused curiosity, which means suspicion. You say the right word, which shows you belong there, that there's nothing in your speech that gives you away."

"How did the Arabs see people like you, who were native-born?" I asked. "Look," he said, "Jews who like my grandfather came in 1882 to the Turkish Empire knew what they were getting into. They kept a low profile politically, socially, and economically. The Arabs could understand them and take them under patronage. That was the Muslim way, it was pleasant, and it was passed down in the families. People who came here during the Mandate weren't under anyone's patronage, and they didn't see the Arabs as patrons. If you ask me, under the influence of my family and the environment until 1929, I actually understood the Arab fear of the pioneers. In this country, we generally behaved in ways that morally were not so justified: we were acting to save ourselves from annihilation, which is even less moral. I wish the Arabs well, but I want them to recognize my right to live."

The more he talked, the more I felt the essential thing was not what he said but the leaps he made between each position and its opposite. He did it naturally and consistently. "Look," he tried to explain, "before 1929 we never realized that we had to live in Jewish areas for security. I sometimes wonder how I intuitively did things that only now I know rationally were necessary."

But what things were "necessary," I wondered. Would a code of behavior, of neighborly relations, have brought about a solution?

Or did he know that in the end the confrontation would only be postponed, and that it was simply the least of all evils? I said: "You had your ears open, you knew what was happening, didn't you sometimes disagree with the policy determined in Jerusalem?" "We didn't carry it out," he replied. "We advised them about the ways and means, the lighthouse they should be sailing toward—sailing, but taking the waves into account."

"Were there cases in which you departed from the policy of the Yishuv's leaders to do what you had to do?" I asked. "Or was there always a sense of harmony?" "I want to make this clear," Palmon said, suddenly insistent. "In the six years before the state, something extraordinary was going on. I don't know exactly what to call it. There was no need for central planning, each person had a sense of what he could do, and particularly what he had to do.

"There was an understanding and agreement about what had to be done, and each person did what he had to," he repeated. "It wasn't a problem. I made decisions at the time that, if I'd made them today, would have triggered ten committees of inquiry."

I asked for an example of such a decision, and he said, "For instance, the agreement with the Jaffa commander to stop shooting in the Manshiyeh area." I asked when that happened, and he replied, "During the War of Independence, let's call it." It was odd that he had added "let's call it"; I wondered what he would have preferred to call the war. "My friend Nimer Hawari was in Jaffa at the time, as commander of the Najada militia. He phoned me—it was in the early months of '48 by then—and he said, 'Your people are holding positions and my people are holding positions, and you're shooting at us and we're shooting at you, and Jewish and Arab civilians are being injured.' These were neighborhoods of prostitutes, where you didn't know what was Jewish, what was Arab. I told him, 'I agree, let's meet.' So I picked myself up and went to his place in Jaffa; there was a large stretch of dunes, with snipers on both sides." "You went out alone?" I asked, and he said, "It's less dangerous alone than with four or five others," and laughed. "I went there on foot. I went to see him, and we came to an agreement that there would be no shooting, and it stuck."

I asked where they had met. "That wasn't a problem. We could go anywhere. There was a large café in Manshiyeh, a very large café with glass walls, and cafés on King George Boulevard, which is Sderot Yerushalayim today. You never saw a woman there. Not a cleaning woman, not a waitress. It was a place for narghille, for card games in the corner." His voice warmed as he described the places, I asked whether he liked going there. He shrugged his shoulders and said, "Yes. I liked their coffee, which was very good. I liked smoking narghille. Whenever I happened to be in Jaffa with a little time on my hands, I'd go to a café. I'd go to one where they knew me and if you met someone, it would be, 'Let's smoke a narghille.' That's where I met Nimer Hawari. At first our meetings were of the 'My brother is stronger than your brother' type. But later I asked him questions I couldn't ask anyone else, about literature, history. His Arabic was fantastic, very rich.

"He once said to me in 1946, 'Between the Jews and us, whoever can withstand the climatic conditions and all the other conditions and grow stronger and take root, that's who will win, and the others will be welcome and blessed neighbors. If we are the winners, we are the winners. If the Jews are the winners, the Jews are the winners.'"

When I asked him what had happened to Hawari after the War of Independence, Palmon told me about his various wanderings in Arab countries and his attempts to organize the refugees and the attempts to assassinate him until he slipped over the border into Israel. "Despite all the risk involved, I brought him into the country and he worked here as a lawyer. Later he was appointed district judge in Nazareth." I wondered whether he could have gotten such an appointment in those years without cooperating in one way or another with the authorities. "He wasn't an Uncle Tom Arab," I half-asked, half-declared, and Palmon said, "He didn't turn into an Uncle Tom, he didn't lose his pride. But with me he was on such terms that he could say, 'Abu-Adi, to you I can say this, at night I cry because I couldn't save my brothers from their plight.' " Then I asked whether Palmon had continued to see him. "Until the day he died," he answered, adding after a moment, "He was a friend without a balance sheet."

"Why do you call him that?" I asked. "I was translating from the Arabic," he said. "In Arabic you say, 'Whatever you tell me, whatever you do, I'll take it well. I won't assume you have bad intentions and I won't keep accounts on why you said this or didn't say that.' It's called *fis-a-klif*." And when I asked how you get to that point, he replied, "It takes time. You can't learn it in a school for spies." As I was trying to figure out the connection between friendship and a school for spies, Palmon continued, "I had ties not only with him, I was on good terms with all. Simply by treating them like human beings. We knew what human beings were and what they weren't." In his tone of voice there was also a warning: "Take it as it is. It's complicated enough as is."

"For example," he continued unprompted, "there were almost monthly meetings with a man named Ahmed el-Einan. He was the mufti's representative in all of the north. I met with him freely. Those meetings were very useful to me, but my status with him was very problematic. He was old and sick, he had a wife, as wide as she was long, who couldn't get through the door of the house. One day I called him and asked whether I could come over. He said yes, knowing very well that all sorts of Arabs might come from Haifa, even without phoning. Once Jamal el-Husseini, top adviser to the grand mufti, Haj Amin el-Hussieni, showed up. Ahmed el-Einan said to me, 'Here's Jamal,' and I could see that he was very embarrassed, so I said, 'If you don't mind I'll say hello to your wife and have some fun with the parrot'—she had a parrot. He was very pleased because Jamal would never go to his wife. It was a complicated business, but we resolved it with honor. Every time we saw each other he would laugh, remembering it."

Palmon said: "You have to take into account—we were nothing at the time, what power did we have? The British were against us. We had endless problems—economic problems, security problems. What could we promise the Arabs? Money? The British, by one concession or another, could promise them the equivalent of our whole budget. But I'm proud that I was a member of that bunch. We were three or four people. And though we had nothing to offer them, they accepted us and trusted us." "Because you knew them?" I asked. And he answered, "Because we were human beings. Because we weren't arrogant, and because we treated them with respect and honor."

"And what about the rest, the Yishuv?" I asked. "How were they?" "Look," he said after a moment, "it's a very complicated problem. I've thought a lot about this ignorance that stood before us like a pillar of fire. If they had seen it clearly, the Jews would simply have left. It was a land of troubles, so what did we have here? I mean other than the mosquitoes and malaria and swamps and lack of budget and all those things, why get into all this trouble?" "Why take into account all those troubles and not consider the people?" I asked. "Which people?" he said. He knew very well which people, but nevertheless I answered, "Arabs."

"The truth is," he said after a silence, "when my daughter got older and wanted to study Arabic, I asked her, 'What for? Study English, French, you'll have something to read.' " He was speaking in the same even tone, dry and matter-of-fact, as though this were the simple logic of it, step-by-step, and not another surprising inconsistency.

Palmon was not an opportunist; he had once found the Arabs captivating, but over the years had come to feel that their interests were not his. He did not really want it that way, but that's the way things were.

CHAPTER FOUR

"Everyone does his best to be a gentleman"

The British government, through its legal authority, set up a uniform legislative and judiciary system for all the inhabitants of the country. The legal system both encoded the Ottoman civil law (Al Megella) and land laws and introduced via "Order in Council" most principles of the British common law and equity, including rules of evidence and court administration. The pleadings were in English, English precedents were binding, and common-law rules of evidence were the guideline.

In law classes in Jerusalem, Arab and Jewish lawyers were educated in the tradition of British law. Ya'akov Shimshon Shapira, the main figure in this chapter, graduated from that school. He led a tenacious legal battle in various courts, defending the ships that brought illegal immigrants to Palestine and that were confiscated by the Mandatory government. The fight was a legal one and was fought according to the rules of law, but was, in fact, part of the political confrontation between the Jewish Yishuv and the Mandatory government.

To be a Crown councillor in Palestine was the most exciting assignment one could have, I thought," said Sir Michael Hogan. "We had the rebellion in Palestine, we had terrorists, there was lots of crime, the whole place was bubbling away.

But the cases on the civil side, on the ownership of land, were fascinating."

He was sitting on a soft sofa without leaning back, legs crossed, trousers perfectly pressed. A lean man in his seventies, reserved in a British way. Still, his Irish origins were apparent, particularly in his fluent speech. He spoke with pleasure about the skirmishes he had had with Jewish and Arab lawyers, but with a slight irony that seemed to curb any obvious enthusiasm. "Practically every acre in Palestine seems to me to have been fought over in the court, and therefore became very precious," he said, explaining the complicated Ottoman land-registry regulations and the fact that Arab fellahin did not register land in their own names in order to avoid Turkish conscription. He then came to the central issue: "When the question of a national Jewish home came along, the title to this land became a matter of great consequence. There were such fierce battles fought as to who really owned what, and to what extent would you disregard the boundary specified in registration and accept the evidence of the inhabitants."

The high Victorian windows behind him in his Chelsea apartment reflected trees in the sun and, beyond, cars moving along the Thames. The room was in shadow, conservatively luxurious, and looked almost unused, perhaps because there were many years he hadn't lived in it. Hogan had returned to England after extended service in countries that had still been part of the empire when he arrived there. He began his service as a low-level advocate in Palestine in 1936.

I asked him when he had left Palestine, and was surprised to hear that it was after the Mandate ended, in the summer of 1948. He had been legal counsel to the forces not yet been withdrawn.

As such he had witnessed what most of the British in Palestine had not—the high commissioner sailing away.

"As the aircraft carrier on which Sir Alan Cunningham sailed passed the foot of Mount Carmel—they had a band on deck—I thought about the last crusaders. I finished up in Hong Kong, and one of the things that attracted me was that it reminded me very much of Haifa. The combination of mountain and warm water."

I imagined him standing on a hill in Hong Kong, looking out into the South China Sea and remembering another sea, and how satisfying that must have been even though the Carmel mountains and that Mediterranean shore had been not only lost but abandoned. He did not deny that the British had left it all. On the contrary: "At the end it was rather humiliating, because it was against the grain to leave without handing over to anybody things that one built up with such great enthusiasm and dedication. And to leave it all in the air—you usually hand over to some other government. It may be a revolutionary government, but you usually hand it over. It was certainly a situation that made one very unhappy.

He added wryly: "There used to be a saying that anybody coming to Palestine arrived as rather pro-Jewish, but after a while became rather pro-Arab, and generally ended as being pro-British."

"Do you think it was true?" I asked. "Well," he answered, "there was a certain amount of truth, because having grown up on the Bible there was a sense of identification with the Jews. Once on the ground, one saw that the Arabs also had a strong case. I suppose that the last stage as pro-British was rather a retreat, away from the front lines of both Jews and Arabs. The lawyers, Arabs and Jews, I found able indeed. The standards there were high on both sides." He told me about the many trials that resulted from an arbitrary action by one of the sultans or a pasha, and how they'd have to burrow into the Istanbul archives to find an ancient signature. I asked him about the cases of illegal immigration that became increasingly common toward the end of the Mandate.

"There was something emotional about dealing with those," he remarked. "It was the situation, and the tremendous amount of feeling engendered by Arab-Jewish conflict, and the Jewish determination to establish a new state, to reinstate what had not been in existence for two thousand years. Quite a decision. It demanded great courage from any group of people to envision what they would have today."

"Was it more of a problem to deal with those cases than with others?" I asked him, and he answered, "No, I don't think so, though you feel inclined to have a liking for one side or the other."

He paused, his pale features withdrawn. Then he returned to law and lawyers in his pleasant, slightly dry manner of speaking: "Quite often we had a journey through history when we were dealing with land cases," he commented with a thin smile. "There were some banana groves near Jericho that at one time had been coveted by Cleopatra. Herod was asked by Mark Antony to give them to her, and Herod sold them for a remarkable price. Everybody was involved in this case, not only Arabs but Jews as well, because they had settlements in the area. The Muslim claim depended, as far as I can remember, on a Sultan Beider, who came that way in the Middle Ages and laid waste to the land. On his way back from Egypt, he felt quite remorseful, and to make his peace with the Lord, he gave the land to the Muslim religious court, the Waqf. They based their claim on ancient inscription. One day in court, I got up to say there was a question of representation. I represented the government of Palestine, and a chap called Goytan, later a Supreme Court judge in Israel, a witty fellow, represented the Jews. After detailing all the representatives in the court, they all turned to Faris Bey, and Bey said, 'Your Honor, who represents God in this court?"

Later, while listening to the tape of our conversation, I realized that I had forgotten to ask him who Faris Bey was. I phoned Hogan a week later, and a woman's voice answered. "Sir Michael died last week." I murmured an apology and some words of consolation. She told me on the phone about the many years she had spent in Jerusalem, and how much Palestine meant to her. The quiet, pleasant talk, so polite, from a woman I had never seen, somehow made his death seem real.

When I mentioned Hogan's death to Ya'akov Shimshon Shapira, who had been a prominent attorney during the Mandate and was later attorney general and minister of justice in Israel, his emotion was audible. I asked whether he had known Sir Michael well, and he replied, "He was a man I respected and admired a great deal."

Shapira received me in a spacious office on the ground floor of his home, which stood alone among Tel Aviv apartment buildings. Another private home along the boulevard of trees was that of David Ben-Gurion, now a museum. The shutters of the room were drawn, set apart from the cars and crowds on their way to the nearby sea and from the street itself. Shapira sat behind a large, uncluttered desk. He was a man of eighty with a severe expression, his chin emerging from a white collar secured with a tie in spite of summer. After a moment of silence, he said, "If Hogan appeared in court, it was brilliant."

I asked him to tell me about a case. He said that answers to such questions cannot be answered offhand. I explained that I was not researching legal cases of the period. His eyes, dark and sharp, examined me from under thick brows, and I could tell that he was not satisfied with my explanation. I told him how Sir Michael Hogan had described a complicated land case that had begun before his arrival and still hadn't been resolved when the Mandate ended.

"Hogan was among the intelligent ones in the British service," Shapira declared. "The law was British and the attorneys were British. The level was high, very high, but still, it wasn't like England. If Hogan had practiced privately, he would also have been a very successful lawyer."

I asked him what he had thought of the Arab lawyers. "Only a minority of them were up to par," he said. "They were a little more on the outside. Well dressed, you know. I was on very good terms with them; there were even Arab lawyers who came to me as clients. You can't ask for money from a client who's a lawyer. In any case, I didn't take money." When I asked why an Arab lawyer would come to him, he replied, "Because he thought I was a better lawyer than he. There might be a case that was a bit complicated, a little bill of sale, or a case where both British and non-British law was involved. Then he would come to me, and not just to me—there were two or three other Jewish lawyers whom an Arab lawyer could approach. He knew I would give him the best advice I could."

"What language did you speak with the Arab lawyers?" I asked him. "English," he said. "I didn't know Arabic. To this day, I don't know any Arabic." I asked whether he had had conversations that went beyond legal advice. He replied, "I didn't look for conversation. I didn't see much sense in it. What would I have to discuss with an Arab lawyer?

"There was more of a mix in those days than there is today, but how many Jews went to Nablus? And of those who went to Nablus, how many slept over? At most you had coffee and you get out of there. I've been in this country since 1924. That's sixty-three years, and I speak no Arabic, I don't read Arabic except for numbers, and I never wanted to study it. It is not only me. It's not for pleasure that you learn this is a cup," and he pointed to the cup of tea in front of him, "and that this is a saucer and this is a table. If you don't need it, you don't learn it." His Hebrew, tinged with Yiddish, was well suited to his manner of speaking—direct, concise, and caustic.

He asked me who among the lawyers in Israel had put me in touch with Hogan, and seemed surprised to hear that Anwar el-Nusseibeh—who had also recently died—had suggested I meet with two Crown councillors to the Mandatory government, Hogan and Sir Ivo Rigby, and had even found me their addresses and phone numbers. For a while we switched roles. Shapira asked me questions and I answered. I told him about the people he had known during the Mandate, what they were doing now, about the meetings in London, and the fact that Rigby had mentioned him as the lawyer who had defended the skipper of an illegal-immigrant boat at a trial that he had conducted.

A faint smile appeared in Shapira's eyes. I asked him about the captains he had defended. "Usually it was a writ by the Mandatory government to confiscate the boat, and then criminal charges were pressed against the captain. I don't think they were naive enough to believe that seizing the boat and jailing the captain would bring an end to immigration. But they thought it would make it more difficult. So the battle in the courts was a battle for and against the immigration."

I asked him to describe a case. Shapira said, "I forget the name of the boat. It was the first case. They seized a boat in Haifa Bay, not in the harbor, but outside. The police prevented the immigrants from debarking and took the captain off. They brought him to court, charged him with trying to bring people into the country who had no right of entry. I tried to destroy their case with facts. At that time the law still didn't allow for confiscation of the ship. My argument was that if they took the captain and sent him to prison, the boat wouldn't be able to leave. They answered: 'We'll dispatch the ship.'"

"And how did that trial end?" I asked. "The judge was actually a man who had some sympathy for us. He asked the prosecutor, 'Why do you want to send the captain to prison? The ship can't budge without him.' The general prosecutor said they would make sure the boat left. After two or three days of debate in court, the judge sentenced the captain to six months in prison. But it was impossible to send off the ship, as it had no captain. So they released him. He left but sailed to Nahariya and let the immigrants off there." When I asked how the captain had managed that, Shapira replied, "He went out to sea. In the sea there's no road, so he sailed for two or three hours toward Greece, then turned around and came back to Nahariya. The British saw, of course. A ship is a pretty big vessel. It was no secret to them. They changed the law and began to confiscate ships.

"Trials of illegal immigrants were held in the District Court," he explained. "When I lost a case and the boat was declared confiscated I would submit an appeal to the Supreme Court. There it would sit for ages. The more ships that came to port, the more difficult it became for them. More of a burden." "Were they, in a sense, political trials?" I asked. "Certainly not," he said. "There were no politics in court. No declarations. No declamations—never.

"The English judges knew very well that I appeared at those trials not because I was looking for additional work," he said. "They knew these were not only my clients. But those immigrants they didn't want to let off the boats were Jews. I'm a Jew. They were persecuting us. Okay, we won't insult you, but you are no friend of mine. We are at war, but we conduct the war like gentlemen."

When I pointed out that there were lawyers of the first rank who did socialize with the British, he answered curtly: "I didn't believe in *kutzinyu-mutzinyu*," a Yiddish expression for whispering empty sweet nothings. "I had some standing as a lawyer. I think I was not a bad lawyer in their eyes. But I don't think I was once a guest in the home of a British judge."

"Someone like Hogan, for instance," I asked Shapira, "did you ever talk to him outside of court?" "I was on very good terms with Hogan," he said. "He was one of the first judges. Another type altogether. He spent his first vacation in this country at Degania. He'd heard about kibbutzim and wanted to see for himself. How many Englishmen like that were there? We, Russian Jews, were some kind of discovery for them. It never occurred to most that I could know something of English literature or that English politics interested me. Sometimes they were amazed that I knew what was written in their books. That I might know something of English law that he himself didn't know."

"When I spoke to Englishmen about Jews from Eastern Europe," I said, "they seemed to feel they were strange birds." "It's hard to say," replied Shapira. "No one likes anyone who is cleverer than he is." "Do you think that the Jews who came here were cleverer than the British?" I asked. "Some were, some weren't," he admitted. "There were some who got on very well with Dostoyevsky without reading him. The average Russian isn't all that steeped in Russian culture, and the average Englishman isn't all that steeped in English culture. Two worlds," he concluded.

"Why," I asked Shapira, "was it important to a man so extreme in his political views as Henry Cattan to emphasize that he had friends among the Jewish lawyers as well as among the British? When Cattan went to London, he had lunch with Hogan and they talked about the good old days and about the cases of the good old days. Or why, when Anwar el-Nusseibeh went to Hong Kong, did he find out that Hogan and Rigby were there and want to visit them? Why did people of the Yishuv, like yourself, have no contact either with the Arabs or the British?"

"There was no contact," he declared. Then he added: "Two days before the outbreak of the Second World War, I was in Lebanon with my wife. For summer vacation we sometimes went to Lebanon. So they called me from Tel Aviv or Haifa to ask me to come back because some Jewish boys had been accused of murder, a very tough case. Three or four of them had been accused." He stopped for a moment and smiled. There was something stoic in the smile, as he came face-to-face with the loneliness of recent years. He was almost the only one remaining of his generation, lawyers who were already well known during the Mandate. I wondered whether he still came down to his office every morning, to the desk that was now almost bare.

"They asked me to defend one of them," he went on. "I said, there are so many lawyers. I have just gone on vacation. Allow me to enjoy it a little. Two hours later I had a call from Eliyahu Golomb [head of the Yishuv paramilitary forces], who said, 'Shalom, shalom. I hear you're on vacation. Having a good time in Lebanon. I wanted to tell you it's a good thing you're in Lebanon, that you don't mind Jewish boys being hanged.' Well, I went right away. All this is by way of preface, because on the Thursday of the trial the war broke out. So Ya'akov Salomon saw the president of the court enter, and he announced to him, 'The Germans have marched into Holland.' And he answered, 'Have they?' Anything not to talk with the native, Ya'akov Salomon. They got off, our boys, but could you keep contact with people like that?"

He gave me a penetrating look. "Can you imagine a Jew appearing—business is business—against an immigrant ship?" he asked, and fell silent. "No," I said. "How could that be 'Business is business'?" he remonstrated. "He would be an outcast, I wouldn't shake his hand, I wouldn't have him in my home. He wouldn't be able to sit at the cinema, couldn't set foot in a restaurant. His wife wouldn't speak to him, his children wouldn't speak to him.

"I was very sensitive to the refugees," he continued. "Even now when I talk about it, it hurts. He was a Jew and I was a Jew, but I lived very comfortably in a well-furnished house, my income was good, and my children went to school. Here he came, sailing in on a ship and drowning in trouble. And he was the Jew who got away, who managed not to be crushed by the Nazis. I could never say business is business. Rigby would expel those Jews, and then adjourn and want to have coffee. Let him choke without coffee." He stopped. "I hoped the intelligent Englishman would understand that for me this was not just a client whose boat I was paid to defend." After a moment he said, "We looked for a little light. We looked for a little light," and fell silent.

Not long afterward I came to see Rigby. I wanted to know more about the illegal-immigration trials that he had conducted up to the last days of the Mandate. This was the second time I had come to see him, after the sudden death of Hogan, a good friend of his. Together they had traversed the shrinking empire—from Palestine to Africa to Malaysia—and finally served as High Court justices in the last Crown colony: Hong Kong.

When I spoke with regret about Sir Michael's death, he remarked simply that the funeral ceremony had been very beautiful. We were sitting in the drawing room, filled with furniture from the Far East. A servant came in to asked whether we would like tea or coffee. "Have some sherry?" Sir Ivo asked, rising. He was a distinguished-looking elderly man. He wore a blue blazer. He had seemed a gentleman who enjoys the good things in life in our previous meeting, but this time he was under the shadow of Hogan's death, which he didn't want to talk about. He poured some sherry and told me about casinos in Macao and the mad gambling practices of the Chinese. As mad as the Arabs and the Jews in the London casinos.

A little later we went to a restaurant near his home. His spirit seemed to lighten as he called the waiter, addressing him by name. He then told me of the last trials he had conducted in Palestine:

"I was in fact the last British judge in Palestine, as president of the Haifa District Court. I was also ending cases in Tel Aviv and Jaffa. I was transferred to Haifa in March or April 1948, but I went down with military or police escort in an armored car to the outskirts of Petah Tikva or Tel Aviv. I never felt any qualm. Those were civil cases. I was ending disputes about property and so forth."

After telling me lightly how he and a few English friends had gone to Jaffa one Sunday, to have something to drink at the deserted swimming club—most of the British had already left— and how, on their way back, they had been threatened by an armed Arab mob, he remarked: "I think I enjoyed the exciting atmosphere. I was sorry to leave. It was a country I was very fond of. I learned law in Palestine, from the hard work and diligence of the Jewish lawyers, and the very good Arab lawyers. There were not many good Arab lawyers, but when they were good they were very good. The Jewish lawyers were completely thorough. It was like a connoisseur eating a beautifully served dinner; you could pick from the superb meal that was put before you."

As we neared the end of our substantial lunch. I asked him: "When things were becoming rather difficult, toward the end, did you look forward to going home?" "Not a bit," he protested with a jovial smile. "I enjoyed my life there right to the very end.

"My last case was too ludicrous for words," he continued. "It was an application by our attorney general to seize a vessel bringing illegal immigrants into Palestine, demanding of course penalties and punishment for the master and captain of the ship. There we were, two days before the termination of the Mandate, solemnly hearing this case, the harbor full of ships, all of which had been confiscated with the knowledge that in a matter of two days they would be handed back to the Israelis."

"None of those ships was a *Titanic*," Shapira remarked when I related to him my conversation with Rigby. "But we got quite decent compensation for them. They confiscated thirty ships and couldn't sell a single one because I was blocking them with appeals to the Supreme Court. When I lost an appeal I petitioned the Privy Council in London. They conducted the game according to the British rules, and everyone does his best to be a gentleman. There wasn't too much I could argue—the ship was a ship, the immigrants were immigrants. They were illegal? They were illegal. And they tried to disembark at night? They tried." He was enjoying his description, telling the story in a Yiddish style, not entirely serious, but sober and real, and I had the feeling that Shapira, when he arrived at court in those days, had entered another world, somewhat foreign but not entirely so.

CHAPTER FIVE

"I suppose you met him in Jerusalem"

Many who lived outside Jewish society did so due to circumstances, halfheartedly, or on the sly. Theirs was a closed small circle, most of which had come to Jerusalem because of the Second World War. The war had brought great changes in the city. The entire country had been filled with armies of sundry kinds, training bases, and auxiliary services. There were no battles in Palestine; the fighting was all on the periphery. Thus Palestine fed the war machine with supplies, industry, agricultural production, and services. Extensive crops were planted; factories were set up or enlarged. Jews and Arabs shared the prosperity, also called the war effort, and enjoyed as well a kind of peace that came along with it. The Holy City became a military and administrative center second in the region only to Cairo, and when Rommel stood at the gates of Egypt, Jerusalem became the primary center. Generals came and went, as did heads of state and flocks of foreign journalists. Exiled or deposed royal families, including Haile Selassie, emperor of Ethiopia, sought refuge in Jerusalem. Princess Irene of the Greek royal family lived in the Talbieh quarter, in the home of the psychologist Max Eitingon, who had escaped from Vienna. King Faisal of Iraq often visited from Haifa. Exiled government leaders—from Poland, Yugoslavia, Greece—came to Jerusalem together with officers of their defeated armies and compatriot refugees. Josephine Baker came from Beirut to sing for the Free French Forces; the generals of the Free French came as well. Wealthy Egyptians came, members of the royal family. Masses of soldiers came and left, and an array of unusual people with unusual jobs. Steven Runciman was sent from Cairo to engage in psychological warfare. He rented a big house near Herod's gate—where Judah Magnes, founder of Hebrew University, once lived, as did St. John Philby, the scholar and adventurer—and there continued his monumental work on the Crusades.

In the Jewish neighborhoods, particularly Rehavia, Jews from Germany and Austria found refuge and there preserved the life from which they had been uprooted, keeping largely to themselves. But there was a small group of well-educated and elitist young Arabs and English who were distinctly Arab nationalist and anti-Zionist, and they too were part of Jerusalem in those days.

No Jew I had spoken with had mentioned Wolfgang Hildesheimer, but his name had come up more than once when I met in England with Arabs and Englishmen, a number of them Oxford or Cambridge graduates, all with a common past in the Jerusalem of the Forties. They were the heart of the cosmopolitan community that had developed during those tranquil years. The war raged around them then; later they went their separate ways to various parts of the world, as academics or in the world of literature, of journalism, or of service to the Commonwealth. Several of them met one another quite often, on occasions like weddings or book publications or anniversaries—all sent regards to one another through me—a kind of Anglo-Arab circle whose members still live in the shadow of the great change of 1948. Wolfgang Hildesheimer was the only Jew among them. He, too, left the country when the group began to disperse. In 1947 he went to England, and from there back to Germany, the country of his birth. Over the years he had become a playwright and author.

I tried to discover his whereabouts, but no one could tell me for certain. Robert Steffens, who sent dispatches to the *Observer* from Jerusalem, mentioned a little village in the Alps, close to a border, but he wasn't sure whether it was in Switzerland or in Germany.

Someone suggested phoning his publisher, since his books had been translated into English, including a widely read volume on Mozart. I continued to ask about Hildesheimer. I was interested in him not as a representative of a period or a group, but rather as someone who had lived outside Jewish society, apparently indifferent to its goal—settlement of the land—and seemed to have had little enthusiasm for its unique qualities. Hildesheimer was an outsider, so they told me, and I heard of no one else like him. I had heard about Jews who became "Anglicized," often employees of the administration or institutions of the Mandate, or with business connections to the British. They often felt guilty about these ties, and usually paid some price for their dual loyalty.

Then I met Christopher Holme, who had been the head of the Information Office in Jerusalem during the Second World War. "It was a kind of Orient," he remarked about Jerusalem, "but it was also very European. If I'd been a bridge player, I could have played bridge. I didn't know Hebrew, but one language I did learn in Jerusalem was mathematics. This was the greatest escape. I lived in an Arab house on the edge of the Old City. One could hear tremendous ringing of church bells, and people called to prayer every morning. You could call it Levant or use any historical term you like for this marvelous assortment of little centers from the old civilized world, and then there were the Jerusalemites with whom I could speak German, people who knew the music and painting I knew, people who'd had the sort of life I had."

When I asked him whether he knew Hildesheimer, he replied that they had worked together at the Information Office and were still friends. He gave me his address, and I wrote to Hildesheimer asking for an interview. A short time later I received a reply in a large, clear hand that he would be happy to see me, but since he wasn't planning to be in London in the coming months, perhaps I would like to visit him.

Some time later, just before the end of winter, I boarded in Zurich, along with groups of skiers, the direct train to St. Moritz, but I left the train midway and boarded a second. The number of skiers had dwindled. I changed again to a small mountain train. Only a few passengers remained, most of them villagers speaking Italian with a Swiss dialect. The train climbed slowly among the huge slopes of soft, sunless white. Suddenly these were vast, stark mountains—no longer ski slopes. From time to time we pulled into stations that were little more than a sign, the track, and a narrow platform. The train climbed slowly through fog interspersed with flashes of valley, mountain, or winter trees in brown and black.

Hildesheimer was waiting for me in the station of the little village. His appearance surprised me for some reason. Perhaps I'd had in mind those thin, spiritual German Jews, or his tall, refined friend, Christopher Holme? I was met by a man of medium height, solid, who clearly worked with his hands. He was wrapped in a duffle coat; there was something bulky in his manner and his movements. Beyond the thick lenses of his glasses were blue eyes.

With the townspeople in a local restaurant he spoke Italian. He addressed his wife from time to time in German, and with me he spoke good English with a marked German accent. I did not ask whether he spoke Hebrew. I had the feeling that even if he did, he preferred to speak with me in a language that was neither his nor mine.

"I first came to Palestine in 1933," he began when we returned to his home after dinner. His wife left, and we remained in the spacious living room. "My father was an early Zionist, of course, one of the generation of Pinchas Rosen. He represented a large British chemical concern in Jerusalem, and I learned carpentry and furniture-making there in a French workshop for three years." I did not ask him why he had chosen to be an apprentice carpenter, if there had been some Zionist influence, with its belief in manual labor. He did not really speak to me, but rather to the tape recorder, as though he were dispensing well-rehearsed details. He had returned to England and studied at a school for the arts there, and with the outbreak of the war returned to Palestine. [He must have been a man in his late twenties then, I calculated. Earlier he'd mentioned a recent large celebration for his seventieth birthday.] He had been an English teacher at the British Council in Tel Aviv, and then worked in the Information Office in Jerusalem.

"I moved in entirely Arab circles," he continued. "Did you speak Arabic?" I asked. "No, no," he protested, "we spoke English, of course. "How do you explain the fact that your great friends were Arabs?" I asked him. "I'd have to think about it," he answered, looking very serious, as if taken by surprise. "Jewish intellectuality was something else, of course. There was the university, and of course there were the scientists, and there was Jewish poetry and Jewish literature. Music was Jewish; I don't think in fact that people of this circle were interested in meeting only other Jews. They were international."

I questioned what he meant by "international," and he raised his eyes from the tape recorder, as if he'd been cut off from his narrative: "When I come to think of it, there was no one with whom I could discuss Joyce or Kafka." I suggested Gershom Scholem or Martin Buber.

"Scholem was another generation, he was a good friend of my parents. I might have discussed Kafka with him, if we were contemporaries, but not Joyce or Surrealism. I was an ardent Surrealist in those days. When I wrote Surrealist letters to an English friend, I was called to the censor. He told me, 'I have a certain understanding for this post-Impressionist style, but you'd hardly find anyone else who has, and I can't pass your letters,' which was probably right."

He spoke slowly, perhaps straining to recall those remote days, sitting now in the large central room of a beautiful house on the outskirts of Poschiavo, in the shadow of the majestic mountains. The high ceiling had disappeared in the darkness, the walls were paneled in old carved wood. A great silence surrounded us, a silence of night enshrouded in snow in a small place.

"It was a period when outer life was concerned with the future, but in our private life we never thought about it. I don't remember whether we spoke about what we did, I didn't really know what I was going to do. If anybody had said to me that I would become a writer, I would have laughed. I went to England in 1947, and then to Germany as a member of the occupation forces. I was a simultaneous translator at the Nuremberg Trials and stayed in Germany. It was very difficult at first and I moved to the country, in Bavaria, where I began to draw and to paint. My Arab friends from Jerusalem came to see me in Bavaria. We never talked about what had happened in 1948."

"Did you talk politics when you were in Jerusalem?" I asked. Hildesheimer answered: "We must have. It didn't interest me, didn't touch me. Even now I find myself absolutely impartial. I can't say that I am for Israel or for the Arabs. My father always said it was a question of right against right, and he belonged to the German Zionists who fought for a national home, but not for a Jewish state. It was a problem and still is. The only thing that embitters me a little is that people speak about 'Palestinians.' There are three hundred thousand Palestinians in Lebanon alone. When they left Palestine there were about eighty thousand, and they are still allowed to call themselves Palestinians? This is quite absurd. Until what generation will they be Palestinians? I had a certain sympathy with Golda Meir when she said, 'I'm a Palestinian.' When I went to England to study I was a Palestinian."

"How did you see the Zionists at the time?" I asked him. "How would you describe them?" And he answered: "I had nothing in common with them." Why is he so evasive, I thought, after forty years? I said: "You were quite a freak." "Yes," he agreed, rather seriously, "I suppose I was. There were few Jews like myself. I don't know. It was not a way of showing off. It was really that a Palestinian Jew at that time had to be less individually minded than I was.

"I was never a Zionist," he continued. "Zionism didn't fit into my system, and I couldn't make up my mind to learn Hebrew academically. I managed to speak Hebrew when I worked in the carpentry shop in the Thirties. I spoke badly, hardly ever read the language." During the Thirties he had also been a member of the Hagana. He said it in an offhand manner.

"We were trained in a village between Jerusalem and Haifa, and I remember one night we were in the mountains, six of us. The night watch was divided, and I was woken up to guard for two hours with my rifle. I fell asleep, and when I woke up it was seven. I wasn't really capable of these things. My career in the Hagana was not very heroic." He gave a hint of a smile.

"Did you feel like an exile in Palestine?" I asked. He thought for a moment, and said: "Well, yes, but to an artist these things do not really apply. You don't think in nationalities, you are extraterritorial in a way. I think the happier moments were parties together with friends, when you forgot where you were.

"It was a period you remembered because it was so unusual. Outer life and inner life were so entirely different, a musical score with several systems that never got together." He went on, looking for appropriate words, cultivated, yet ducking the unclear, the unstated.

"It is possible that Jerusalem might have bred a certain view of life, in all of us. Jerusalem was a place where one felt time pass. You must remember that the Arabs I was friendly with were pro-Arab, of course, but they had no Arab friends. They felt more themselves in my company and in that of our English friends than they felt among the Arabs." Was that really so? I wondered. To them he was a friend who accepted them unconditionally, but they were political people who accepted him on condition that he remain apolitical.

"I don't know how it looks now," he said, "but the atmosphere was amazing, and the bar, especially the bar of the King David, was something absolutely magnificent. It didn't have the glamour of the great places in the world, but it was unique, a center of intellectual small talk. To think that the English would have governed a country like Palestine, where half the population was as civilized as the Jews, German immigrants who would never have left Germany, who came to Palestine because Palestine was the only place they could come, who gave parties where Goethe or Matthias Claudius or the German Romantics were read. It was unique. It was the Near East, not Europe anymore. It was a civilized world in danger."

It was late, and I asked whether he didn't want to stop. He raised his eyes from the tape recorder. His expression had changed. There was a flash of unexpected feeling, and he said: "I remember an evening at some Arab friends' house in Jerusalem, where I gave a poetry recital. I don't know whether there was another place in Jerusalem in which it would have been possible to read one's works not in Hebrew."

His blue eyes looking steadily at me from behind the thick glasses: "It's about time we admitted that these people, especially the Arabs I mixed with, dreamed of a cosmopolitan way of life, which the Jews did not. The Jews had Zionist ideas. The Arabs were in Palestine anyway. It was not their primary aim to create a Palestine and to make something of the country. There was no member of the Jewish community who could have shared that feeling."

Is that really the way it was, that no one could be found in Jewish society to share this existence with him, I asked myself that night in my room, in the great silence, between the regular pealing of church bells. Was it possible in those days to give up the idea of a shared fate?

Back in Israel, I went to see Lotte Geiger, a woman in her late sixties with smiling, curious eyes. She came to Palestine from an assimilated Jewish family in Berlin in 1933, worked for the Mandatory Administration, and had many English friends. "I came as a non-Zionist to a land I didn't know," she told me one summer evening in her flat in Jerusalem's Talpiot quarter. "I didn't know a soul, but I saw that here you could leave your suitcase in the street and still find it a few hours later. You could leave your door open. You walked down the street on Friday night and you heard music and you could just walk in. It was a classless society. For someone coming from Germany, where classes were no less than in England, that was the challenge, the vision. I was very enthusiastic about that. I even was silly enough to write my sister in Germany that everything was going to be wonderful here, so long as they didn't let others in, so that those who were here could find their feet." She spoke in a lively manner, in fluent Hebrew with a slight German accent. "I had complete faith in Brit Shalom, the coexistence, the binational movement. I was eighteen, and I thought that it would have to go slowly, but that this was the right direction."

Like many Jews of German culture, Geiger felt a greater affinity with the English, who were part of Western culture, than with the mainly Eastern European Yishuv, which they considered inferior. "The Jews of Eastern Europe had always been alienated from the ruling powers," she said. "Those from Western Europe were another story altogether. " She had worked in the Mandatory Administration as an assistant to the head of the Public Works Department. "That was a high position for a native; I had control of the safe and their secrets. I also stole all their geologic maps."

She had many friends among the British and also the Arabs, but her most intimate friends were German Jews, and the intellectual life of Jews in Jerusalem attracted her.

"You had the feeling you were in a cultural center. Life was less mundane, more spiritual. At that time, before El Alamein, wherever you went, to a café or someone's home, people talked about important things—how the war was going, what you could expect of the future. There was a sense of relief that there was no war here, and no riots and no troubles. Every day we were grateful that it was quiet. People went to Café Vienna to play chess and to Café Europe on Ben Yehuda Street, a big café, with a garden and palms and waiters dressed as waiters ought to be, with music in the afternoon. That's where the Arabs sat, and lots of Jews, of course, and British, too. It was a meeting place. And there was a café on Gaza Road that I loved going to. Jewish writers would be there and they would really talk, not just about what was happening that day, but everything, mainly about literature. They spoke only Hebrew."

I also spoke with Michal Zmora-Cohen, a musicologist, daughter of Moshe Zmora, the prominent lawyer. "We had a very big house on Ben Maimon Boulevard in Rehavia, she told me, it was an open house, always crowded with people from Yishuv circles and German Jews, both those who had come to Palestine early, like my father, and those who came later with the rise of Hitler. There was always something, someone lectured or someone played music, or there was a concert of newly arrived records. If you weren't invited, you came at any hour of the day or night. You were always welcome, you could always sleep there. There were no hotels at the time, there was no such thing as going to a hotel. There weren't many telephones, you rang the bell and there you were. As a result there were all kinds of friendships and love affairs and betrayals. You felt that life was being lived to the fullest, the full measure. My mother was from Russia. My father and my uncle, Blumenfeld and Scholem, they all married Russian women, who were much gentler than the German women, more romantic. My father was very sentimental, the Russians pitched into that feeling, he loved it."

She continued: "At home they spoke German and not Russian, because Father didn't speak Russian. My father's culture was German, though he had wonderful Hebrew even before he got here. I speak German perfectly even though I've spent only two weeks in Germany, I know Schiller and Heine and Goethe by heart. For him that was the epitome of expression. He didn't read Russian and he didn't know Tolstoy. He read German, there was nothing like Goethe's poetry for him. He died with that book in his hand, but he took his cues from those Russians who were definitely lower-middle-class people who drank tea from a glass. They were the model."

"I remember three or four kibbutzim," said Albert Hourani, "especially Ein Gev, where I spent a few days as the guest of Teddy Kollek. I remember how physically exhausted everyone seemed to be—it was summer, and very hot—and how preoccupied and not very willing to talk. Perhaps they were tired, or perhaps few of them spoke English or Arabic. But perhaps they were engaged in an enterprise in which the outside world was irrelevant. I got the sharp feeling that they were deliberately turning their backs on that world, and on their own past, to create something new. I found this both admirable and frightening."

In Jerusalem, though he was not a native, Hourani felt he understood most of the various neighborhoods of the city. But as he walked through Jewish quarters, he had the feeling that they were now impenetrable: "The Jews withdrew into themselves—a community talking to itself. They had intellectual intensity that was frightening for those who did not share it. Another breed altogether. As if they were a secret society."

The King David had been the refuge of Hourani and his friends. I thought about this one spring day, as I arrived at the hotel. It was afternoon; there was a good breeze and iridescent light on the pink stone, at the time of year when usually many tourists descend on the city. This year, because of the uprising in the territories, tourists hadn't come. The doorman stood in a corner, arms crossed over his uniform, lulled by the slow day, not even bothering to push the revolving door for me. The lobby was empty. Only the friend I was meeting awaited me in one of the large armchairs with the golden hoops, designed in the imaginary style of the biblical kings. Opposite, in a straight, dramatic line, was the large, central window that looked out onto the Old City. A heavy curtain had been drawn theatrically to the sides. As I advanced into that famous lobby, the reception clerks, passing the time, followed me with their eyes.

I sat in a corner and no one approached—no hostess, no waiter. From outside came the faint sound of a piano. Afternoon music was being played on the balcony. A number of guests were sitting out there. It was a good point from which to survey the hall. The color of the pillar reliefs was intense, as were the turquoise and gold of the high corniced ceiling, and between cornices, squares of glass discreetly covering fluorescent lights. The wood on the armchairs gleamed. The multicolored marble floor was polished. So it had looked back then, I thought. I went out to the balcony that overlooks the garden and the Old City wall. The pianist was still playing. Here and there people sitting around. A group of English with a good-looking blonde woman.

The tabletops were white plastic. The thick cups bore a "Dan Hotels" stamp. The wind ruffled the poplar trees that blocked the view of the Old City wall, planted after the Forties. But the tall, elegant Washingtonia palms had been here then, and they now reached tremendous heights. The pianist was playing Israeli tunes, the kind you might hear in an El Al plane before takeoff. Toward dusk, the lights went on at the edge of the balcony, brilliant in the clear, darkening sky. I walked through the lobby past the new bar, which was empty, and then down two floors to the grill room, La Régence. Rachel Eliachar had said of the grill room: "It was the only place I liked. Even today when I'm invited out, I want to go to La Régence." Near here must have been the old bar, I thought. The doors were already open and I asked a waiter, an older man, where the bar had been. He explained that the bar was still the same bar.

I returned to the empty bar. Not even the barman was there. And I thought of the description of the bar by the journalist Gabriel Zifroni, a *Daily Telegraph* correspondent at the time: "At eleven-thirty the barman, François, was already on duty, and between twelve and a quarter to two you could meet people from all corners of the empire who had found their way here. The King David Hotel was the gathering place between the Atlantic and the Indian Oceans. This one came from London and that one from Calcutta and another one from Chongqing. Farouk's mother—where did I meet her? In Egypt I couldn't have met her, or her younger sister, Farida. When the British asked, 'Gaby, where were you born?' I used to say, 'Born in Tel Aviv. Educated in the King David.' "

On the other side of the corridor, beyond the bar, was the doorway to a conference room—a long golden table down the middle of it. Here everything remained almost as it had been. I sat down in a corner. Nearby was a large, closed fireplace: on its marble mantle, a bronze bust of Moshe Dayan that seemed in place. I thought of the Old City, the heart of this place, so many thousands of years old, and of Jerusalem even before the Old City, the stone plateau of the Temple Mount and now the mosques—the primordial Jerusalem, as the author Soraya Antonius, daughter of historian George Antonius and Katy Antonius, wrote in her book *Where the Jinn Consult*:

"Perhaps this Jerusalem, before the first, sprang only from its sitting on the shallow platform straddling the watershed between the Mediterranean and the Asian plateau. But it is the one place in the world where this platform—so small and insignificant—appears. Perhaps this is what the Neolithic tribesmen were describing when they first called the low rocky site cupped by its hills the navel of the world. But then how did they know? They hadn't travelled—how did they know there was no site like it in, say, Turkey? Or hidden in some fold of the ante-Lebanon, several days' planning away from them? As it has turned out, even the satellites have proved them right. There isn't another configuration with its great sloping rock like it anywhere else, even in the desert, which is strange when everything seems to be repeated, somewhere or other, nature evidently abhoring singularity as much as emptiness."

It occurred to me that the British, too, set up their Mandatory rule like a huge tent over the Temple Mount and the Old City and its surrounding neighborhoods. And in that tent, during those years, everyone accepted the existing order, with a sort of tolerance that Jerusalem had never really known before. Knives were not put down; they simply were not sharpened. Zealotry, hatred, conflict did not disappear, but in the meantime there was a kind of acceptance of one's fellow man, of one's rival, of the foreign and the different. There was a temporary respite, and Arabs and British and Jews lived quietly among themselves and with one another. Struggles were deferred while the labor of a bigger war was carried out. An entire wing of the King David was taken over to house the military and civilian administrations. Officers and officials who worked there were served by the same tall Nubians decked out in white robes who served high-ranking guests and short-term visitors and members of the three large groups—British, Arabs, and Jews—who went about their ordinary lives, the way the people of any cosmopolitan city go about theirs.

But it was the British who were allowed to rule. They did their job with great dedication. They kept mostly to themselves, often meeting at the Sports Club in the German Colony. English women gathered there in the afternoons, they played tennis there and met for cocktails. It was for the British only, as was the custom throughout the empire. But the British, even those not greatly involved in the life of the city, felt that Jerusalem was different. I recalled something the writer Taqui Altounian-Stephens, who came to Jerusalem from Aleppo, had said to me: "When I tell my children about a friend they say, 'I suppose you met him in Jerusalem.' It's true. You made very good friends in Jerusalem.

There were so many parties, and they were different from parties anywhere else. The setting was extraordinary. We had strange parties on the roof of the Monastery of the Cross [Golgotha]. We had moonlight parties on the walls of the Old City. We went to concerts on Mount Scopus, at the university, overlooking the Dead Sea."

Whenever I talked to people about Jerusalem, the name Katy Antonius came up. She had a regular table at the King David where she entertained her English and Arab friends, the regulars of her salon. "I was among the few Jews who went to Katy Antonius,' " said Zifroni, the *Daily Telegraph* journalist. "It was a political salon in the home of the mufti, which she was renting. That was the place to hear the latest Arab propaganda. Anytime a new British commander arrived, he would be invited first of all to Katy's. She was from the Nimr family, Lebanese, owners of *al-Muqattam*, the influential newspaper in Cairo, and she married George Antonius."

"Her house was not primarily a political salon," remarked Hourani. "It had been so when George Antonius was alive, but when he died she could not keep it so. She did not know any of the Palestinian Arab leaders well except Musa Alami, and they may have regarded her as not being wholly discreet, and as not knowing enough about politics to be drawn into their confidence. She loved entertaining for its own sake, and did it very well. The house was full of beautiful objects. The food and drink were always excellent. Conversation was mainly in English and French, there was a lot of music and dancing, it was all high-spirited, innocent, and very detached from the realities of Palestine and the world, and somehow old-fashioned, an echo of London or Paris in earlier days. She had a gift of finding and attracting men and women of taste and intelligence, bringing out the best in them. But by the time I knew her, very few Jews except those who were rather detached from the Yishuv.

"Jerusalem was a small town," he said, "with small-town intellectuals, with small-town politics. You saw the same people. It was a special place for only a limited number, for that group that gathered there due to the war and the circumstances of those years of fragile tranquility. I had no doubt that it would end in tragedy. For us, Jerusalem was a dream. It was too good to go on."

CHAPTER SIX

"We were never airborne in Palestine"

After the Second World War, the Jewish Resistance Movement was founded to oppose the British rule in Palestine. It was a common framework for the three underground movements: the Hagana, the Irgun, and Lehi. To fight its terror and sabotage activities, the 6th Airborne Division, one of the elite units of the British Army, was brought in from Gaza. The division soldiers were not paratroopers but landed in special gliders, towed by bombers to their destination into enemy territory. The division took part in the great battles of Allies in Europe—the Invasion of Normandy, the Battle of the Bulge—crossing over the Rhine into Germany and suffering heavy casualties.

They fought no battles in Palestine, but took part in large-scale operations against the Jewish inhabitants. They searched houses, put a siege to cities and villages, looking for arms and suspects, controlled curfews, removed by force Jewish refugees from incoming ships, and were called in to face enraged crowds, using bayonets and sometimes firearms. Most of them hated their duties, but they fulfilled them with dedication. The actions of the Jewish underground organizations escalated, and the confrontations became fiercer. As the soldiers of the division wore paratroopers' red berets, they were nicknamed calaniot (anemones) by the Jews as a gesture of derision.

"We had been through a war, we had finished a war, we were preparing to go to Japan, but then Japan collapsed. So, thank God, war was finished. We didn't want any more war. We didn't want to shoot at anything. Suddenly we were told to go to Palestine, and then we found that we had to be armed again."

Colonel John Tillett, retired career officer, was a company commander in the 6th Airborne Division, sent to Palestine in 1945 to deal with a Jewish population rising in rebellion. By the armchair in which he sat were two canes he used for walking. The canes and his lameness emphasized his height and his sturdy build. Strong features, jaw firm but the mouth relaxed, a collected look behind his glasses:

"We were glider troops in the war, we were the Red Berets. We did two major air landings during the Second World War: one in Normandy, where didn't have too many casualties. The second major air landing was in Germany over the Rhine, where we had half the battalion casualties." He stopped, awaiting my next question. Cautious and reserved, he preferred waiting until I asked, so that he could deliver carefully considered answers. Both he and I knew that sooner or later we would get to the difficult question: the Red Berets, after all, were the soldiers most hated by the Jews living in Palestine.

"One was proud to be in the Airborne Division?" I asked.
"Very much," said Tillett. "The Red Beret was something to be valued. We were allowed to select our soldiers and officers on the strength of their mental and physical capabilities. We had many volunteers and many we rejected.

"While in Palestine," he continued, "we were taken out of the Airborne Division after six to nine months. We were almost in tears. Glider battalions were given up because they were very costly in men and matériel. They only retained parachutists. We joined a normal infantry division that did exactly the same work in Palestine as anybody else; we were never airborne in Palestine, we just did ordinary 'internal security,' as we called it, in support of the police."

On the table at his side were an open file, a notebook, and various documents. Tillett had come prepared to this interview, which took place at the London flat where I'd been staying that winter. I too had done groundwork for the meeting. In England procedures are formal and not quick. Letters are always preferable to phone calls, and we had exchanged a number of letters. He had agreed to speak to me only after the widow of a comrade-in-arms, another officer in the Airborne Division, had put in a good word—and even then only after making in-depth inquiries regarding the purpose of the book. All my other formal requests, to the units themselves or to the veterans' association, had been turned down.

"When we first arrived in Haifa, we went down to Gaza. Occasionally someone would blow up a bit of a railway line—nothing very much—and we didn't go about armed. Way down in the south nothing happened but flies." He summed up the scene drily, as if intending no irony about the peaceful, simple south—sea, sand, Mediterranean flies—versus the complex north: European and dangerous. "Then we moved to Tel Aviv. But the first year, I would say, things were fairly peaceful. Early in 1946 I would go down with friends to Tel Aviv to have a meal in a Jewish restaurant. I have a feeling we went armed, but we were pretty free. We were trying to get down to peacetime, really.

"I was in Kfar Vitkin in February 1946, and we were attacked by a gang of Jewish terrorists," he went on. "I think they were the Irgun. We were attacked at night. I got a platoon of my soldiers and sent them to counterattack, as we called it, but I read in my history book here"—he resorted to a file he had brought with him—"'Lieutenant Andrews went off with his platoon in entirely the wrong direction.' So we didn't find the terrorists. On part of the perimeter wire there was an orange grove that led right up to the wire. Here was where the raiding party got in. The next two days we had a bulldozer and bulldozed away that orange grove, and I can remember the farmer being in tears at that."

"You were sent to a place where people were not too friendly toward you to begin with and became more and more hostile," I remarked, and he repeated slowly: "Became more and more hostile. But never, I mean, we didn't have sympathies. Some may have had. We weren't pro-Arab or pro-Jew. We were doing what we were told to do and we didn't like doing it." "Was it difficult to do?" I wanted to know. "No, we were soldiers," he answered. The voice was clear, with a modulated accent no longer popular in an England that is trying to eliminate class distinctions. That voice was coming to life. "Did you talk about it with other officers?" I went on, and he said with a slight smile, "Not much. We were busy with peacetime activities. It was a job to be done."

"How did you spend your time?" I asked after a silence. "We did a lot of training," he replied dutifully. "We did a lot of shooting on ranges, we did a lot of sports and games. I might have one platoon of thirty men manning a roadblock on the main road from Tel Aviv to Haifa, and their job would be stopping vehicles and checking for passes. I might have another platoon in Haifa guarding, say, Barclays Bank, and then I would get an order to go to a settlement somewhere. There were many emergency cases, and we always had one platoon fully dressed and ready to leave. They were named the Lightning Platoon.

"In later stages we had three hundred men of the battalion on duty every night, every day," he explained. "We were called in when required by the Palestine Police to cordon areas, to disperse crowds, to guard roads, searching constantly for members of the Palmach or the Hagana or the Irgun, and searching for arms and ammunition."

After a moment he added: "The worst of our period was in Atlit, because that was a clearance camp for illegal immigrants. There were Jews behind wire, and we were the guards. Atlit was a nice location, and it was lovely to go for a swim in the sea, but to see these poor people, whom we knew suffered so much, to see them put behind wire was ghastly." "Why?" I asked, and he replied, "Because I with my company had actually liberated a concentration camp in Germany, and I had seen what had happened there, and then to see so many Jews coming to Palestine and having to turn them away, arrest them. I thought it was ghastly, but that was government policy, and therefore we had our duty, and we did it.

"It was an individual feeling, I suppose, but I know that quite a lot of my friends felt the same. We did have to carry people off boats in Haifa harbor, because they wouldn't come off. We had to force them at times. We had to guard the place, make sure that no one broke out. We also had to make sure that our soldiers didn't break in, particularly to the women's quarters, because they had been offered all sorts of bribes to let people out. Those women were desperate." He was speaking in the same formal manner, still enclosed in his military shell. He was not apologizing, but bringing to my attention another set of facts, as if to say, aside from your version of things there is our version, which includes our difficulties and our honor.

"Didn't it bring up questions about the whole business?" I wondered. "I'm sure it did," he agreed. "But we tried to ignore them, we tried to go on with our job, do what we were told to do. We were soldiers. I do remember wondering when, for goodness sake, would the British government take us out of it," said Tillett. "It was a question of getting out; it was not a question of 'Are we leaving it to the Jews or to the Arabs?' We didn't care, I don't think. It was their affair. It was not our problem. Our problem was to make sure that no one shot us or anyone else. It was nasty, at least for those of us who had been in the war. The young soldiers didn't understand.

"It was those things in the middle of 1946 that made the whole situation change from being really a peacetime situation, as it were, to much more of a wartime situation," he went on. "After that we had to go out armed, two vehicles always had to go together, we were not allowed to go into the city except in groups of at least four people. And we had to watch our backs a bit. But even so," he added, smiling, "we still went on playing cricket. We still would go to cafés. I suppose in Jerusalem we might chose an Arab café."

"Was it difficult not to feel bitter toward the Jews?" I asked. "If my brother officer or soldier had been killed, I would have felt bitter," he answered. "I, personally, was never shot at, and my battalion had only four casualties in two years—one killed and three slightly injured. No, there was not a bitter feeling except when eight soldiers were killed in Tel Aviv in a parking place. Or another time when two sergeants were hanged near Netanya. We were near Netanya at the time. It was Camp 22 nearby, and it was very difficult. It took a lot of discipline to hold our soldiers in camp. Some of the battalions did break out to go and smash places up. Not in my battalion, because the officers kept going around the soldiers saying, 'You damn well stay here.' They were bitter, naturally. I had no great bitterness.

"I remember we found arms in a potash factory down in Jericho," he continued. "And I remember our commanding brigadier, who was very tall, calling the manager of the potash factory, who was very short, and saying, 'Naughty little Jew man, you have been hiding weapons.' And then we went to a kibbutz just outside Jerusalem and my company did a search there. We did a lot of searching of settlements. Half the troops would form a cordon, the rest would go in and search, separate the women from the men. It was fairly late on, and we had our little search, and then the *mukhtar*, the Jewish organizer, asked whether we join them for lunch in the common dining room—myself and one of my officers. Would one do it? Would one be poisoned? Would one be shot at? I joined him for lunch. I liked him. I took one of my officers with me and had a very nice lunch with them, and a very nice conversation. Would I have done it without my soldiers outside? Probably not at that time, 1946."

Kibbutz members are capable of all sorts of things, but not of poisoning the food served in their communal dining room. I asked him his impressions of the kibbutz, and he answered: "They had a marvelous determination to try and build, and build in every sense of the word, not only the land and the country. For someone who has spent one's life in the army, in an organized society, it seemed marvelous that people could in fact get together and organize themselves and discipline themselves to build up that sort of thing." If he didn't regard them as dauntless savages from some distant corner of the empire, I thought, why did it occur to him that they would put poison in his food?

Was he taking into account what had happened when soldiers from the Airborne Division marched on kibbutzim and searched them? What happened, for instance, on November 26, 1945, during those days Tillett claimed were fairly quiet, when, following a Hagana attack on the radar station at Givat Olga, a great siege was laid to the settlements in Emek Hefer, during which soldiers of the Airborne Division and armored units attacked Kibbutz Givat Haim? Hundreds of people from the surrounding settlements turned out, and with members of the neighboring kibbutz, Ein Hahoresh, they came to the aid of Givat Haim. In the open fields between the two kibbutzim, soldiers of the Airborne dug themselves in, and in heavy automatic fire from one of the positions, five people were killed and about fifteen wounded. All in all, eight were killed and seventy wounded during that siege.

"You, the Airborne, were the most unpopular troops," I said, "and I suppose you knew it." "Yes," he agreed with a broad smile. "Absolutely. We trained to be harder, fitter, tougher, and we had to be. My own battalion was mainly country boys who didn't get very excited." "How was it, finding oneself at the center of hostility?" I asked. "We didn't care," he said. "We in a way wanted the Hagana or the Irgun or the Stern Gang to be frightened of us. The more frightened of us they were, the less likely they were to attack us.

We wanted them to think that we were constantly alert and that if they fired one shot we would fire back. We wanted them to know that. We may have earned the name of animals, but we didn't mind that because with any luck it would stop us being shot at.

"We were doing a dirty job that no soldier would have liked. It was neither one thing nor the other; not battle, not fighting, not peace..." and he stopped. Perhaps it was still difficult for him to switch from the simple state of mind of a soldier reliant on his sense of power to one in which nothing is simple, least of all the use of force. "If you talk today to Israelis," I said, "they will tell you that they were lucky to have the British Army; British soldiers didn't like doing these kinds of things." Tillett said, "Some did." "You always get the odd one," I said, and he remarked, "Some are vicious." He grew silent. For the first time he seemed troubled, and I was going to ask him about something else when he said:

"We cordoned and searched settlements somewhere down the coast. I don't remember where, but it was a big operation. We arrived at dawn and we were part of a cordon, my company, in open country, and other people, military police and special police, went in to search. Our job was to make sure that nobody broke out and nobody broke in. Well, about ten o'clock, I think, a great crowd of Jews from other settlements gathered about one thousand yards from us, and I should think eventually there were about two thousand people, and my company was very stretched out, with one soldier here, one soldier there. I'll always remember it because a man on a white horse assembled the Jewish party and got them all together. The idea was that they were going to break through the cordon and stop the search, a very alarming thing. There were a lot of women and children, and we could see them through binoculars, and although we had our weapons and everything, you know, this is a thing that a soldier in peacetime is very frightened of. You have to make the terrible decision whether to actually shoot at somebody unarmed, and that is not nice. And he got them all marshaled up in a great sort of phalanx, I remember, and they started to advance toward us."

Uncharacteristically, Tillett talked at length, still involved in the event so deeply etched in his memory—a man on a white horse rallying masses of Jews against them—until finally, so he explained, the soldiers had heaved smoke grenades at them, and there was great confusion and most of the crowd dispersed: "But the small group that did get through the smoke in an organized manner had a lot of women and children, which we didn't very much like because they were in the front. My fellow company commander on my right, he had the job of stopping them, and there were probably two hundred. How was he going to do it, since he could not physically lean against them like some English bobby? He decided eventually to fix bayonets and to present a row of steel, saying, if you wish to walk into that row of steel, that is your problem. Had that group advanced, we would have had to let them through, unless somebody fired at us, but we wouldn't fire at women and children. They in fact dispersed."

I asked him whether he remembered when it happened, and he replied that he didn't know exactly, as forty years had passed, but that it was at a later stage, apparently in 1945, when the struggle had turned fiercer; from among the photos in his file he chose one—a small one, like all the photos from that period, and unfocused. It showed a flat expanse, sand or fields, soldiers here and there, their backs to the camera, and he said: "Funnily enough this was that little operation, when I said that a whole lot of Jews formed up with a man on the white horse, and that we happened to take a photograph of it. Way in the distance you can just see them coming toward us."

Captain Hugh Clark—Tillett put us in touch—told me a slightly different version of "that little operation." Clark had been drafted in 1944; he was a religious man who used to meet with a small group at an evangelical church in Jerusalem. In the Forties he returned to civilian life and today works in the finance department of a London construction firm and keeps in touch with his comrades-in-arms. A pleasant, soft-spoken man who told me when I visited him at his home in Surrey:

"There was one particular cordon we had to do regarding some immigrants who had come ashore. I think it was near Hadera. It was fairly near the coast, and again, it wouldn't sound very good for an Airborne soldier to say this, but I found it quite frightening to face a mob. They were a disciplined mob of civilians, slowly advancing toward you, and you are spaced one every five yards, knowing that if they get too near you have got to shoot, and that I found hard. On this particular occasion there was one shot. One of the leaders was a man on a white horse, and something that we did out there that seemed quite brutal. But if it looked like it was getting out of control, we gave a warning that we were going to shoot, and we didn't shoot indiscriminately. We didn't shoot high or low, we shot at the ringleader to kill. That sounds terribly cold-blooded and brutal, but the regulation was that we had to give a warning, and in fact we gave two warnings, and we picked the ringleader."

"The man on the white horse?" I asked. "Whether it was the man on the white horse who got shot that day I don't know, but someone got shot that day. You got to a stage where you had a thin line of troops with perhaps three hundred people moving toward them, and I suppose that in the army wisdom this was the only way to stop them, and, I think, probably it saved lives, because had they got among us there would have been fighting and bloodshed." "Was the ringleader killed that day?" I asked, and Clark answered, "Yes, he was, and after that they pulled back and dispersed."

"Who gave the order to shoot him?" was my next question. "That would be the company commander," was his answer. "Had it been in my sector it would have been my orders. You would have a sniper, someone who was a good shot. You couldn't take the decision lightly because we were under very strict control. Every round of ammunition you used, you had to account for. You couldn't just shoot off indiscriminately. We fired single shots, we didn't use machine guns." "Were the people moving toward you armed?" I asked. "We were never sure of that," he replied. "I don't think they could have been. They might have the odd club. We realized we were shooting unarmed people. But it was not done lightly, because there would have been an inquiry afterward, you had to give a full report." "Did it happen more than once?" I asked. "Not when I was involved," he said. "It probably did happen, yes. But that case was spoken about for a long time afterward—the man on the white horse."

Why had they continued to talk about it for so long? Had something happened there that was not in keeping with orders, something that gave rise to a number of versions attempting to cover up or, alternatively, to explain how it happened? And perhaps they did, after all, follow orders, and killed in cold blood a man who might have been guarding the fields but who seemed to them the ringleader of an organized mob, and who was or wasn't on a white horse—and they were glad that the matter had ended with the death of only one man and that the Jews had returned to their settlements and they, the soldiers, to their camp. Everything was all right, and yet, with time, it had become an incident outside the order of things, a story still haunting about a man on a white horse.

The story was told to me early in 1987. In March 1988, back in Israel, I received a letter from Tillett that read in part as follows: "Hearing the sad news of the disturbances in your country has brought back memories. I hear some pretty stupid, cynical comments from people here who had not had to face unarmed aggressive adversaries. My sympathy goes out to your army having to act in present conditions. In 1947 I was lucky enough to command experienced, highly trained, mature soldiers, and in more than two years we were never forced to open fire with our weapons. But had I been commanding partly trained eighteen-year-olds, the story could have been very different."

Once again he is defending the honor of soldiers, I thought, and he must know very well that this story could have turned out quite differently. He had worked under those same emergency regulations that today are applied only to the Arabs of the occupied territories. Regulations that David Ben-Gurion, Moshe Sharrett, and Dov Yosef had called "Nazi laws" in the Forties. Regulations under which all of Tel Aviv had been put under curfew after the bombing of the King David Hotel by the Irgun in June 1946. The heat was intense at the time, and during the curfew, soldiers of the Airborne Division had broken into a kiosk to get soft drinks.

The matter was brought before the House of Lords and the secretary for the colonies, and they had to apologize.

"At the same time," Tillett added in his letter, "in ignorance of being at this distance, I do feel that Israel has got to do something for her Arab citizens to improve their lot, as long as Israel can maintain her territorial integrity. How very easy for an outsider to say! And coming from a British ex-imperialist it must sound even more strange. But age does mellow one's opinions, I expect.

"I had lunch with Sergeant Major Bill Bailey last week," he wrote in his last paragraph, "and he asked to be remembered to you."

Bill Bailey had arrived one day at the flat where I'd been staying in London. Though he had been working for a long time as the administrative head of a firm of solicitors in Covent Garden, his gaunt face bore evidence of long years in the sun. His face grew animated as he spoke, and he spoke well, with a sprinkling of Cockney here and there, but he kept off the subject of politics or encounters with unarmed crowds, preferring to talk about peacetime, about the bars they used to frequent in Tel Aviv: "The Jewish bars had more in common with continental ones, so those of us who swarmed across Germany or Europe would get the odd two days off and would go to those places, and there were nice ones. You could make a drink last quite a long time. You might be talking to a girl, but that didn't last for long."

After a moment he added with a jovial smile: "I liked Palestine. I have often said that the only place where I served and could have settled comfortably was Palestine. Sometimes in the East, in the tropics, you get some fantastic green, but I always think that the green in Palestine was green as nothing else. It was the combination probably of orange groves and corn or something similar. If I compare my stay there with Kenya or Malaya, the Palestine stay had more in the way of unpleasantness, but I remember bits and pieces about Palestine that I don't remember about Kenya."

I asked him whether any of those "bits and pieces" came to mind, and he said, "Well, I suppose it was the aftermath of the King David Hotel bombing, when I was absolutely furious. Captain Clark took me in the old jeep and rode off to one of the hills. I was furious, and there was nothing I could do about it." There was a moment of silence, and then I asked how he had been affected by the prolonged stay in a hostile environment. "It created a sense, I suppose, of aggressiveness. Remember, we were young and fit. And then there was the term *fear*, which Englishmen usually don't like using," he remarked with a sly look.

"Life in Palestine was quite pleasant at the beginning," he went on. "It was peaceful. No doubt there were undercurrents, but you did all the things that the tourists nowadays pay a lot of money to do. You got to the Galilee, to Bethlehem, to Tel Aviv to swim. That was a bit later than when we arrived, but these were still the early days when it was very much the business of doing duties. Generally speaking it was a British battalion being posted and making the best of it.

"Later on if you weren't on duty, you were semi-officially on duty, so you couldn't relax and sing or dance if you wanted to sing or dance. What you could do, you could form a party and drive down to the beach and have a swim, protected by others who were not swimming, you see. And when the weather is warm and the sun is bright, things become a little more menacing, if one can put it that way. That atmosphere is not there during what we would loosely call the winter months. It is a personal feeling, you see. I experienced it in the streets of Jerusalem and later in one or two places in Tel Aviv, and later still in Nicosia. An atmosphere slightly menacing, especially in Jerusalem.

"And when things happen that way, I don't know why, but I always think why things are so damned awful, and it always seems slightly worse than on a miserable winter day. Somehow it became more oppressive with the heat and the sunshine, and usually it is quite calm at that time of the day, most people resting. I haven't discussed it with anybody else, so I don't know what their feeling would be, but to me it seemed to be part and parcel of what was going on: the heat, the sunshine, those dark shadows under the wall. It is an atmosphere that I did not find unbearable, but I used to think, 'This is a sort of afternoon when something is going to happen.'"

Baron Martin Charteris, head of British Military Intelligence in Palestine in the years 1945–46, felt no menace. When I met him in his London office, overlooking Westminster Abbey, I thought I would meet an old and distinguished gentleman—the former secretary to the queen, the provost of Eton—but the man who sat near me in an armchair was agile, his speech was fluent, and his eyes were curious and a bit mischievous, as if he did not take the subject seriously. He said: "In Jerusalem I stayed for eighteen months, and I felt as if I were at the center of the world. It was in fact a small place. A large problem in a small place. But I think that for me these were wonderful days, really exciting days, and I was friendly with both sides. I was really in the midst of it.

"There were lots of parties in Jerusalem, and everybody always talked politics," he continued, "always about what was going to happen, what we have to do about Palestine, about new ways to solve the problem. They were not interested in anything except for the Palestine question. In a certain way the Arabs belonged there more then the Jews. Most of the Jews came from outside, not so?" He opened a small box, snuffed some tobacco, and closed it delicately. There was something abrupt in his movements, something that did not fit with his light manner. "The Jews were united in their passion to return to Palestine, something pushed them there. I think that the Jews are really different from any other nation. They excel in debate, isn't that so?" He laughed. "They can never understand the other side's point of view, only their own. And how are they now?" "Most of them are still like that," I said, after some hesitation. "Sticking to their opinions," he agreed with a smile, as if dealing with stubborn children. "Did the Arabs seem to you as extreme?" I asked. "I wouldn't say so," he answered, "certainly not people like Musa Alami or Albert Hourani. Those I met were highly intelligent and they found themselves helpless facing the torrent of Jews who had flooded the place they thought was theirs. I had lots of love for them, and at the same time I identified with the ambitions of the Jews. A problem without any solution, of course."

I did not ask him why he thought there was no solution, and he did not go on. But this avoidance, this silence, made the problem more acute: a dispute that started in those distant days when it still seemed that there were various possible solutions, and when everybody was still sheltering under the wings of the Mandate, and when Charteris brought the manager of the King David Hotel some eggs for a wedding cake, and for his honeymoon went to Tel Mond, where there was a large ranch raising cattle and sheep, and he and his young wife would go riding in the orchards of the Sharon.

"Was it difficult to remain impartial?" I asked. "No, I don't think so, both sides were fascinating," Charteris answered. "Most of our actions were, of course, against the Jews. They fought us, as you know. For me being impartial was not very difficult, but I think it was extremely difficult for others. I think most of them were against the Jews, against the idea of a Jewish state, and some of them were even, in fact, anti-Semitic."

And he started telling me about his friendship with Chaim Weizmann, who was an intimate friend of Lord Balfour, who was, in turn, an intimate friend of his own family. "Weizmann was a wonderful conversationalist. He hated violence. He knew how to use it but preferred to get his demands by negotiation, with the help of personal charm, convincing arguments, even bribery, and not through murder. He used me as a mailman to transmit his messages to the government." It was as if he were emphasizing that impartiality for the British was not only the basis of proper rule, proper colonial rule, but a value in itself.

"Did you think, when you retired at the end of 1946, that the British would leave?" I asked. "I can't remember what I really thought. On principle I am for the partition plan," he said, as if the partition were still a subject for debate. "I thought we should leave, but at the time I was there I don't remember that it was seriously discussed. Our main occupation, day by day, was to prevent the bombs from exploding and to deal with 'illegal immigration.'"

I knew that the major part of Charteris's work in those days was to find and take over the refugee ships, and I wanted to ask him about what an enlightened man like him thought about the deportation of the Jewish immigrants, but he went on telling me about the enjoyable hours he had spent with Teddy Kollek, who at the time was an intelligence officer for the Jewish Agency. "I must not talk too much about it, for Teddy has his own secrets and I have my own," he said with a smile. "I continued to deal with the problem in London. When I returned I worked in the War Office." And I wondered whether even then, when the War Office decided to deport the ship *Exodus*, he could still maintain his impartiality.

"Though I was not a party to all the details, I went on being interested in the subject," he said. "I don't think I still know any of the personalities involved except for Teddy, who goes on forever, just like me." He laughed a short laugh and asked how Jerusalem is today, since he had never returned. I told him about its new buildings, and he commented, "What was beautiful in Jerusalem was that this was not just a colonial life with tennis and golf. Everybody talked politics with great intensity." I asked him whether that intensity was not in some way the source of the tragedy, for it had no solution. "A tragedy," repeated Charteris, as if suggesting that this is a word one must be careful of. After some thought he added, "I think the tragedy is that it still continues to be so terrible."

We were silent for a moment and he took another sniff from his tobacco box. His thin nostrils widened and suddenly he seemed again that young man, an intelligence officer in a conference room of the King David. "I was not there in that turmoil at the end," he said. "I left just at the right moment." "When you look back at your period in Palestine," I asked him, "how does it look to you now?" "Full of glamour," he answered, as if it were the most natural thing to say. I asked, "Why?" "I don't know. I am a romantic, probably. It was an exciting and romantic period. The Zionist idea, even if you don't agree with it, has a romantic element in it. And at the same time the Arabs, too, are a romantic people." I thought that it would be really nice to be able to look at things that way, but that it's a pity that after all these years only an English gentleman like Lord Charteris can still view them as romantic.

"I think it was an exciting affair, the idea of the return of the Jews to their homeland," he added, and it seemed to me that it was a harsh remark, toward both the Jews who wanted to return to the country and the Arabs on whom this return was forced. Charteris, it appeared, had great enthusiasm for bettering the world and a sense of being a partner to a great adventure, but it was a limited partnership. He always had the option to not take part anymore, to step aside and look at the whole unfinished business from the sidelines. For he who can call the conflagration of Israel an "exciting affair" is not really involved in it. I sensed his sadness, but even so, there was a note of indifference, touching on cruelty, in his words.

CHAPTER SEVEN

"The nuisance value"

Only one Jewish underground organization, the Hagana, was active during the first years of the British Mandate. It was founded in 1920 in order to protect the Jews from Arab attacks. Over the years it became a large premilitary force. It was subject to the instruction of the moderate political leadership of the Yishuv and the Zionist Organization. More extreme groups that wanted to start an armed conflict with the Mandate authorities did not find their place within its framework. In 1931 such a group left the Hagana and founded the Etzel—Irgun Zevai Leumi. During the Thirties, the Etzel opposed both the Mandate rule and the containment policy of the Hagana during the Arab Revolt. Its members attacked Arabs. At the start of the Second World War, the Etzel declared a cease-fire with the British. As a result of this decision, a group splintered off from the Etzel and created the radical Lehi underground movement, which declared war on the British, notwithstanding their fight against the Nazis. Lehi was a small group, many of whom were intellectuals, like their leader Avraham Stern ("Yair"), a scholar and poet. They perpetrated political assassination and hundreds of violent attacks against the British. They were called by the British the Stern Gang and were mercilessly pursued. In 1942, Stern was killed by the British, and Lehi went into hiding until 1944, when its members joined the declaration of revolt by the Etzel and intiated various murderous terror operations. It was in these years that Nahum Nimri, the main character in this chapter, was an active member of Lehi.

"When I came back to Jerusalem in 1946," said James Livingstone, deputy to the head of the British Council in 1946–48, "things became so difficult after a few months that more and more our social life was with people in the British community. At that time I was introduced to something called the Middle East Society of Jerusalem, and it was run by a man called Nimri. He had Arabs and Jews and British on his committee. Lectures were given by prominent people, and he set up competitions for the entire Middle East, including the Sudan, which schoolchildren would be invited to. I wondered why he was doing this, and I thought the Jewish Agency was doing it for good public relations. But after the murder of Count Bernadotte [the UN mediator who tried to make Jerusalem international and was killed by members of Lehi in 1949], I think, he and others hastily left the country, and he was believed to be the head of political intelligence of the Stern Gang."

Livingstone, whom I interviewed in London, later served as a British Council representative in various parts of the world. But in the Forties he was a young Scottish socialist whose only wish was to move from Cairo to Palestine. He came to know many of the Jerusalem Jews, but when I asked him for additional details about Nimri, he realized that he knew little more about him than that he worked as the public-relations man for a potash company, and was well connected in Jerusalem's British and Arab circles. When the city was divided into sectors fenced off with barbed wire, Nimri was always able to move from one sector to another, and if you wanted to send a message to someone in another sector or to obtain something you would always go to him. But Livingstone knew neither his first name nor where he was from, and had heard nothing further of him over the years.

On my return to Israel I heard about Stanley Goldfoot, who had been the treasurer of the Middle East Society and, like Nimri, a member of Lehi, known for its extreme terrorist acts. The were called the Stern Gang by the British, who had killed their leader Yair Stern. Goldfoot, who made his appearance in Jerusalem during the Second World War as a correspondent for South African newspapers, addressed me only in English when I walked into his flat in an Arab house in Jerusalem's German Colony. He talked at length about the society and its activities, but did not mention Nimri's name until I specifically asked about him, and for every question I asked about him he had almost willfully short answers: Nahum Nimri was suited to his job. He was educated in Palestine and dealt with Middle Eastern affairs. When I asked what the area of Nimri's Middle East dealings was, he replied:

"It was a research society, and on the surface of it we looked very serious. In 1946 the empire was still run on societies, learned societies that they had everywhere—the Royal Asiatic Society, Chatham House was another one—and when we founded one here they said, 'Middle East Society—sounds wonderful.' We used to have lecture meetings, and we gave fantastic receptions afterward, usually at the Villa Rosemary or at the King David, in the garden. Hundreds of people would come."

He went on to talk about a journal the society had published and a diary of events in the Middle East that was one of its regular features: "Now the detailed events of the Palestine section were given the kind assistance of General Staff Intelligence Headquarters, for British troops in Palestine and Transjordan. They helped us. We could go in and out of every army camp, headquarters, anywhere. Under the auspices of this society we could discover British troops' movements, their intentions and plans, their intelligence-office communication, we knew it all."

I asked whether I could see one of the diaries they had published, and Goldfoot presented me with a faded gray pamphlet. I asked what kind of information they would pass on to Lehi. He replied: "Oh, how long a curfew was going to be enforced, which areas were going to be under curfew, how many troops were being moved from one place to another, what time a convoy was going, when it would be safe to travel on certain roads; if we wanted to move some men from one place to another, what the best time to do it would be. Their files were open to us, we listened to their discussions, and the head of the General Staff Intelligence, the Right Honorable Martin Charteris, who became private secretary to Queen Elizabeth, he was the head of it all. We became personally very friendly with him. It was all based on friendship. They didn't have an idea of what we were doing."

I asked Goldfoot how long the society's activities had lasted, and he said until the end of 1947, that it had served as one of the few meeting places for Arabs and Jews and British—those "interesting" people who had long since vanished from Jerusalem. I asked whether he regretted their departure, and he replied: "I don't miss them at all, but I think that the English did leave us a justice system that is almost gone now, and their sense of fair play has also gone, and that's a pity." He added that the period before 1967 had not been a good one for Jerusalem. I asked him: "Which Jerusalem do you prefer, the one that was or the one that is?" "The future one," he said with a dreamy smile, a spark flaring in his blue eyes. A thin man, short, with a carefully tended gray beard, agile movements that contrasted with the slow, deliberate speech that always betrayed some excitement: he described with enthusiasm the activities of the Temple Mount Faithful, to which he belonged. Only when I asked whether he could put me in contact with Nimri was there a change in his manner. He replied with reserve that Nimri's residence was in Geneva. I asked for his address there, and Goldfoot gave me a telephone number in Tel Aviv, telling me that I could reach Nimri there during his visits to Israel.

From time to time I tried the Tel Aviv number, and there was no answer. On occasion, people mentioned his name—a few Englishmen and a few Jews from the extreme right wing—but they said little about him. They usually made do with something like, "Yes, I remember him from Jerusalem," as if the man had retreated to some corner of Geneva and everyone was quite relieved.

One day it occurred to me to phone the international operator, and with no trouble at all, I received the Geneva telephone number and address of Nimri. We exchanged two or three letters, and late one afternoon, on a rainy winter day in early 1988, I arrived at a high-rise in a quiet, unfamiliar northern part of Yehoshua Bin Nun Street in Tel Aviv. Judging by the name, I was expecting the door to be opened by a man of Middle Eastern appearance. But I was received by a tall gentleman in his seventies who spoke Hebrew with a slight Polish accent. His white hair was well cut and painstakingly combed; his athletic build was apparent through the expensive jacket. He led me into a quiet room whose eastern wall was made up entirely of large windows. "Usually you can see Judea and Samaria through them," he pointed out, but at the time there were low clouds between us and the view, and they were quickly darkening. The room was luxurious and bourgeois: immaculate, perfectly kept, and clearly little used. With excellent manners—slightly stiff—Nimri questioned me slowly about the nature of my book and the people I had met. He wanted to know who had mentioned him, what had they said about him, and he repeated the questions during the conversation. After pulling up two small tables and bringing us tea, he asked where we should start. I replied that the order was of no importance. But he did not agree; the order was important to him. Ordered talk is controlled talk. I asked him how he had joined Lehi.

"It was actually my right-wing leanings, though I never use that term, *right-wing*—I consider myself a nationalist," he began slowly, paying deliberate attention to the choice of words and their pronunciation. "But my right-wing leanings started back at the Reali School [in Haifa], from the time, at the end of the Twenties and beginning of the Thirties, that there were active Communist cells. That was the peak period for Communism here, and I was among those who rose up against that whole thing, though I wasn't antilabor. Most of my teachers were Mapai people. At first I was in the Hagana, like everyone who went through this. My father was active in the General Zionists—too ready to compromise, too mild for me—and after the riots of 1929, when there was an argument about *havlaga* [self-restraint], I was against it. All this despite the fact that Ernst Simon of Brit Shalom also figured in my youth. He taught at the Reali School, and I was his favorite pupil. He opened his huge library of all the nineteenth century nationalist movements to me, all the secret orders. 'I hope,' he said, 'that you will read this with an open mind.'"

He chuckled, somewhat drily, and added, "But I was never a member of the Revisionist Party, and when the Etzel [the second, much larger terrorist underground] seceded, I didn't join them, but stayed outside any framework, neither here nor there, just thinking at the time. We were a small group of intellectuals, and we set up a circle that we called B'nai Horin—Free Men. With a symbol that was influenced a bit by all the fascist movements. National unification—that was the subject."

"What were you looking for, if I may ask?" I interjected, and for a brief moment he focused his narrow, searching eyes on me. "I was interested in archaeology during the course of my architecture studies," he said in Hebrew, which he spoke well but carefully, hesitating from time to time. I had the feeling that sometimes he was translating phrases from another language. "And when we did our first tour I had a Bedouin guide and he called me Abu Nimre—Father of the Panther—to show his respect after I shot a panther that he had tracked. And from that nickname came my name—Nimri. I spent about a year among them, and then I understood the difference between them and the urban Arabs whom I knew mainly in Haifa, and who didn't make much of an impression on me, not as nationalists and not as people you could deal with. In contrast to them, the Bedouin were much more authentic, purer, had much more character—proud, with a kind of majesty. That attracted me, and I said, why not go and see who they are? After all, they're in our territory.

"I enlisted in the British Army in 1938 at the time of the Arab gangs," he went on. "At first I was a translator from Arabic into English, and later a liaison officer between the military authorities and the Arab population and all the Jewish institutions. My base was in the Galilee, and when the war started I was loaned to central headquarters. [Abba] Eban [the eminent Israeli stateman] was in Cairo and I was in Romania, in Lebanon, and for a certain time in Damascus. We had the same commander, Colonel Elphinstone, who was an Arabist like that whole band of them who dreamed of Lawrence and the men of Arabia, the ones who tried to speak Arabic and read Arabic and believed all the Arab lies. Those were the Arab experts. And today we have Jews like them, who believe everything they read about Arab affairs." I thought to point out that he, too, had gone out among the Bedouin like one of "that whole band" and that in his eyes, too, they had seemed authentic and pure, but I was wary of getting a long explanation on the matter of "Arab lies," so I asked:

"If you had been an Englishman here in the area, and had met the Jews and the Arabs, what would you have thought of them?" and he answered: "Look, there were some Englishmen who weren't taken in by that Arab exterior, but almost all of them loved that grandeur and friendliness and politeness, the I-am-your-servant bit, and they knew exactly what it was, just the way letters end with 'your obedient servant.' The large majority of Jews had none of that, which was, unfortunately, the syndrome of our behavior. We didn't know how to be cruel, but we certainly could be crude." The way he linked crudity and cruelty was unexpected: if you're going to be crude, then better to be cruel, in his opinion, or perhaps cruelty was a necessary trait?

"Did you have friends among the Arabs in Palestine?" I asked. "Friends you meet for a cup of coffee or a shot of whiskey," he replied. "The ones with stories, the ones who used to quote a line of Abu Nawas, who was a kind of Arab Rabelais. Very spicy poetry, and whenever I met with them I used to quote from his poems, and that would dispel their suspicions. There isn't an Arab who doesn't know these poems, from peasants and Bedouin to great pashas. And when you get down to this level of poems and stories, everyone starts telling his own adventures, his loves and his betrayals, stories like that, and this, after all, is one of the things the Arabs do well—*One Thousand and One Nights*—and they'll repeat the same story hundreds of times."

After a moment he remarked: "There was a man like Nagib Abu Sha'a, who was a prominent lawyer in Jerusalem, with whom I met after the UN proclamation. There were already battles with the Arab gangs and he proposed to me, 'Come to Amman for a few months, we'll smuggle you quietly.' There were also those with a moderate, humane approach, but in all their Arab history the Jews were second-rate, and to this day they don't accept that there is such a thing as Jewish lordship." I was wondering about the choice of the word *lordship*, when he went on: "They weren't stupid. They were friendly. Very sociable. Very kind. They didn't have a firm belief in the justice of their cause, though when they spoke they were very persuasive. I had British friends in the army who knew the Bible better than I did, and with whom I used to have long talks, and one of them said to me: 'Tell me, why is it when I speak to an Arab, even though I know that he is a bloody liar, I believe what he says, and when I speak to most of the Jews, even though I know that maybe they are right, I can't believe them?'

"Many of the Arabs were playboys," he said. "I played the part, but they really were." "Did you enjoy their company?" I asked, and he said yes in a laconic way that made me feel the need to add, "Did you feel some affection for them?" "Certainly," he replied, and after a moment remarked: "To me they were objects." That last remark suddenly raised an old childhood fear I had had of the members of the Etzel and Lehi. There were none in my neighborhood. In my home they were condemned in words not entirely understood but very impressive, like *secessionists*. To me those Jews were more frightening than the Arabs. You didn't ever see them, but they were definitely there and flashed into view with bombings, or the hanging of one of them, or handbills out of nowhere stuck on walls. But in Tel Aviv, on summer visits to my uncle, everything was different. The adults whispered about them sympathetically, and children talked about them as heroes. In the house across the street a neighbor disappeared, and his daughters spoke with pride of searches. To me they were part of Tel Aviv; they belonged to the streets and were truly urban. There was some kind of natural connection between the crowded cafés and those unidentified people with their black magic.

"I was of the opinion that talks with the Land of Israel Arabs could only take place indirectly, through some country that had nothing to do with us, or through minorities who could be enlisted in opposition to what was the Sunni Muslim world," Nimri went on. "One of my first postings was in Jebal al-Druze. I had a few friends there that I spoke to about cooperation. Among the Druze there were people who impressed me a great deal." And here he went on at length about the families he knew there. "The emir of Jebal al-Druze, Hasan al-Atrash, was a close friend of mine," he said. "He was heir to the dynasty of Atrash, the strongest tribe in Jebal al-Druze. At that time I was in the headquarters of the Ninth Army in Lebanon, headed by General Wilson—he was commander in chief of Palestine and Transjordan, and in 1941 he commanded the campaign in Syria and Lebanon—and he called me in and said: 'Since you know some of the Bedouin from past experience, I want you to go and write us a handbook on all the Bedouin tribes and give us an appreciation of the nuisance value to our war effort.' Which meant not how friendly they could be but to what extent they could get in our way.

"I began then to gather material on the 135 Bedouin tribes that live in the Fertile Crescent. Of course I had to visit them all. On one of my trips I met a tribe that lives in northeastern Syria and northwestern Iraq that is called Yezidis, and they believe in the devil. They believe in God also, but they pray mainly to the devil in the form of a peacock to which they bring sacrifices, and that's because their basic philosophy is that God is a good divinity and will do no evil, and the devil is a bad divinity and therefore you have to"—and here he stopped and seemed to be looking for the right expression. "Appease him," I suggested, and he said, "To grovel before him and to ask his favor, to repent, and to pay him off. That was also the line of the English here. They tried to get into the good graces of those who most got in their way.

"That's why on my first home leave I tried to get in touch with Yair Stern, in order to find a way that we could be more of a nuisance than the Arabs. During my army service, up to that meeting with Wilson I'd had no contact except for periodic meetings with Jewish Agency people who dealt with intelligence and contacts with the British. I had a very long talk with Yair, the first time I met with him, and I decided to switch and fight the British." "And before that?" I asked. "I thought along the lines of [Etzel commander David] Raziel," said Nimri, "that if we worked with the British and showed them how good we were, we'd win their cooperation toward independence. Raziel was killed, and the Etzel was on its way to a compromise.

"And then I went to Yair with a proposal to prepare a rebellion within two to three years, assuming that the war would continue that long. To pull off a kind of putsch," he went on, "all this under the influence of all the history books I'd read on different putsches in different countries, with the main element being total surprise. That is, to prepare under cover a small camp, a small army, so that one day, at a certain hour, it could seize some twenty strategic positions in the country, including a few hostages, and sit down to negotiate with the British when we're holding such strongholds as the radio, the railroad, a few major police stations. I knew the British were not the Germans and their responses would not be German, but Yair told me that if the condition for success was we keep it secret for two to three years, there was no chance a thing like this could be accomplished. So he favored small-scale attacks. My line of thinking was that we had to harass the British in order to turn them into allies. His line was that this was foreign rule, and foreign rule must be fought." His tone was matter-of-fact.

I tried to imagine that meeting between the man most wanted by the British and the intelligence officer in the British Army who was also a proud Jew. In the eyes of Nimri was this just a change of direction; was he aware that he had come to the point where one must bring into being something visionary and absolute? Nimri, after all, was also a practical man; his encounters with reality were many and manifold. And here he was, jumping to a grand conclusion, terrifying in its simplicity; from this point on he would no longer be his own man, seeking his way in the Revisionist camp, but one of those fighting the fight as Yair defined it, one of the ranks who could be released only by death. And perhaps this leap in fact resulted from his knowledge of the place and its people, I suddenly thought. Perhaps intimate knowledge of the maze with no exit pushes people to take leaps like this, and conclusions that are beyond all possibility then look like suitable plans of action.

"Well," said Nimri with a kind of smile, "we had only ten pistols in all, and my first mission was to locate the arms depots of the Middle East. That was in the last few months before my demobilization from the British Army. And I was busy then with the final editing of the book I'd written on the Bedouin in the Fertile Crescent. The book was printed under military guard at the Lipschitz printing plant, in one thousand numbered copies. I was taking an afternoon siesta between bouts of proofreading when my landlady, a German Jewish woman, came in, in a panic: 'Two Englishmen are here to see you.' They had heard something about weapons, which of course I carried as a military man, and while they were in my room they asked, 'What do you have in that box?' I said it was army material, and they said, 'We'll take it, and we ask you to come to police headquarters tomorrow morning at nine.' Only when they had gone did I wonder whether they were really from the police. In any case I went to the army command and immediately called Damascus, Colonel Elphinstone, and asked him to inform the police of who I am and what I do. I didn't sleep all night because inside the box were the plans of all the camps of the British Army, and I was supposed to give them to Yair in a few days; this was to be the first big supply of arms for Lehi.

"In the morning I get up and my hair has turned white here," he continued, in the same dry, controlled tone so reminiscent of the understated manner of the English, but without their light touch. "At nine o'clock I go to the office of Captain Scott, who receives me warmly and apologizes, saying he has received explanations from the army command, but just to be on the safe side perhaps I should tell him a bit about myself. I see that the box is still sitting there with the lock on. And he says that after taking down the details they will hand the box over to the army headquarters. Then I say that off the record, I'll give him a few classified details, and I tell him about my meetings with the Kurds, adding, 'Let me show you,' and bring the box over to the big desk, and open it in such a way that he can't see what I'm taking out, and give him a few documents, and he reads them very attentively, because the moment someone reads secret documents he considers himself privileged. And after we chat in a friendly fashion, he asks, 'Can I get you some coffee?' and I say, 'Certainly,' and he goes out of the office and with the greatest possible speed I put the maps under my shirt."

I asked Nimri whether he had remained in Jerusalem after that unpleasant visit to the police, and he recalled that he had moved to the Villa Rosemary in the German Colony, explaining that it was a complex of six villas with a pension and reception rooms in the center; today, he noted, there was practically nothing left of the place. Before the regulations on preserving the beauty of Jerusalem were passed, ugly apartment buildings had been put up there. "Colonel Elphinstone, when he came to Jerusalem, used to stay there with his wife and Robert Graves's sister, who served as my secretary for editing the book on the Bedouin. And then I, too, moved to the Villa Rosemary, and many Jews believed I was one of those Anglicized types. It's an image I cultivated.

"In 1942 I resigned from the British Army and started working as one of [Moses] Novomeisky's advisers on Arab and British affairs at the potash company," he went on, without saying a word about the elimination of Yair Stern a short time later and about the survivors of Lehi who went deeper underground. "We started launching reprisals for every British action. At first against installations, and later against people. And that's how the struggle against the British began. There were some who used a different word—*murder*—but it was killing in the course of war." He said the words "killing in the course of war" quietly, in his usual manner, but with an emphasis that restored to the term *terror* its original meaning. For those actions by Lehi and later by the Etzel brought the element of terror to a place that the Second World War had quietly bypassed, a place whose inhabitants had begun to enjoy the peace.

"With Lehi, it was a matter of total faith in the justice of our cause and in our ability," recalled Nimri, "despite the fact that we were a small minority and that feelings ran high against us. We were men of complete faith, and for that reason there was never any traitor planted among us. So, when I found out in those days that Teddy Kollek thought I was an Etzel man, I realized he hadn't the slightest idea. Among us were lots of leftists and also some Agudat Yisrael, a whole unit of fighters, who were terrific fellows. We were above all that narrow factionalism. The idea was that this was an alien occupation—Yair's term, if you want to put it that way. All the others, and me, too, before I came to Stern, still thought we'd have talks with the British."

In 1946 Nimri set up the Middle East Society of Jerusalem: "Each month the Middle East Society would convene in the Villa Rosemary for a lecture/party on historical, social, economic, or political subjects related to the Middle East. Among those invited to the meetings were consuls-general in Jerusalem, heads of the different churches, heads of the British civilian authority, the upper echelons of British Army General Staff, and senior British police officers, as well as prominent people and Arab and Jewish notables.

"When Lord Charteris gave a lecture at the Middle East Society," recalled Nimri with an amused smile, "there was a young intelligence officer of the Royal Air Force there, and we were good friends. And he gave the kind of glance that made me think he was hinting that they suspected me. One of his tasks was to follow my activities and to check on who was behind me and what made me tick. When I found out he was on my tracks I decided to let him in on the secret of my success with the Arabs, and in fact I later found out he had reported that I was 'mad' about research and English-Arab-Jewish cooperation and that I had no underground ties. He was a very young man, but he knew Shakespeare backward and forward. He was also a great mimic, and we had lots of good times together. After the plot against Bernadotte, when I was imprisoned with the rest of the Lehi people, my name was published in all of England in September 1948 under the headline 'The Man Who Fooled British Intelligence—Among the Heads of the Stern Gang.' When I was released as a result of the collective hunger strike staged by the rest of the prisoners, I found a letter awaiting me from that same Royal Air Force intelligence officer. In the letter he asks how I am and what my plans are and concludes:

'Pleased to hear that you are free again. Please let me know if I can be of any help, or shall we say, again.'

"Among the English there were lots of friendly people, lots of interesting people, and I learned a great deal from them. They had that credibility, and mainly the belief in their position and in their self-respect. They also derived a lot of pride from the Bible, which had a great influence on me, and when I was in the uniform of a British Army officer, I also had this sense of power. There I am with a little stick, and all the others are standing at attention awaiting my every utterance. My feeling was that this is the way a healthy, self-respecting nation acts, a nation that fulfills its task—ruling the world. I had great admiration for a small nation that for hundreds of years ruled a world on which the sun never set. How did they do it, how did they bring it off, how did they lie without ever showing it, always in the name of that British sense of fair play, that facade of civilization?

"For instance, there was the brother of Robert Graves," he went on, "who later became governor of Jerusalem. They were people you could talk to about anything."

I asked him what Charteris had lectured on at the Middle East Society.

"In a moment I'll tell you exactly," replied Nimri, and produced an old booklet whose format was already familiar to me. *A Year as an Intelligence Officer in Palestine.* "That was in September 1946," he explained, and read: " '*A Year as an Intelligence Officer in Palestine.* What, first of all, is an intelligence officer? And is he in any way a different variety in Palestine than elsewhere? Well, my experience is that everything and everybody in Palestine is slightly different, and an intelligence officer is no exception to the rule.' "

He read carefully, in a pleasant accent, slightly Polish, which actually lent a certain elegance to the English.

He examined the booklet for a moment, and traces of a smile played across his introspective face. "When the story broke in the papers, I was told that Charteris was shocked. I wrote him a letter when I got out of prison: 'Dear Martin, I was amused to read the article by Clifton Daniel, the prominent journalist and the managing editor of the *New York Times*, but I can assure you that you were too valuable to us to harm you.'" "Did you get an answer?" I asked, and Nimri shook his head: "He was a nice guy, Charteris, but he was an object for me, and I had to be careful not to let anything slip. I knew he'd never hesitate to have me hanged."

I mentioned to Nimri that Charteris had told me he was in favor of a partition plan and a Jewish state. "There were people who supported us, as it turned out," he said. "One of the heads of the fight against terrorism, a senior officer who was on loan to the British police from one of the crack Scottish regiments in the British Army. During his time in Palestine one of his men murdered a member of Lehi. That was in 1946. Our man was kidnapped on a Jerusalem street and never heard from again. Later it was found that he had been tortured to death during his interrogation. I invited that officer to lunch at Hess, which was open to the British during the period when Jerusalem was partitioned with barbed wire. Before that I had lent him a book based on the correspondence between Pontius Pilate and the philosopher Seneca [which contained comparisons between the Romans and the British and their respective troubles in ruling the stiff-necked Jews], and I said to him, 'Read this.' I didn't hide my nationalist feelings from the British, but I expressed them, let's say, in a rather civilized way, without speeches. That's why they considered me 'one of our reasonable Jews.'

"He read the book with great interest and wanted to return it to me. We arranged to meet for lunch, and that was to be his Last Lunch. On the morning of that day, a messenger arrived with the book and a note attached: 'I can't keep the appointment. The ground is too hot for me.' And he left the country.

"When I was in Scotland one summer during the Sixties I asked about him, and then called him: 'This is a ghost from the past. Nimri is speaking,' I said, and after a moment of silence he asked: 'Nimri el-Kudsi?' We spoke on the phone a few times."

"Did you tell him about the Last Lunch?" I asked, and he said, "No." "You weren't the one who was supposed to kill him, were you?" I said. "No," he confirmed. "I was the host. It was planned so that there would be no hitches along the way. They were supposed to lay an ambush and attack him as soon as he left the restaurant." "And wasn't it hard for you to be the host?" I asked. "From the human point of view I had no hesitation, because if I put myself in his boots for a moment—thinking how he would have responded if he'd known of my membership in an underground fighting British rule—he wouldn't have hesitated a moment, despite our friendly relations and the somewhat intellectual understanding."

Nimri was right, I thought: had he fallen into the hands of that Scottish officer, he would have been dispatched without a blink. Still, I felt that there was some difference between the two possible murders—not in the act itself but in relation to the man it was planned against. For in some fundamental way Nimri saw the world as a place in which the devil must be appeased—the view of the Yezidis tribe that had left such an indelible impression on him.

Evil prevails in the world, and one can only confront it with absolute faith, preferably of an ancient type, and not with such ephemeral, disposable creatures as human beings. But those who don't feel the need to save the world through absolute faith of this sort put a different value on human life. Even when life is cheap—as it was during that period—and even when it was a matter of a tough Scottish officer who had come to eliminate terrorists, even then the life of the eliminated is the life of a particular person, and not of an object. Is that why Nimri did not tell the Scottish officer what had been awaiting him after the lunch at Hess? It makes sense to assume that the officer might have known, or at least suspected, and in any case was not shaken by a plan that was never realized. Perhaps Nimri didn't have the nerve to admit to the officer that for a time he had been a target for murder because in his heart he knew that the man had always been only a target.

"He was marked for murder because he had eliminated some of our men," he saw fit to explain. "Even so, I liked him personally because he was a great clown. But again—if I'd fallen into his hands, the human in him would have given way to the British in him—and in that sense I learned a lot from the British." Here Nimri stopped. I didn't ask him about the episode again. In the large windows with a view beyond the Green Line there was darkness. The lamps gave off a soft light. And again I noticed that muffled silence of hidden chambers, as if you left the country the moment you set foot inside.

CHAPTER EIGHT

"There are two Englands"

During that period, the Jews in Palestine prepared themselves for a struggle with the Mandate rule. Their leaders preferred to act politically but turned to armed combat in order to protect Jewish settlements and immigration. Yitzhak Ben-Aharon, one of the leaders of the labor movement, was part of an activist group that believed there was no contradiction between building the country and using force to protect it. Both Sir Harold Beeley and Yitzhak Ben-Aharon appear in this chapter.

"Would you mind waiting here a moment?" said the elderly doorman of the Reform Club. He went off across the room to a man resting in a straight-backed chair near the window. Total silence prevailed. The crowds and traffic of central London were neither seen nor heard, though they were very near and surrounded the large clubs sequestered with their members and their furnishings and their customs in the grand white buildings. The cab drivers who brought me to the clubs would identify them not by signs, which for the most part did not exist, but by their numbers on the wide, imperial street, Pall Mall.

From the chair in the corner a man in a dark suit pulled himself up to his full—considerable—height, adjusted his glasses, and welcomed me with a smile. "Let's go upstairs," said Sir Harold Beeley, who had been an adviser to Ernest Bevin and was one of the chief shapers of his Palestine policy. "It's quieter there," he added, observing with some reluctance the waiters laying tables in the huge entrance hall, and explaining that the Reform Club was having a jubilee celebration that evening.

We sat on the uppermost level, near the balustrade that wound its way around all the floors and down the stairway. The small tape recorder seemed out of place in the old gallery, which looked out on the palatial interior. Beeley ordered us tea and listened attentively to my explanations. A man in his seventies, dressed in the conservative suit of a senior British Foreign Office official but not looking the part, not in his manners and not in the eyes observing me from behind the thick glasses, studying more than examining. When I asked how he had come to deal with Middle Eastern affairs, he replied: "Oh, Chatham House asked me to write for them about Palestine in 1936, and my first instructor in Zionism was Walter Eytan [spokesman of the Jewish Agency and a senior diplomat]. We were both teaching at Oxford, and I went to Eytan to learn about Zionism. Jamal Husseini [second to Mufti Haj Amin el-Husseini, leader of the extreme nationalistic movement in Palestine] was the first Arab I met in London." And he waited with a wry look, ready to be assailed with questions about his distinctly pro-Arab policy.

"If you think about Arab and Jewish intellectuals and political figures you have met through the years, if you think about their outlook, were they very different from each other?" I asked. "The Zionists, of course, were much more articulate," he said, "and on the whole, the more sophisticated. Also there were far more of them."

"Would you say that the Arabs were more emotional?" I wanted to know. "No, I wouldn't," he answered. "They were emotional, but not more." And after a moment he added, "I always thought that the best book written about Palestine at the time was *The Arab Awakening* by George Antonius. I met him twice in 1938. He was the most impressive on either side." And when I asked him why, he explained, "Because of his grasp of problems, his command of the subject, his eloquence."

I wondered how it was for a man like him, an Oxford intellectual beginning to take an interest in the subject, to meet people already immersed in the struggle, people who must have talked to him with great fervor, while he sat back and reflected on the issues. But Beeley was going on to tell about the political figures of the Middle East, both Jews and Arabs. He had served as a diplomat in Iraq and in 1961 was appointed Britain's first ambassador to Egypt after the Suez affair; he served once again as ambassador after 1967, and had gone to Jericho many times to visit Musa Alami (a prominent figure in Palestinian politics, who founded an educational farm in Jericho), with whom he kept in close touch. Once he had met Moshe Dayan there: "I was on the board of the Alami farm. As minister of defense, Dayan was responsible for the occupied territories, and I was sent to talk to him and try to persuade him to help in the repair of the wells. He was—*cynical* perhaps is not the right word—he was very detached and could be very amusing. When I put this to him, he answered, 'My job is destruction, not construction.' I must say, I liked him."

His tone was light, and I wondered what it was exactly that had so pleased Beeley—the direct answer that prompted a smile, or Dayan's style? Had he found the Zionist leaders he met in the early days devoid of style? What was it that appealed to him? I asked him how those Zionist leaders had seemed to him, and he replied jovially: "They were obsessed, many of them. I think that Zionist people I met were more obsessed with the problem than the Arabs were. The Arabs were pretty well obsessed, but they seemed to be able to forget it more often than the Zionists."

Yes, I thought, that was certainly true, but had he considered the fact that the problem of the Zionists was very hard to forget during those years? Yet I had the feeling that despite his decidedly anti-Zionist policy, despite the fact that many Jews of the period had seen him as the foe's emissary if not the foe himself, what bothered him was Zionist policy, and not the Jews. I said: "I found the British still very emotional about Palestine. Why?" And he said: "It's associated, don't you think, with partisanship with one side or the other. I can't think of any colony or mandate that was as demanding intellectually and emotionally as Palestine."

After a moment he remarked, "There are not too many British people, I think, who have emotional links with Zionism as those who have emotional links with Palestine Arabs." And when I asked why, he replied, "I don't know. One clue to it is that the majority of people who went to Palestine when it was under British rule went on the whole with sympathy for the Zionists, who were progressive, modern, European, and came home with sympathy for the Arabs. That was the commonest experience, I think."

Again I asked why, and he laughed. "I haven't thought about that," he answered, somewhat surprised, as if this British attitude were a given. "I suppose they thought that the Arabs were the indigenous people and that the Jewish claim was historically not terribly convincing. This is the big divide. The Jewish people on the whole take the connection with Palestine for granted. They regard it as a basic truth that it is wrong to challenge."

"Was the Holocaust a turning point in British policy?" I asked. "Yes," he acknowledged. "But for that, there would have been a different settlement." "When did you become aware of it?" I asked, and Beeley answered, "We became aware gradually how decisive it was, I think, but not immediately. Because Bevin used to say, 'If the Jews can't now live in Europe, what did we fight the war for?' And that had prevented the significance of the Holocaust from influencing people as much as it had otherwise done."

"Do you think it should have influenced you more as a policy-maker?" I asked. He thought for a moment. "I suppose it did not sufficiently. The effect was indirect. It came to us through America. We thought of the American attitude as being rather perverse and misguided. We didn't really appreciate the enormous effect of the Holocaust on the United States."

How could he have possibly thought about the Holocaust in terms of power politics with the United States and then based a policy on political considerations alone? He made no excuses. I recalled a footnote I'd read in a publication by Gavriel Cohen, "British Policy on the Eve of the War of Independence": "About fourteen years after the event, one of the British experts on the problem of Palestine after World War II, who had been in charge of the Palestine issue in one of the policy-making offices of Whitehall, and was even an active party to the decision to force the ship *Exodus* back to the shores of Germany, said about the affair: 'It was a mistake. To tell you the truth, I think it stemmed from the vanity of princes. This wasn't a matter of evil intent, but of an angry, unbridled outburst. . . . But I understand that it was a serious mistake. Today it seems strange, but none of us accurately gauged the intensity of the feelings Jews had regarding immigration.... We did not comprehend the special situation of the years 1946–47 and the significance Zionism held for the displaced and the immigrants of that period.... Perhaps it's peculiar, but we had no idea of the depth of feeling and identification. The truth is that I can't recall anyone opposing the decision on expulsion.'"

Since we were treading a fine line—one slips quickly and imperceptibly from ruminations on the political climate into political argument—I did not quote the footnote to him. Instead I mentioned the book Richard Crossman wrote after participating in the Anglo-American Committee of Inquiry, which examined the situation in Palestine in 1946 and recommended a solution; in the book he notes that only a visit to concentration camps and displaced-persons camps had made him perceive the reality of the Holocaust. Until then he had comprehended nothing. And Beeley, who had served as secretary of the committee, said:

"Crossman was a friend of mine. He set off without strong feelings for either side, and he came off rather a convinced Zionist. What converted him was, I don't think it was the camps, what determined Crossman's final attitude was the kibbutzim, the socialist character of the Jewish community. At the end of it all, when the report was finished, Crossman asked me which, had I thought, of the twelve members of the committee, had understood the Arab case best, and I said, 'You did.'"

"There is almost an inner contradiction," I said, "in becoming a converted Zionist and understanding the Arab problem better than the other members." And he laughed and said, "Yes, I suppose so, but again, one had to make up one's mind!"

"Quite often," I said, "when people make up their minds they can become insensitive to the other side," and Beeley murmured something. His face was suddenly blank, and I asked him whether impartiality had in fact guided British imperialist policy, and whether that had been of concern to him in Palestine. He replied: "I don't suppose I did retain my impartiality. I tried to, but most people won't regard me as impartial, and there comes a time when you can't remain impartial, I think, unless you are purely an observer and nothing else. If you are taking part in political activity, you can analyze a situation or try to analyze a situation with the greatest possible impartiality, but when you have to act, to do something, you have to come down to some extent on one side or the other. So impartiality is not politically a practical attitude."

"When did you find that you had lost yours?" I asked then, and we both laughed. "When I had to chose between supporting one policy or supporting another policy," he admitted. "Was it early?" I kept on, and he said, "Yes, it was quite early, and of course it always happens. The side that thinks you partial to the other side drives you further in that direction. You become more committed as you get more involved."

I asked whether he had visited the camps. He said he had been detained in London and visited only Vienna, leaving from there for Jerusalem. Then he told me about his stay in Jerusalem in 1946, and his visits to Arab villages and to kibbutzim. When I asked him whether he too had been impressed by the kibbutzim, he answered frankly: "When I went to the kibbutzim I was impressed with them, but the people we were meeting in Jerusalem were not so different from the people we knew at home."

"I was wondering," I asked Beeley, "whether the British understood the nature of the Zionist struggle. Were they aware that many of the Jews in Palestine didn't think of a state until circumstances forced them to do so?" He replied: "The British were aware that for the Jews in Palestine after the war, there was no other way but a Jewish state. When we talked to people like Ben-Gurion and Moshe Sharett, this became very clear." "What did you make of it?" I went on. "Did you think that again they were just being emotional about it, or did you realize that one had reached a point of no return?" And Sir Beeley answered with a wry smile. "Neither, really."

"In 1946–47, if the Arabs had been prepared to work for a compromise solution, we would have worked with them, I think. But we had no cooperation from the Arabs. The Arabs rejected of course any form of compromise." When I asked him why they did so, he answered: "A number of reasons, I think. First of all, the difficulty of imagining what sort of compromise we were suggesting. Second, a feeling that the battle was not lost. There was I suppose still some prospect of maintaining their position by force. One must remember that the Arab rebellion had been fairly successful, and the strength of the Zionists had not been demonstrated before 1947. And then, I suppose, there was an element of fear. Every Arab leader was afraid of being the first to accept a compromise."

"One does wonder why the British didn't accept the hundred thousand certificates for refugees and keep the Mandate much longer." I had come out with the inevitable question. "Accepting a hundred thousand immigrants in one year would have been such a radical revolution in our policy—the White Paper Policy—at a time when we were looking for a settlement," explained Beeley.

"Had you done it," I pointed out, "the Americans would have calmed down." "Would they?" he asked, and his tone changed. It was not as detached as before. "I don't think it would be final, as we didn't think that partition would be a final solution." After a moment he remarked: "When the Arabs were not prepared for any solution, we abandoned the problem in the middle of 1947."

"When you say 'abandoned the problem,' do you really mean 'let go of the whole thing'?" I asked. "Yes," he said. "How do you feel about that?" I asked, and he burst out laughing. "I was not against it because I could not see any alternative. We came to a point where we could not very well see in what way we could perform honorably and sensibly without doing things either to the Arabs or to the Jews. But until it became clear that the Arabs were not prepared to consider any serious form of compromise, we hoped." "When did it become clear?" I asked. "Oh, I think, in February 1947, when Bevin made proposals to the Arabs in London and they turned them down," he answered.

"Did the Jews 'read the map' better than the others?" I asked. "I think it is probably true," he replied. "I think that their estimate of the possibilities was more accurate than either ours or the Arabs'. And they calculated their force rather well. Our military advice given to the government at the time was that the Jewish community is quite capable of defending itself against the Arabs, and in fact may very well prove to be militarily the stronger. So we didn't expect a decisive victory for either the Arabs or the Jews."

I asked Beeley when they had stopped hoping, and he said: "Oh, when it was clear that the Russians would vote for partition. We expected the Russians to take the Arab side, not only because the Americans were on the Jewish side, but because we always expected the Russians to take the opposite view on every question. We therefore thought that the necessary majority couldn't be found in the UN. So we didn't really know until quite fairly late in the proceedings what the outcome would be. But when it was clear that the Russians would vote for partition, that was the moment we recognized that we had come to an end of a kind we were not happy about."

"Did you think 'Good riddance' then?" I was curious to know. "No, we certainly did not think that; we were extremely interested to see what would happen next," he replied with a grin. And it was that grin and the eyes flashing behind the glasses that conveyed how profound his involvement had been, even after the English had "abandoned the problem," as he put it, but had not yet abandoned their rule, and still hoped for some unexpected development in the power games they no longer controlled.

"Beeley and I walked in Hampstead Heath; it was 1948," Sir Isaiah Berlin, the philosopher and professor of the history of ideas at Oxford, had once recounted to me, "and Beeley was convinced that the United Nations would not resolve it, and that they would come back to the English." I wondered whether this could happen only in England or whether there were other peoples who never lost the ability to speak to their enemies. In those very days they could stroll in Hampstead Heath and talk about what was to happen out there in a Palestine already engaged in civil war—Berlin the confirmed Zionist and Beeley the militant anti-Zionist, who apparently was making no concessions yet.

"I am most definitely of the opinion that the English forced the state on us," said Yitzhak Ben-Aharon, who had served as secretary-general of the Histadrut labor federation and as a government minister. It was our first meeting. Ben-Aharon preferred coming to my place; he was a man in his early eighties with bright, curious eyes, wearing a white shirt, the collar open, and light khaki trousers.

"Weizmann and Ben-Gurion wanted the English to stay," he continued. "Ben-Gurion pleaded with them up the very last minute, 'Let's come to a settlement on the business of immigration, transfer immigration to us, to the Jewish Agency, and stay here as long as you like.' Even in Bevin's time they tried to come to a settlement. When the matter of partition came up of course they seized on that and said, 'Statehood now,' but they were prepared to do without it. Partition wasn't such a lovely thing. What we could have gotten would have been something very minimal, and there was lots of opposition here and we weren't really set up for independence. What did we have, what were we? There were five hundred thousand Jews: is that the time to become a little statelet with an army and titles and a bureaucracy, but without settling the land, without pioneering? The main problem was not governmental, the main problem was Jews and settlement, shaping a nation here, and it didn't matter who would be in charge, Bevin or someone else," and he spoke in packed sentences with a vigor that had not diminished over the years.

During one of our talks at his home, in a room looking out on the tropical vegetation and the lawns of his kibbutz, Givat Haim, he told me about his years in a Nazi POW camp: "I was a second lieutenant when we fell into the hands of the Germans in Greece. When we reached Piraeus, who was on hand to greet us? German officers who stood there writing down every plane and every tank. By the time we got to the camp near Piraeus, all the phone lines prepared for us had been cut. Not a single British plane got off the ground. The evacuation was halted. The Germans had control of the air. At 2 a.m., the brigadier got his command together and announced: 'We're surrendering.' All the British officers disappeared. They went to British units. No one wanted to fall prisoner with the Jews. Early in the morning I called the whole bunch together. There were fourteen hundred of us in the Engineer Corps, and I was responsible for them in no small measure. Most of them had followed me in enlisting. I was their leader there, secretary of the Tel Aviv labor council. I got them together and I said, 'We're being taken prisoner and we have to go together, and go honorably. The firmer we stand, the less we endanger our lives. We shave, we clean up, we brush.' All of us were dirty by the time we got there. We lined them up in threes, and I was the highest in rank there, so I walked at the head.

"We went to Kalamata, a harbor town in the southern Peloponnese, a very pretty town. We came to the square, one of those beautiful piazzas, and the German command was waiting there. Some colonel arrived, and 'Halt'—like a wallop on the head—there have never, never been any parades like that one. And I give a salute and announce, in English, of course, 'Reporting for duty, units such-and-such at your command.' The German colonel with his translator looks at me and says to the translator, 'What's his rank?' and I answer, and he says, 'So that's the state of the British Army: a second lieutenant commands a brigade.' I hear this in German, before the translation, and I say, 'I'm sorry, after the surrender there was an order given to get out of here, and anyone who could, got away.' He translates this bit, and the colonel looks at me and says, 'Don't be childish, you'll meet them all in a little while.' And he was right. Next thing, a command was given to line up by country, and of course they separated officers from enlisted men. That was the end of it, I never saw them again, the rank and file. I was the only one left from Palestine, and then a roll call, again they were doing me the honor, I was standing alone, an orphan. Along comes an officer, a translator, and tells me, 'You must be shaking a little.' And I say, 'Of course,' so he says, 'Take it easy, Germans abhor kosher meat.' That was for starters.

"With a gentle shove I was attached to the senior British officers, who were treated very badly because, according to the stupid international treaties, officers taken prisoner don't work. Enlisted men worked. Besides that, they had an obsession that went on for the whole war, that we would be the core of an anti-Nazi underground. The worse they were doing in the war, the more nervous they got, because they had a huge camp full of slaves, tens of millions, and they were sure we were organized, with instructions to lead the insurrection the moment the Allies got near. And they simply starved us, the Germans. In the end, when a drunken American sergeant entered the camp in a jeep full of booty, he happened to come across our section and we were liberated, famished as dogs, and then this American comes over to us and says, 'There's food here. What do you mean, there's nothing? What else could you want?' There were one hundred thousand Red Cross bundles in the storeroom. The Germans never gave us any of it, but they didn't take it for themselves either, the food and the coffee and the tea, which you just couldn't get by 1945. And they had a register, and everything was written down.

"I knew German," he went on, "and I played a pretty central role in the whole anti-German intelligence and smuggling scheme. I was also the translator and decoder of anything we could manage to get from the Germans, and we passed it on to England in all sorts of ways. So I had very close ties with those people who served in their career army and fell prisoner in Greece or France or some other place. [David] Stirling, my closest friend, was the head of the Western Desert commando before [Bernard] Montgomery. At the time of the British Army defeats he headed the long-range commando that broke into German airfields. That was a conservative elite, and I was great friends with them.

"In all the contacts with them, there was something interesting. Those aristocrats who moved from feudalism into urban life, when they became businessmen and stockbrokers, they came across Jews, and usually it was not a pleasant encounter. Basically, they were anti-Semites. They couldn't have talked with an English Jew the way they talked with me, and they said that very clearly. As far as they were concerned, I was not a Jew. Not in the way I talked, or my attitude toward Jews or the diaspora, or my negation of the diaspora. I talked to them about ideological matters," he added with a laugh. "What we were in Eretz Yisrael, what we wanted in Eretz Yisrael. And they saw me as part of some other nation, no relation to Cohen over there in England, or to someone like Greenbaum or the whole bunch that they knew—not Sacher and not Marks—there was a spark of anti-Semitism among all the non-Jews, and no less among the aristocrats, and they could talk to me because they had decided that. I was not a Jew. 'Bloody Jew,' they would say the way the Scotsman would say, 'Bloody English.' So our contact was really free and very intimate, with no boundaries.

"When I got back from the war I was half-English," he continued. "The Yishuv here after the war was really turning into a state-in-the-making. I was still a soldier, not yet demobbed, and for a time I was also in the hospital, but right away the clashes became more frequent, right away we had the great search, the siege, which I was involved in, and this was war, quite simply, war. A whole division attacking with rifles and bayonets. And those four to five years that I had been an ally and worn the same uniform and gone around with the same paraphernalia of the King's Commission, and now all of a sudden I'm the enemy. That confrontation was especially hard for them. After a few months' leave, they had gone back to the army and suddenly found themselves here, in a war against the Jews. Some of them were career army, of course, and saw this as a profession, a job to be done. They weren't such delicate souls, but there were some who had a tough time indeed coming face-to-face with one of their own war heroes.

"They got us together on the lawn. It wasn't only our kibbutz, it was all through the Sharon region. There were big searches throughout the Sharon. They put a table up there, and then they brought Sharett and Greenboim and Remez, and I was among them, up to the table. An informer sat there with his head covered. And we passed by him and then passed by some major who said, 'Name, please?' and I said, 'Jew from Eretz Yisrael,' and he: 'Mr. Ben-Aharon, what do you assume we are?' and introduced himself. He had been with me in the prison camp, and he said, 'How embarrassing that we should meet under such circumstances, but understand that I am doing my duty'—and once again I was supposed to express compassion. And from then on, twice a day, the orderlies would come with cigarettes, with canned goods.

"After the siege they had me court-martialed for perjury, for the fact that they had found reinforced positions and an armed population here. That was a serious transgression. And I accused them of murder. They had killed people without any provocation. I was still a military man. I was on paid leave. I argued in court that I had come home after a war and prison camp and found my kibbutz under siege—ruined, laid waste. And why? Because the survivors of Hitler had returned to their home. I pleaded the usual Zionist case." He smiled faintly, as if he could still see the English before him, listening to the plea. "I received a grave reprimand. After the trial, two or three of them came for polite visits. Later they started to put me in jail every time or in a detention camp despite the fact that, after five years, I was no longer an active member of any political body. It turned out that they had a file, and this is interesting, because although I was an ally and I was an officer in the British Army, they had a file on me as a potential enemy, because as an army man I had acquired the data and the knowledge that would enable me to fight them with their own weapons. They were sure that I was one of the biggest fish in the underground, and whenever there was an incident, they would haul me in.

"And then, after all this, I was told, 'Go ahead, go out there and do some political work.' I went to the Zionist meetings in London, along with Weizmann. By then there was a Labor government, and I, the socialist, actually had connections with the British Army. They tried to use my connections with the Conservative elite. They specially arranged a meeting for me with [British foreign secretary Anthony] Eden. The whole thing in Greece had been Eden's failed strategy, in their opinion. It was Eden's fault that we had been taken prisoner in Greece. And we barely got out alive. After we were taken, the prisoners talked for four years straight about what they were going to do to him, and they were all colleagues of his. And when I got there they decided they had to have a face-off between him and me over this. So they arranged a cocktail party, whiskey flowing, and Stirling and a few others brought Eden and me into a little room and said to me, 'Shoot.' They took him to task over his strategy and what he had done."

"Wasn't it strange for you, switching like that from Palestine to England?" I asked. "No," he said, "that's the whole thing. There was a kind of symbiosis. Englishness was not something foreign—not mine, but not foreign; it was something that I understood very well. It was quite organic, I knew it to its depths. After life as a POW—you have to know what it is for people to live together with no barriers, eight to ten people in a room like that with triple-decker beds—what years of that shared life are for people. I couldn't see them as enemies. The cards were all in the open."

"And you didn't have the feeling that you were different when you were with them, apart from your regular life?" I asked. "No," he said. "Aside from the tie and jacket and all that, there was nothing special. Some of them were gentleman farmers, with large estates in the English style, not ours, and we also talked business as farmers. Others were scholars at Oxford, and there were conversations about philosophy, sociology." Amused, he added, "There was no need for a concerted attack or for any Zionist dialectics. Over a glass of whiskey, you'd have a joke, a bit of good cheer.

"In the summer of 1947, before the UN declaration, they proposed that I go to England for political activity of a practical sort—to use my connections to get to Churchill, Macmillan, Eden, and all of them, and in fact we did have some important political meetings in which I tried to get a sense of them and pass it on to Weizmann and to Sharrett. I was very warmly received by my POW buddies. They were still celebrating their demobilization and return to civilian life, and I could have spent months at their festivities. "Were the celebrations in your honor?" I asked. "Yes," he said. "The phone calls went like this: 'Ben is here. Come and have a drink.' " His voice was suddenly different, and his intonation changed as he quoted them. "And out would come all the nostalgic stories of prison life, everything replayed, and of course I tried to talk with them as well, but their response to politics was not what it had been before the war. 'Let's leave politics to the professionals,' they said. 'It is a dirty job anyway.' But they said, 'Give it to them. If you've got the strength, you'll do all right; if you haven't got the strength, you won't.' When you come right down to it, they weren't particularly shocked by the actions of the extremists like the Etzel and Lehi.

"It was a group I'd been brainwashing for four years," he added with a look of amusement. "We were a very intimate group that spent hours upon hours together, day after day. Those who were hostile to Jews and to Zionists weren't in this group, they wouldn't bring them in. They would say themselves, 'This one is an anti-Semite, that one's involved in oil.' They had categories of their own. While we were starving there I sat and wrote a book in English about that doubleness, the Jew in the hands of the world and the Jew as British soldier in the hands of the Germans. A bit of fiction and a bit of autobiography." *Letters to My Son* is the title of the book, and in those fictional letters to his eldest son, Ben-Aharon tells about his childhood and about life in Nazi prison, and conveys his world outlook. An English officer published the book in Britain in 1949.

"Did they all hold conservative views?" I asked. "Yes," he replied, "clearly—but they were feisty. They were relatively young people who had come back from the war to a ruined empire. Anyone who could get himself a job outside of England did so. The war had a great impact on them in spite of everything. It dragged them out of their complacency, and they asked me then, what's the struggle about—the Americans on one side and the Russians on the other. Their mood was defeatist, and all they could advise was 'Give it to them,' give it to the Brits in the teeth, that was the standard formula. 'They don't understand any other language, eventually they have to get out. And there's no point, in any case they have to get out. You want it, take it.'"

"Those you met in Palestine," I said, "some of them were part of the same circle," and Ben-Aharon replied, "Almost none of them, they were almost a different nation, a different kind of people chosen for a special job, and they suited the job and the job suited them. They were the rulers and we were the subjects, the rebels. Any way you look at it, those were not relations among equals. The same ties could never have been formed here, even when they brought in special people who had to deal with the special problems, with the Jews and with the Arabs. Don't forget that the Arabs at the time had a first-rate intelligentsia." After a moment he added: "Before the war, before I had lived with them, I assumed all the British resembled those in Palestine. When I returned from a shared life with them, the English in Palestine seemed the exceptions. My estimation of them was the same as that of the British themselves: They were colonial elements no one had any use for, trash with which England filled the empty spaces of the world. But there are two Englands.

"That didn't prevent me from taking an active role in getting them out of here when the time came," he pointed out, "but that was in fact what gave me the faith that they could be gotten out. Because I knew them, I realized that they would not mount the barricades if they had to pay a high price for staying. Those who didn't really know them, who only knew those who had been here, accepted. They were in a very sorry state. Like any great power fighting a liberation movement and unwilling to pull out all the stops, and unable to. When we followed a policy of restraint, that gave us some moral advantage, and they admitted it, they couldn't wipe us out. Strong-arm tactics just united us all. A softer touch, and we climbed all over them. What made the question more profound was 'What for?' They had no way out, there wasn't any way out. Have we found a way out? They couldn't either."

TOP: Leaders of the Arab Revolt on a visit to the Prime Minister of Egypt, Cairo, Late Thirties. BOTTOM: Kibutz Ramat Hacovesh after a military search by the British army, November 1943.

TOP: Training of naval units of the Palmach commando in guise of aquatic sports. BOTTOM: Party at the King David Hotel, Jerusalem 1946.

A group of English women, residents of Haifa, in an afternoon party thrown at the occasion of the closure of the British soldiers canteen, Haifa 1944.

An attack by Lehi(Stern Group)at the Lions Gate,
the Old City of Jerusalem, 1946.

Mass Jewish demonstration against British policy,
Habimah Theatre, Tel Aviv, 1946.

TOP: British soldiers leaving Palestine, May 1948. BOTTOM: The French and Belgian Consuls entering Jerusalem for the first time after the end of the British Mandate.

CHAPTER NINE

"A twenty-inch stick, a knife, and empty hands"

In 1941, the German Panzer Division of General Erwin Rommel was advancing toward Egypt. The French army of the Vichy regime (under Nazi Germany) took over Syria and Lebanon. It seemed that Palestine was about to be conquered as well, and the British government was making preparation for a retreat. The leadership of the Yishuv was set for a last battle with the Nazis, and decided to create a special fighting force of the Hagana to oppose them. Those were commando units—the Palmach. After the victory over Rommel at El Alamein, the British had no more need of the force, and the Palmach went underground.

The Palmach members were volunteers. They were sent to kibbutzim, where they divided their time between training and agricultural work. From time to time they were called up to take part in major operations related to the illegal immigration of refugees from Europe and the founding of new settlements in strategic areas. They were also deployed, by command of the Hagana, to operations such as attacking British police stations or blowing up bridges.

At the beginning of the War of Independence, the Palmach played a central role in the defense of settlements and transport on the roads. After the establishment of the state it was a leading force in most of the battles, and twenty percent of its members were killed. During the war, Ben-Gurion decided to dismantle the force and to *disperse its fighters among other military units. But the inheritance of the Palmach spirit was apparent for years after that in a certain way of speech, in stories and songs, and its battle tradition was kept alive within the Israeli army. A number of its company commanders became leading generals, like Yitzhak Rabin and Moshe Dayan.*

Every group, even thieves, has a language of its own—chimney sweeps and anyone you can think of. An army unit, certainly. Listen sometime and see whether you understand a quarter of a conversation between two soldiers." Shimon Avidan, a Hagana man who had commanded a battalion in the Palmach and been head of operations during the War of Independence, was talking about Palmach lingo. "We had no doubt, yes, that as soon as the war ended our struggle would begin. We had no reason to think it was going to be easy. How does any self-respecting young man protect his flank? With jokes, or half words, or he doesn't talk at all. He whistles, yes. He doesn't even know how to drink. Stepping on a cork is enough to make him drunk. They were good kids in that sense."

Avidan was also commander of the Palmach's German company, the boys who were trained in guerrilla tactics when the army of the Third Reich was about to invade Palestine; I preferred to hear about the Palmach from someone who had been part of it but had come from the outside, from Germany. I was hoping that through his eyes the Palmach would appear different to me—less familiar and less worn, less like people whose time the passing years had not favored. And yet, I felt, the people of the Palmach had something that time could not touch, like a book from childhood that you read and reread—out of love and out of boredom—until you'd memorized the very shape of the letters and the placement of passages on the page. For a long time I postponed the encounter with these people who had told and sung too much about themselves, had too often retraced the years of those stories and songs. I wanted to ask who they had been before that, before they retraced and before they recounted.

I met with Avidan in Tel Aviv, at the headquarters of the left-wing Kibbutz Artzi movement, a rather tall office building not far from the stores and cafés of Ibn Gvirol Street—not much different in appearance from the building of a bank or investment firm. When he left the army after the War of Independence and returned to the kibbutz, Avidan had served as secretary of Kibbutz Artzi, among other roles, and now he led me to one of the offices that was empty at the moment. He sat down opposite me, across a desk, his face in the shadow. It was an office overlooking the courtyard, untouched by the white noon sun. Before we started talking, he took his watch off and put it down in front of him—the habit of a meticulous man who budgets his time. He gave brief answers to my opening questions. In 1934 he had come to Palestine from Germany via France, joined Kibbutz Ayelet HaShahar and the Hagana, in which he was active for many years. In 1940 he moved to Kibbutz Ein HaShofet and in 1942 joined the Palmach. He spoke in a quiet voice with a slight German accent, at a rather labored pace—question-answer, question-answer—like someone filling out a form.

I asked why he had joined the Palmach. "In 1942 Yitzhak Sadeh [the founder and first commander of the Palmach], was looking for ways to counter the German threat," he said, "and he arranged with the Hagana command to set up a platoon of German speakers within the Palmach, whose task would be to appear as Germans and to work behind the lines in the event of a German invasion here. The Germans were advancing on El Alamein at the time, and the British had made plans to evacuate Palestine and retreat as far as Persia, where they would be back-to-back with the Red Army. If they were to retreat, they were interested in leaving behind some forces that would be able to halt the German and Italian advance, if only temporarily, and so they contacted the Hagana and assisted in setting up such units. We worked with British advisers who took charge of our training. That was the period when every Oxford graduate worth his salt was setting up his own secret unit. We had contact with all sorts of units like that."

"Can you tell me a little about what happened?" I asked with some hesitation. Despite his kibbutz informality he was a bit intimidating. "What happened?" he said. "I can tell you. To my delight Rommel was thwarted and we had no need to fight for our lives here. Our basic plan was to concentrate the Jewish population in the Carmel area, including part of Haifa, to gather the entire population there, to add to that the Jews serving in the British Army, arms and all. In such an event there was little hope that we could do what the Allies hadn't done—defeat the Germans—but we would have sold our lives at a better . . ." And here he stopped, as if it was obvious how they would have sold their lives and he was not inclined to pathos. "A kind of Masada?" I suggested. "Call it whatever you like. The art is not to die but to kill the enemy," he said, putting both me and the matter in our places. "There are lots of ways small units can delay and obstruct, particularly when they're wearing German uniforms and can at least for a short time resemble German units, carrying out intelligence operations or bombing airfields at a depth of hundreds of miles behind the lines, or blocking some advancing division for half an hour. The British were in a bad state all around and they would try anything. That was over as soon as the German threat subsided, but we, meanwhile, were not wasting our training. We had sent people to work with British units behind the lines. Later that platoon was drafted into the British Army, and they were also involved in the Bricha [moving illegal-immigrant war refugees south]."

"You commanded that platoon?" I asked, since he was waiting, withdrawn, for my next question. "Yes," he said. When I asked how he had recruited people, he replied, "I recruited among the various circles I knew, and those in the Palmach who fit the bill." As we talked about Jews from Germany it occurred to me that I had been expecting to meet one of those German Jews who was both refined and exacting, one of those in whom kibbutz life had brought out the spiritual qualities. Shimon Avidan was not like that. A short man, sturdy, solid, even now he seemed built for hard work. His eyes were a lucent blue, made paler by his white hair, cut short in military style. His face reflected a different kind of asceticism, like the face of a farmer turned monk. I asked whether he had been the same age as the people he recruited, and he said, "Maybe five years older. I was more aware than they, but I wasn't so much older that I couldn't deal with the questions and the conflicts young people had.

"And so, it went all right," he added. I had the feeling that those last words had been translated or somehow transferred from German. "My special tasks put me in a certain situation. Playing the role of a German officer twenty-four hours a day, for instance, is not easy. I had to do all those things that I love to do," he continued in the same tone, with the same dryness, as if he really meant to say "that I love to do" and not "that I despise," and then I said, "For instance?" "The language, curses, forms of address, orders, speechs, songs, yes. People met the challenge and were able to play German soldiers successfully. They would put people in a German prison camp so they could discover which of the prisoners had lied about his particulars, who was an officer, who was a pilot. And they'd stay as long as two weeks without being discovered. In the event the Germans discovered a plant in the camp, he'd be found the next morning covered with blankets and quite dead."

"Did they have longer training periods than other platoons in the Palmach?" I asked. "No," said Avidan, "but they made fuller use of the training." "If you think about a day of such training, what was it like?" He thought a moment and said, "For instance, this unit had to operate in the field according to German commands and German training, so we put emphasis on form. Saluting, delivering a message, how you start it, how you end it. Beyond that, we practiced all the things that had to do with explosives. We added lots of nighttime exercises in infiltration, breaking into buildings, storehouses." And when I asked whether they had also carried out acts of sabotage, he said, "Yes. We destroyed planes, about eight of them, in Libya, and carried out observation and intelligence operations against the German army on the coastal road to Egypt. Everything is written down, recorded."

"In the camp they spoke only German?" "Yes," he said. "But it wasn't only a matter of which language, it was a very particular kind of language. German got shorter during the war—every excess word dropped out, and anything foreign was eliminated.

Also, young Jews usually didn't know the curses and the vulgar talk that were part of any army unit. It wasn't simple for a Jewish boy, even if he had the Aryan look." After a pause he added: "To go back and behave and express yourself in a language and a manner that you hate—you really have to be mentally prepared. Although, as I said, our aim was to strike and escape, we realized that we had to know everything—including the nature of relations between them and the Italians, including they way they sit or lift a cup— dozens of things that enable me to tell you who's German and who isn't. We had to put heart and soul into preparing people to carry out the mission."

"It must have been very strange—that training." "Yes," Avidan agreed, "very strange and extremely difficult." "There's even something sinister about it," I ventured, and he said, "Quite sinister, yes, it was a bitter task. Particularly because you have to be on your guard, see that someone doesn't get carried away and start enjoying it. There are those types, too. Some of the best soldiers were Germans. Still Jews, but Germans by nature." And when I said something about the special situation of German Jews in Palestine during those years, he said, "I'm not a prototype of the German Jew. I'm not from one of those families. My father was a carpenter. At the age of fifteen, I went out to work, and I didn't bring along the culture of the piano and the tasteful room. What I did bring with me, certainly, was the memory of my grandfather, and of my grandfather's grandfather—who were not Jews. That's it."

He lit a cigarette. My next question was a long time in coming. His concluding "That's it" had steered me away. In any case, I did not dare ask him whether he wasn't Jewish and what besides socialism had brought him to Palestine. "Did the platoon have a name?"

I asked. "Yes," he replied. "Among ourselves we used the name of one of our boys who had fallen in action—Peter Haas," and after a moment he added: "Later they charged me and, through me, the German platoon with setting up a Balkan platoon. That is, people who could appear to be Romanians, Bulgarians, Czechs—and among them, the paratroops. For about six months I commanded special units, including airmen and seamen, all the dirty work. The German Department was of assistance with all that because of its professional level. Every one of them performed at the level of officers during training." "Did they feel driven to prove themselves better because of their different background?" I asked. "I would put it another way," he said. "There's a difference between someone who was born here, whose spiritual world has deep roots in this land, in the sunset and in the stillness and in the language and defense, and a young man who saw the rise of Nazism, and perhaps felt it physically, or saw someone close to him experience it. An order is an order and, yes, carrying it out is carrying it out. Beyond that"—and here he paused to search for words—"beyond that they had no illusions, and none of that youthful mischievousness, yes, that was part of the Palmach."

Beyond that they had no illusions, I repeated to myself, and I wondered whether the others, the ordinary boys of the Palmach, those who had "deep roots in this land, in the sunset and in the stillness and in the language and defense," did have illusions. I asked, "What was really your impression of those native-born Palmachniks?" "Look," he said, "whoever came here came to fight. That is, my experience has been that the percentage of fighters in any nation is next to nil, one or two percent at most, and all the rest, if they can only find some way of existing with a modicum of what passes for honor, will do so. Here you had young men who were looking for a framework in which to fight against everything they found insufferable, whether it was the British or an external enemy. So, if you ask me how they looked to me"—and here his words took on the tone of a kibbutz member talking about the younger generation—"some of them, through their love of the land and their closeness to nature, had already turned into natural soldiers.

"For instance," he started to explain, "it was clear to us that any fighting would be at night, since during the day a hostile government prevailed and there was a potential local enemy who was many times stronger—the Arabs. If it was a matter of the German army, clearly the daytime advantage in observation and equipment. Anyone moving at night could do so only in small units, and in small units, each individual has much greater responsibility: nothing forces the night fighter into battle; he can also curl up in a corner. So everyone has to say to himself: I owe it to my friends, and then he gets up. What it means is that you have to educate, that the image of the commander is different, that you have to teach a fighter what night is. A city person used to streetlights doesn't usually feel too good out in the middle of nowhere."

And he coughed—a smoker's cough. "The weapons at our disposal," he went on, "were always of the sort that you had to conceal, so they had to be light, and light means short-range, short-range means you have to get close up. What that means is you have to develop very sharp teeth in these people, and what is more important, you have to develop in them a readiness to move across that distance. Those are some of the qualities. I could go on and on. We were terribly poor. Everyone was poor. But we were especially poor. There was a period when I had a pair of pants with only one pocket, because they wanted to economize. We couldn't give them heavy weapons, not the weapons that were required. And often enough, no shoes. Going barefoot can be disastrous or it can lead to great things. The Palmach knew how to turn what it lacked into advantage. The offset, that is, had to be in the person. To me there's nothing worse than enforcing authority or discipline without an attempt to win the person over.

"During the War of Independence I was appointed commander of what was then called the Givati Brigade. 'Givati' was my nickname in the Hagana, and this was a southern brigade. That brigade had had encounters with both the Arab Legion and the Egyptian Army, and very quickly had to be made into a regular force. We did that successfully, but even in the framework of a regular army we tried to win the soldier over as a partner and retain the image of the commander as a friend. In the Palmach you were a commander only because you happened to be older, more responsible, with a sense of justice. After every action there was an open discussion, and the commander was fair game. To me a good soldier is a thinking soldier, yes. A soldier is also a person who will not leave a wounded comrade, because he shares the sense of responsibility. A natural soldier, you know, is a kind of animal in the wild, someone who once picked up a handful of earth and felt it run through his fingers and realized that felt good. It's a person who will naturally notice the tiniest spot.

"We taught a lot of close-range combat," he added. "That means fighting with a twenty-inch stick, a knife, and empty hands. The military value is questionable—any bullet has a greater range and more penetrating power. But the educational value for what you would call aggressiveness is inestimable. Beyond that, no one had much experience in the Palmach. There had never been a Jewish company or battalion commander under those conditions. And we didn't have anything to learn from. We were lucky enough to have a number of people at the forefront; I don't want to call them leaders because they weren't leaders." Here he paused in his efforts at precision; the more important the matter, the greater the difficulty. "They had no doubt about what awaited us," he continued. "They set down one principle that can account for the fighting and the victory in the War of Independence, and that is that fighting is not conditional but goes on under all conditions and unconditionally. Beyond that, they established that you have an obligation because you are aware of it, and that you take the mission on yourself, no one forces it on you."

"In the summer of 1944," said Meir Drezdner, who had been a deputy battalion commander in the Palmach, "four of us went on a big outing through the whole country to little-known places like Gaza and Jericho. It was a big trip, like a bachelor party in America. We had just graduated from school, so it was kind of trip you take before you go into the army or to kibbutz training—a farewell trip." His tone was jocular; he was in his early sixties, but his manner did not match his age. There was something youthful about it, simple and very familiar. The road to his house was also very familiar: he lives in Haifa, not far from my parents' home.

Today he is an engineer, dealing mainly with water and agricultural development. A good part of his work is done abroad, but Drezdner looks very much the local, as does his wife, Miriam, who was a medic in the Palmach and today teaches biology in high school. They dress simply, and in their spacious and simply furnished apartment, nothing is around for show. The light tiled floor suggested summer: long undemanding days, sandals outdoors and bare feet indoors. Children played a game in the street, which was familiar and yet whose name I could not recall.

"I guess it was in July or August that we went out for kibbutz training," he continued. "It was what they called mobilized training. That's the way it went—Palmach and ploughshares. We went out to Kibbutz Alumot, which was then in old Poriya. Members of the kibbutz lived in basalt houses and in sheds, and they set up lean-tos of woven mats for us. It was very pleasant. As I recall, we started quite a long period of work, and no one at all from the Palmach command turned up. Here we were, signing up, eager for battle, and what did they mean, we were supposed to work? Where were our training exercises? 'We've been working for three whole weeks and no training, a month by now and no training?' There was always that kind of agitation.

"In fact, this business was not so simple. There was a problem with places to train and weapons for training—this was an underground. Besides, we had to take the kibbutz into account. If it's a matter of learning to use a gun, you can always do that some other week. But the harvest won't wait. The kibbutz was small, and there were thirty of us. I worked in the dairy barn, and that was purported to be a great honor, but at Alumot, because they were poor as church mice, they didn't have a superb herd of Holsteins. They had a Damascus herd, Arabian, and mainly they were beef cattle. So I was less a dairyman than a cowherd, going out day after day in the dewy morn, before dawn. The Yavne valley was my grazing ground: eighty head, a bitch, and yours truly." Colloquial speech had changed, I thought to myself, but this style, blending formality and heightened speech with the colloquial, persisted.

"There were some things I learned and some things I never managed to get straight," Drezdner continued. "I tried playing the recorder, but just couldn't do it, I wasn't really dedicated. I learned to smoke, on the excuse that I used to meet Arab cowherds and they would offer me a cigarette, and I had to have some on me to offer them. My second course of study was the slingshot, not just a stone flung on the end a string, but a genuine David-and-Goliath affair. In 1944, just to remind you, World War II was still in progress. And there were hordes of British soldiers in Palestine and in Egypt, and these soldiers were fed on cattle raised in Syria and taken to Egypt on foot. It was a journey of a month or two. There was an English company called Steel Brothers, and they were contracted by the army. The herds were theirs, and they had Arab herders. They would do a head count when they got them, near Aleppo somewhere, and they'd count them a second time on the other side, when they got to Ismaïlia. They would be debited for anything that died on the way and credited for any increase, whether from calving or anything that happened to attach itself. They would go with huge herds of five to six thousand head, covering the whole countryside. And when they saw a small herd like mine they would coincidentally mingle in, and by the time they'd passed I was short five or six head, and that was most unpleasant. You couldn't throw stones at them because there were ten of them and one of you, and they'd kill you. You had to throw stones at your own cows to get them away, and the best instrument for that purpose was the slingshot, which allowed you to shoot from a distance of sixty to seventy yards.

I'd throw a stone at a cow and she'd run to join the herd. If my herd was massed on one side and theirs on the other, and I was standing in the middle, one of the herders would come up to me and then it was *ahlen* ["welcome" in Arabic] and shalom and a cigarette." "Do you speak Arabic?" I asked. "I knew a little," he said, "because I grew up in Haifa, which was a mixed city and there were always Arabs around."

"With whom did you feel more comfortable, the city people in Haifa or the herders?" I asked. "To tell you the truth," he said, his eyes smiling, "I didn't feel comfortable with either. Although we grew up in a mixed city there was some feeling of being a tourist abroad when you went to eat hummus in an Arab restaurant near the Armon cinema, which was in the border area between the Arab and the Jewish neighborhoods. Don't forget that that was just a year or two after the riots ended, and I won't say there was hatred of the Arabs, because in our generation there wasn't, not even afterward, during the War of Independence. I don't remember there being any hostility, but there was a feeling of foreignness and of danger." "And of fear," added Miriam, and he said, "You weren't allowed to admit it was fear."

"Didn't people want to get to know them better, if only as a source of fear?" I wondered. "I grew up in Jerusalem," said Miriam. "Our neighborhoods were separate, the Arabs were over there on the other side, and there was a tremendous sense of foreignness. We studied Arabic at school, but beyond that we took no interest in them as people." And yet they wound kaffiyehs around their necks, I thought, and they had campfires with coffee in a *finjan*, a special small pot for brewing coffee on a campfire, and they annexed many Arabic expressions into their Hebrew.

"We were so involved with ourselves," said Meir. "Scouts and the Hagana filled our lives. From scouts we went to the Hagana, and in scouts from the age of fifteen you lived with the awareness that you were preparing for kibbutz life, and somewhere in the background, behind the scenes, were Arabs. But that didn't occupy us particularly, though in scouts we had lectures on Arabs, and part of the ethos was the belief that we in fact would be a great boon to them." "And you accepted that?" I asked. "I think we pretty much believed that, since there wasn't any hostility," he said. "It seemed quite clear that we had to behave morally. On the other hand, we were eager for an engagement. Without a doubt."

Again the heightened language that puts a dusting of irony on the lofty expressions of those days. But they do something else, I realized then; they distance the stark meaning of those expressions. "Eager for an engagement" sounds better than "dying for a fight." "What exactly do you mean?" I probed. "Look," he explained, "we were in awe of weapons. The Hagana was everything to us. Whatever the squad commander said was holy writ. Their willingness, devotion, was without reservation, of a kind that only young boys and girls are capable of. There were problems with the people of Israel, and the Holocaust, but there was also this simple matter of—I don't know how to say it—a kind of joy among young men at the prospect of an engagement. There is such a thing."

"I can easily see how the Palmach and the underground and all that attracted you," I said, "but what about the kibbutz and the farmwork that came along with it?" He replied: "There was something about the kibbutz that repelled me. In my discussions with myself it turned out that I didn't want to work in the cow barn all my life, and that was actually the decision that I made, not to join a kibbutz. The kibbutz was a kind of taken-for-granted thing, topped by a big question mark. But work was one of the principles of the faith, and what made you respectable in society was not that you were a big fighter during training; if you didn't work, you were in disgrace. A good-for-nothing wasn't someone who did nothing, but someone who avoided work; he was simply not a member of the human race." "That's still the case," Miriam pointed out, laughing. "Yes," Mair agreed. "We've been brainwashed."

"And it was really good to be in an environment like that?" I asked him. "You know what," he said, "it was fantastic, it was extraordinary. I look at my daughters now—they had to blaze their own trail, they had to answer the questions themselves and to make decisions. We were exempt from decisions. What we were to do was perfectly clear. Today when they talk about kids finding themselves it's silly but it's legitimate: they finish army service and they have to decide what to do. For us it wasn't like that. For us the War of Independence came and threw everything out of kilter."

The War of Independence that threw everything out of kilter is central, an unfinished story, understood only to Drezdner and his friends. Caution was advised here, I thought. No point in announcing that there was something noble about foregoing decisions, when it also had an aspect that was bleak and restrictive. Still, I couldn't help but ask: "Wasn't there something stifling in all that?" "Yes," he agreed. "Certainly, from time to time. Look, we used to kick a little." A moment later he corrected himself. "Let's put it this way: I didn't feel it. On the contrary, if I'd had to leave it I would have felt completely lost." So he claimed—a man with an open face, speaking with assurance, with no apparent need to prove his existence. His place was well-defined. He was centered in the world, and radiated a sense of confidence and consistency, the feeling of a pleasant environment with no hidden corners. It occurred to me then that the word *family* had never come up as he spoke, but it was inherent in what he said. Whether he was saying "I" or "we," he always spoke of himself as part of a specific family, a body from which everything else issued. And this large family of friends who had gone through everything together during the Palmach years was the crucible of the world. All the rest—however beloved, attractive, interesting, and important—all the rest was outside.

"Imagine that *Emil and the Detectives* [a well-known German young-adult novel by Erich Kastner] is official and formal and you have the backing of the entire Yishuv," he said. "Could anything be better? It was a bit of a game, but not entirely. It was full-time, it contained us. We did it the way a good Jew says his prayers, with all his heart and soul." His last words reminded me of something Yitzhak Ben-Aharon had said: "We were Jews through and through, raised on the commandments, studying in the heder, in yeshivas, and because we had absorbed it all, we could also deny its relevance. But we didn't splice the next generation to those same roots. We spliced them to secularism." Is that the way it really was, I wondered then, and what happens when you try to create such grafts?

"A second generation is formed differently, there's nothing you can do about it," said Gavriel Cohen, who had been a member of the Palmach and was now a professor of history researching the Mandate period. "In fact, education at the time saw in each individual a thinking person. It gave each person the feeling that everything was on his shoulders. And they looked for political leaders and competed for them, and wherever they heard that there was someone worth anything, they sought him out. But in reality, and it's the reality of every national revolution, the decisions of a revolutionary magnitude were the preserve of the first generation, and you got used to that without realizing it. You were not going through it. The smoke-filled rooms of the Zionist Congress were not part of your experience. And yet, every week whole evenings would be devoted to discussions of the kibbutz, of existence, of everything. The quantity of thought and mental exertion we invested was astounding. But there was a feeling, nevertheless, of something convenient—that's what I called it—something dictated from above that released you from the necessity of deciding.

"The problem of that generation that came to be expressed in the Palmach was that it learned to live with an unusually powerful leadership that was making all the moral decisions," he explained, adding, "They lived the struggle of that leadership, but they grew up implementing its decisions. Their test in the eyes of the leadership and in their own eyes was implementation, and implementation is a world unto itself. Because the process of Zionist realization was one of discovering something new each time that would not be done if you didn't do it yourself. At a certain moment it became clear that there had to be a permanent mobilized force, but at the same time some people were fearful of having such a force, and there was the idealistic view that there were dangers in having such a professional army. And the relationship between the Palmach and the kibbutz movement did not develop smoothly either. There was a constant struggle. And since it was so complicated—the agreement with the kibbutz movement, the argument with part of the political leadership over the very fact of the Palmach's existence and whether it wasn't better to join the British Army—the concept of a working army crystallized, two weeks of training alternating with two weeks of farmwork as a way of supporting the Palmach. So they turned necessity into an advantage, including the ideology that grew up around it, which said you were something special, you were not a professional soldier, for instance: you had been called on to fight for the most sacred thing in the world, most sacred to the Jewish people, but you were not an ordinary soldier.

"It was a special framework," Cohen said, "which caused the average man to turn out above average. It was a group of people who gave full expression to some common denominator that was much higher than usual despite the fact that its members were quite usual. Something elitist was definitely being nurtured, in the sense that you were encouraged from outside and you also knew inside yourself how to nurture this feeling, this faith that at every stage they were destining you for the central task of Zionism. But to the extent that we really were a select unit in battle, to the extent that we really had the qualities attributed to us, it was due to two things—a sense of shame and camaraderie. You can put the ideology last. Even in battles where you know that the fate of the state rests on your shoulders. What made me leave the hospital two days after I was wounded though I could have stayed there another two weeks? Two things: friendship, in the sense that you don't want to miss one of the group experiences, and shame."

"I have a feeling that it was a very intense and full period, but maybe one in which you didn't ask too many questions," I said to Meir Drezdner, and he replied: "Look, the questions were rhetorical questions. There were lots of fierce discussions. And we talked about everything, but the answers were known, it was an exercise in indoctrination. It never happened that we discussed equality and then voted it down. That was inconceivable." He was using that easy tone of self-irony that brought to mind the style of the upper-class English, whose self-irony also is tinged with a certain consciousness of status. "And that didn't bother you?" I asked. "It wasn't disturbing?" "Let's say that to me it wasn't," he replied.

"Does this mean you were willing to carry out this business—if there's something to do, let's get it done—but that you didn't really want to bother too much with the theory of it?" I asked. "I don't know," he said, hesitating. "What it comes down to is that our parents believed in those things, and they were the ones who sent us out to do them. We were all of one mind." He thought for a moment and added: "I can't speak for everyone. You know, some of the people were recent immigrants, from Austria, from Germany. Imagine that for many of them this was foreign and peculiar and created a lot of tension—and today we hear about outbursts that occurred. But the interesting thing is that they were superconformists at the time. They were the ones singing loudest, leaping highest when they danced. They wanted very much to belong because the group was very strong."

"What did you think of the people who were not like yourselves, who were more urban or involved with the English?" I asked him. "Look," he said. "Girls going out with the English—that was bad. But the English themselves—I never met any besides the soldier who asked me for my papers at the checkpoint. We had the newspapers, and we were always having mass meetings where they explained everything and gave speeches, and I accepted what they said, that the English had betrayed us and all that, but I had my own interests."

"And what did you have against them or for them that remained somewhat abstract?" I asked. "We felt that the English were foreigners here and none of this was any of their business, and they'd played a dirty trick on us, but I didn't have any really strong feelings on the matter. Look, I was in a course for platoon commanders, which was a very underground course, because it was after the June 29, Black Sabbath, the day leaders of the Jewish Agency and the Hagana were arrested. We stayed in the Kfar HaHoresh guesthouse, and we went out to train in canvas-covered trucks. A new tactical structure was set up that was more suited to regular actions against the British. Fewer guns, and ammunition that was suited to urban warfare. All the training was for raids and blowing up installations. Everything was for war against the British, and our conviction was so strong, and the confidence—not confidence in our strength, but confidence in the cause—was such that we could actually fight them. I didn't hesitate for a moment to go out there with explosives and blow something up. If you have to, you fight them."

Sounds a bit like the English soldiers, I thought, fighting without overinvolvement. The point was to fight, the point was if you had to. Neither the Arabs nor the English occupied them very much. They didn't hate them and they didn't like them. They didn't dismiss the others: they were human beings, but they might as well have been from outer space. The world was themselves and their parents' generation and various adjuncts, but the main thing was themselves—new, with no diaspora: only with Hebrew, with the Bible, with what was here, at the center. Did they take for granted that they were the center, was that a given like their training and their raids, like the questions answered in advance, like their absolute faith in the answers?

"Did you have the feeling that you were an elite unit?" I asked Drezdner, and he thought a moment. "There was something strange in this elite unit," he said. "People weren't chosen for it. That is, there was practically no screening; whoever wanted to join could come, including people who for health reasons would have been rejected by the army. That was one aspect. The other thing was that, until the War of Independence, the Palmach was the most highly trained unit. A member of the Hagana in the city would come in the evening, train for two hours in some grove or on the grounds of the Technion, and go home. We lived under field conditions, you jumped the fence of the kibbutz and you were in the fields, and if something had to be done at the spur of the moment, there was no need to start from scratch to organize it. So we trained more, and the commanders were busy with this twenty-four hours a day. Most of the commanders could, at a given moment, with a gesture of the hand or a change in their tone of voice, let you know, 'Okay, this is over, now we stop being buddies and change gears.' And it worked very well, because in those days a Palmach commander had support and immense credit. He would have had to do some pretty stupid things to lose that credit. From the start they put their faith in him, and if they made him a squad commander or a platoon commander or a company commander it was a sign he was worthy of it. But the moment he lost his credit, he was finished. I used to stay up half the night thinking about how I would get the lesson across the next day. I went over it in my mind day and night. If you met other people you'd talk about that, lots of discussions about Company Five's operation in the south or two squads that went out and cut power lines—what they did and how they managed to pull it off. It went on like that all the time.

"It was something we believed in. We believed that we were the trailblazers, we were the standing unit of the Hagana, they called us Strike Forces and expected us to do certain things. We were capable of doing them, and we would do them. It was inconceivable that we wouldn't, that we would fail at something. It's true that when we went into action we turned out to be not nearly as good as we'd thought, much less well trained and not such experts at war after all. We made up for much of what we didn't know with total devotion."

"To be part of such teams—such an elite community—is a state of grace, but all so temporary," I said to the Drezdners. "Did you think about what would happen later on?" They both said no, and then Meir added: "First of all, we were very secretive, but the whole country knew that anyone on the street in a certain kind of coat was Palmach. There were two kinds of coat, both made out of British Army blankets, like a peacoat. One was gray and the other black or dark brown. We had a poet who said those coats had the majesty of tents in the desert. That's as far as grace is concerned. Regarding what would be afterward, I didn't see myself finishing service in another year and leaving. I didn't think about it. There were always other things, the dangers and where were we headed and what did the future hold for us, and I was in the future, I was always there."

"On the door of our room we had a big sign: 'Eat, drink and be merry, for tomorrow we die,' " said Miriam about the early months of 1948, when they were on Mount Canaan. She talked simply, without embellishment, about people who were killed, about the cold, about a bullet accidentally discharged. But it was clear that she had told these stories before. From time to time Meir, who had been the commander on Mount Canaan, would join in with some ironic remark, without disturbing the flow of the story. They were reciting together a familiar text, a text they needed to impart, doubtless a genuine need to tell, a way of meeting the world. It was also a way of being presented in life—within the story that took place then, in that rare period when the present contained the future.

"On May 14, at night, I was walking at the head of a company on the way to blowing up a bridge on the Litani River [Lebanon], which today is called the Khardaleh," said Meir. "It was a pretty difficult business, far away, and we had to walk about ten miles over hills carrying a huge amount of explosives—sixteen hundred pounds. That night there was also the last attack and finally, finally, the successful one, on Nebi Yosha. Not long before that we had gotten communications equipment for the first time, radio transmitters, and so, because Nebi Yosha is high and we were walking along a ridge, I could talk to our unit there. The battalion commander said over the radio, 'You know, this afternoon a Jewish state was declared,' and I said, 'So what.'"

"That 'So what,'" I said: "Wasn't it a way of telling the previous generation that there was more than a difference in style between you: they would never have gone so far as to say, 'So what'?" "No," he said, "it was only a matter of style, changes in expressions, all kinds of things, but I have the feeling we were much closer to the previous generation than the next generation was to us. We were really of the same flesh and blood." "What I meant to ask," I said, "was whether Zionism was not, even in your time, something said a bit tongue-in-cheek." "It wasn't a question of Zionism," he protested, "but of talking Zionism. It's the talking that was scorned, not the Zionism. Zionism was not at all in quotation marks. It's just that it was embarrassing to talk that way.

"What do you do if you're on a bare mountaintop, carrying a guy who's got a bullet in his leg? What do you do, stop everyone and sing 'Hatikvah'? At that moment, when they said that over the radio, I was very worried. I was on my way back from an attack and I had one casualty who had to be carried, and as was usual in those days we were late and it was already getting light and we were stuck in some hole in the middle of Lebanon. I knew there was a Syrian pillbox near Metula and that I had to cross the border. I was preoccupied with weighty matters. And I had known they were going to establish a state. That's what the whole thing was about."

When I left the Drezdners' house it was already dark. The children who had been playing in the street were gone. A scent of pine needles and dust hovered over the sidewalk. On foot I would have found my way immediately, but I was in the car, looking at the signs that had changed—one "No entry" after the next—and I lost my way in the small neighborhood of small houses and small gardens, like other such neighborhoods, now surrounded by apartment buildings better built and bleaker, and as I passed them I recalled a Palmach song we used to sing when I was a girl; whole lines came to mind.

"How the road goes on, winding or straight / The paths slip by, the wind is great. / At eve we'll take up arms again / As a Hebrew village glimmers afar." The village is has no name. What counts is that it is Hebrew. "Come north, my friends, the border's nearing / Ready for battle at the clearing." The song goes on at a marching pace, not overly military, the language elevated and slightly archaic. But at the end there's one short line that contains a simple question and a simple answer: "What a song, what a *kef* ["hashish" in Arabic, "fun" in Hebrew], who's riding high? Palmach." There is little use for the expression "riding high" these days, but *kef*, which was taken from the Arabic because the Palmach loved to take words from the Arabic and maybe couldn't find a suitable one in Hebrew—that word has stayed in everyday use.

CHAPTER TEN

"A sporting chance"

Great Britain conquered Palestine in the last months of 1917, toward the end of the First World War. This was not just another military conquest. The army commander, General Edmund Allenby, did not enter the Old City on horseback. He walked on foot through Damascus Gate at the head of his force. The officers of the Mandatory Administration regarded Palestine as a special place to serve. This was the land of the Bible, the Holy Land. Quite a few among them saw themselves as the followers of the Crusaders. They called the conquest of Palestine the Sixth Crusade. They were thrilled to serve there, but it did not take long for them to realize how difficult and complicated this service was. The Mandatory rule was supposed to prepare the country for independence. But who would rule in Palestine—Arabs or Jews—remained an unanswered question. The conflict between the two peoples began, in fact, during the Mandate years.

Many of the Englishmen came as pro-Zionist, but after some time became pro-Arab. The Arabs were part of the exotic Orient, as well as the underdogs. The Yishuv was generally seen as the source of trouble. Those were strange foreign people, becoming stronger and stronger while the natives, the Arab fellahin, were being expelled from their lands. As the hostility between Jews and Arabs grew, the disappointment of both sides with Britain deepened. The English lived more and *more within their closed community. But Palestine remained for them a significant place, and a feeling of guilt toward the Arabs, whom they had abandoned, grew deeper with time.*

I think that we did them a great wrong. We gave away a country that wasn't ours to give, we made it possible, and I think that many Jews forgot about it. I don't think that the Balfour Declaration, of which I have a copy in that desk, I don't think that Balfour ever envisaged the Arabs being turned out for the Jews." The speaker was Faith Lloyd-Phillips, widow of Ivan Lloyd-Phillips, who had been a district commissoner and district officer "from Dan to Beersheba," as she put it—from the north of Palestine to the south. Ivan had gone to Palestine in the Thirties, and Faith had joined him there a few years later, the two of them remaining until the end of the Mandate. Before we met she had warned me on the phone that she was very anti-Zionist, so I would know how things stood, but she received me warmly.

"I never knew I could feel as strongly about a country apart from my own as I feel about Palestine," she said as we ate lunch in her home. It was an old cottage on a small river near Oxford. Lloyd-Phillips was wearing a good tweed suit that emphasized her height and slimness, and an attractive Victorian pin on her lapel. In her appearance there was something well groomed and unfeminine, the air of a rider in high-quality boots, coat, and hat.

When I asked her how she became an anti-Zionist, she answered willingly: "The first time I went to Palestine, I went in the Thirties with my mother, and we stayed at Government House, and I came away very pro-Jew. I really was, and I came back to Palestine, and my husband did not influence me one way or the other, and I hadn't been there very long before I got very irritated—I am sorry, but I did—with the Jews. Because I thought they were so unnecessarily grasping. Well now, we lived in a very nice house belonging to the Melchetts. It was a Mandate, and unlike the colonies, they did not buy houses, and Ivan rented Villa Melchett on the Sea of Galilee. It was a lovely place but terribly lonely because my husband went off and I was left there. It is the little things in life that often influence people in what they like or dislike, and one of the things that infuriated me was, we rented a house with a charming garden, very nicely kept. But on Saturdays, if I was there—my husband worked till lunchtime—I would be overrun by Jews from the nearest kibbutz. I was not used to this."

"Why would they come?" I asked. "They just came because it was a very nice place to come to. Not into the house but into the garden, they did, and I would say to them, 'Look, I am sorry, we live here, you can't come here, we're here.' And they spoke English and they said, 'But this is ours. It belongs to the Jews. It belongs to us.' And you know, this absolutely maddened me. Because in the garden there was a sort of a little place way down, and there were two seats, and you would sit and you would see to the other side right on the lake, and I used to take my book and sit down to read. Well, I didn't want all these unknown people jostling all around me. And they would come and sit on the seat, and they would say to me, 'This is our land and we will come when we like.' It would happen pretty well every Saturday."

"Do you think it was political?" "I don't know. It was communism to me. I thought the Arabs were not communists, I must go to the Arabs. You know, this was the beginning of it, and I thought, Zionism—I have had it."

She laughed merrily, and I think I must have laughed with her out of embarrassment. I had been told about people like her, and the history books described in depth the reasons that many English disliked the Jews in Palestine. But still, it was different to meet, for the first time in my life, someone who talked that way. I was surprised by the intensity of my response as I listened to this enthusiastic, spontaneous delivery: "There was something very delightful about the Arabs, and I didn't feel that the Arabs were as foreign to the English as the Jews were in their approach to life. I don't think that a lot of the Jews who came to Palestine had any respect for anybody. What their background had been I don't know, but they were all out for what they could get, and you never had that feeling with an Arab. I am sorry, but that's the truth," and she laughed. "That's all right," I said, but it was not all right. Because I realized then that what she was saying stemmed not only from anti-Zionism but also from something deeper and more primary—a nonliking for Jews, let's call it.

Apparently Lloyd-Phillips felt uncomfortable as well, because she went on to tell me how much she liked the Orthodox Jews who used to come to the offices of the Red Cross in Jerusalem, where she worked in locating missing war refugees. I asked her, "How did you sort it out for yourself, the fact that those Jews wanted to come to Palestine after the war, and they weren't allowed to?" She answered promptly, "I couldn't see why they should." I went on, "What did you think, where did you think they should go?" And she said, "I don't know whether I thought at all. I don't know because I think that the countries where they always had been living, those countries should keep them. Why should they have got rid of them? We have got Jews in this country."

I did not respond. She had spoken with complete honesty, hiding nothing for my sake. I could have gotten up and left, I could have answered her, told her at least that many Englishmen who thought the way she did in those days had since changed their minds. We changed the subject to figs and jasmine and the wildflowers that bloom on the hills of Palestine, and she talked about that, too, with great enthusiasm. Only a few hours later, when I returned to London, did I realize what I should have said to her. What I had to say departed from the role I had set myself when I began this search for people and for a period. I wanted to listen to them, to see them, I wanted to remain on the sidelines as much as possible, watching, not interfering with the tale as they told it. And here, now, I could no longer fill that role. I could not but intervene, returning first of all to a point that had been taken for granted until then, the confrontation between the Jewish people and people like Faith Lloyd-Phillips. The clash was very immediate, not something that had taken place forty years earlier.

Edward Horne told me: "I never felt a stranger in an Arab place or house, whether it was a university man or a doctor or a fellah, whereas I felt a stranger in a Jewish house. I don't know why."

Our conversation took place over lunch at the Royal Overseas League, near Piccadilly. He was a man in his sixties, carefully dressed, with an old-fashioned air about him, mainly his large, fair mustache, meticulously curled at the ends, and his impressively straight back. There were traces of the former empire in the spacious rooms, in the large crowd of elderly English who had come to town for the day. Ted Horne, too, had come in from New

Milton, which is on the sea. He had retired there after serving in the London Police. At the time he was also editor of the *Palestine Police Quarterly*, and had written a book on the Palestine Police called *A Job Well Done*.

"My generation of schoolboy in England learned everything about India, the Zulu, the noble Zulu. An English boy up to 1939 had a pretty good knowledge of the empire, which meant the world at large. We could tell you a lot about China. Well now, there are dark areas in the British system, and one of them was the Balkans and Eastern Europe. Total incomprehension and absolute ignorance. I remember a boy saying to our geography master, 'Sir, where is Bessarabia?' and his answer was, 'At no time in your entire life are you likely to meet someone from Bessarabia. Let's go back to the subject at hand.'

"Now those boys were confronted with people who came from those countries. Every month there were a few thousand more of them, and those Jews came from countries where the relationship with the police was rather different. And so the friendly bobby was totally alien to them, and the British thought, 'Well, what are they? They are vaguely European.'"

When I asked him whether he spoke Hebrew, he told me that in the training camp they had been taught only Arabic. A policeman or an employee of the administration could not advance without passing a test in Arabic, and so all of them—police officers, clerks high and low, British Council workers—learned Arabic.

That was the language of the place, and the language they used to communicate. "Arabic was spoken right across the country," Horne explained. "Hebrew was spoken only in certain parts. Mainly in Haifa it was not an 'in' language at all."

Because he had mentioned Haifa, where I was born and spent my childhood, his words evoked some surprise. To him, I was one of the recent arrivals, though in my own eyes I was entirely native. I had never known another place. Perhaps because I had been a little girl and there was a war going on around me, it seemed to me that that was the way it was in the world—among the natives there were many foreigners, and there were foreigners who were not entirely foreign, and natives who were not entirely native; naturally there were always Arabs and British and Jews who came of their own will, like my parents, and others who were refugees.

I asked him to tell me about the Criminal Investigation Department's work. Everyone could be bought, it was just a question of the price, as he put it. The main work among the Jews was catching Etzel and Lehi people who had escaped to the Sharon region, mainly to Netanya, where he had an office. The office in Jenin dealt with crime, and occasionally with smuggling:

"The problem arose of how to move at night in Arab areas without looking conspicuous," he said. "And there was this wonderful man, Kamal Irani, who was an inspector, and he would teach us how to walk like an Arab. The fellah tends to use the whole of his foot rather differently from an English military stride, and an Arab can see half a mile away whether someone coming is an Arab or a non-Arab. So we learned this and must have been quite successful, training daily, going slowly, roll on, foot down, roll on the ball and lift it off, and the thing is you had to do it in sandals. And no Arab smokes a cigarette quite like an Englishman, and you had to learn that. The nearest thing you can get was to manage a long time in prison where they had their clandestine cigarettes. You had to memorize. An Englishman says, come here, and his arm is crooked upward; an Arab says come here, his arm is crooked downward.

"Another thing Irani taught me that lasted me all my life is how to climb a hill without being puffed up on top," he explained enthusiastically. "We had our own training at the top of Mount Eival, which is about one thousand feet high, and you could imagine that the average European soldier would arrive all puffed, winded. That's not the way to do it. No Arab shepherd is ever winded when he scales the mountain with his goats. So how do they do it? It's hard to describe, but basically, bend your knees, and you walk as if your knees are in a fixed bent position, and you use your hips. And I have never forgotten that, and take two steps at a time.

"An Arab could lie in bed at night, and when his dog barked he could really tell whether it was an animal or a human being, and often they could tell whether that human being was menacing or not. To get into an Arab village you had to get into this charade for a quarter of an hour, half an hour, and then you would have a straightforward situation of a shoot-up or a seizure of smuggled goods. Translate that into a Jewish area and there were problems. They would say something but you never got precise information. You go to the *mukhtar* of a Jewish village and you get no cooperation. He would suddenly get amnesia. He couldn't remember."

When I asked whether he had learned the Jewish habits for his work in Netanya, he replied: "In the rural areas the Jews knew one another, and if there was a stranger, whatever they thought we never knew, but it would conceivably be 'He is a stranger,' much as an English villager would recognize a stranger, so you could not overcome that. What we used to do with the Jews was to keep our traps shut, not say a word, or only speak in German or pick up some Slav words because so many Jews didn't speak Hebrew, some didn't want to. Therefore you could get away with being blue-eyed and fair-haired as so many Ashkenazi are.

"But the thing that gave you away with Jews if you were not very careful was clothing. If you got yourself a blue shirt, blue was considered Jewish, and very short shorts that would bring tears to the eyes, and no socks, you could probably get away with it, and if it was a local shirt made in Petah Tikva, so much the better. You could not have the sartorial elegance a lot of our chaps had. You had to study the art of being clean and scruffy, and it didn't come easy to them.

"Also, you would put on some cheap shoes. They were good at making shoes but they looked like Mediterranean shoes, you never saw them in England. You would invest in these. And you would put your hands in your pockets, which no Englishman would do in those days, and certainly not a policeman, and you studied how to be decadent, as if you just came out of an unemployment exchange. And I suppose short hair would give someone away. It actually worked but it was not easy, and I don't pretend I mastered it." As he spoke there was a faint smile in his small blue eyes, which seemed alert and expressionless at the same time. "Even in Tel Aviv, I felt an alien," he added, "perhaps because in the East you expected to find something vaguely Oriental, and you found something of the backstreets of Warsaw. The British don't like people moaning and grumbling, that's not the way to get things done with the British."

✧

I didn't respond. But when I met Isaiah Berlin, I asked him about relationship between Jews and Englishmen in Palestine. Berlin, who had been a close friend of Chaim Weizmann's and used to visit Palestine frequently in those years, met me at the Athenaeum Club in London and responded to disturbing questions with good-humored pronouncements:

"The British imposed the pattern of public school wherever they were. If an Arab makes trouble we kick him downstairs. If a Jew made trouble there were no rules. The headmaster would get a note from a powerful relative. For the English, the Jews were hysterical, troublesome, completely alien. I don't think that any Jew really got friendly with the English in Palestine. Even for the British Jews, things were changed over there. Only some of the old wise English thought the Arabs were a bore, only they appreciated the Jews. The Arabs were thoughtful and dignified. The Jews were undignified, ugly, cunning. The Arab women wore lovely colors. Their food was good. Jewish food was awful. The Jews were a nuisance, the refugees were a nuisance. There was anti-Semitism, not active, not violent, but once it found an outlet . . ."

I was in Palestine from 1942 to 1948 but was not unfortunately, keeping a diary at that time. However, I do still have some memories of those years and should be very willing to give any help I can. It is unlikely, I am afraid, that I shall be coming to London in the near future, but if you thought it worthwhile traveling this distance, I should be very happy to see you here.

Sincerely yours,
Oxford.

The Earl of Oxford and Asquith was writing in response to a letter I had sent him at the suggestion of Harold Beeley. When we had agreed on the date and time of my arrival, I set out from Paddington Station for Bath. There, as I left the platform, I looked for an old green Morris, as Lady Oxford had insisted on coming to pick me up. But before I could find the car, I saw a tall thin woman with a slight stoop coming toward me, walking quickly with a barely perceptible limp. She was dressed in old corduroy trousers and a black sweater. Parked beyond the taxis was a green Morris, its rear end elongated and sitting low. The bottom of the car was covered with mud and dry leaves. We took the side roads, among hills cloaked in mist, and Lady Oxford, who had been Anne Palieret in those days, told me she had been recruited into Military Intelligence in Jerusalem, under Martin Charteris. "I worked in the King David," she said, "and very often I used to go on duty, I used to meet my friends down there for drinks." Her voice was somewhat husky, her tone direct and lively—youthful-sounding. There was also something young about her appearance. A refined woman without the mannerisms of a lady. The gray hair, upswept, was thick and glossy.

"I saw things from the Arab point of view," she informed me. "The people I got to know intimately were the Arabs." Was she trying to caution me, or was she just saying that it was natural for her to be on the Arab side? She was still talking about the Arab friends she had not seen for such a long time because they came to London so rarely when we approached the avenue of tall, old trees leading to the family estate. It had been the home of Prime Minister Asquith, grandfather of the present Lord Oxford, and was a fifteenth-century manor house, modest in comparison with the homes the aristocracy had built since, and adjacent to the small village. There was scaffolding along the high walls, and she explained that they were repairing the roof in stages.

Lord Oxford greeted us at the door and led us into a high-ceilinged room with high windows that did not let in much light on that drizzly late November day. Old Persian rugs flanked the large fireplace, which, though blazing, could not dispel the chill in the room. Anne Oxford went off to prepare lunch. Julian Oxford poured us some sherry, suggested that we sit by the fire, and joked about their not putting on the central heating and about the cold one could never escape in these rooms. I told him about the book I was working on, and the fact that it had no particular political slant. But when I asked to record the conversation, he was reluctant. For him, recording a conversation was an invasion of privacy, and only after I had argued on behalf of precision and English—that it should be his and not mine—did he acquiesce.

"I was in the army then," he began. "I had been on the staff of General Spears in Lebanon, and when he went back to England, at the end of 1941, I went back to more regular army duties, and found myself in Safed, in a unit of Royal Engineers, which is my calling, building roads for what was called the Fortress, which was constructed in the hills of Safed. The nearest Germans at the time were about a hundred miles from any direction. It was thought that they might come closer, and those underground fortifications were built so that we all could go underground if they came. That involved lots of spadework and road building and excavation and so on, which kept us fairly busy on these rather menial pursuits, but did enable me to see quite a bit of the country and get absorbed in the beauty of it. And so it happened that the government representative there, a man called [Harry] Pirie-Gordon, became a great friend of mine and was very hospitable, and it was a great comfort after the rather spartan conditions, being in a half-finished hotel on Mount Canaan.

"Anyway," he continued, "I had this opportunity of talking a great deal to Pirie-Gordon, who was the assistant district commissioner, and getting to know a bit about the country, and after about six months the Palestine government approached me, prompted a little by Pirie-Gordon, to ask whether I would join the administration, and I agreed to do so."

His simple way of telling the story reminded me again of the unequivocal presence of the English, rulers of the land, rulers, in fact, of the world. The man sitting next to me, now about seventy years old, with a shock of white hair, had been offered a position the way young lords were offered such positions. In keeping with the old, unstated rules, it was suggested to him that he join the Mandatory government, and he agreed.

My host and I had been in Palestine together for a number of years, it occurred to me, but I, like my parents, had been suspect natives as far as he was concerned. Our existence was marginal, whereas he, in my eyes, was among the lords of the land. There was something imperious about the English; they had a natural confidence that was lacking in the leaders of the Yishuv. What could those leaders, with their muted, shapeless authority, offer us in comparison with King George, who was a king, first of all, and whose birthday was a holiday and, since it was in June, marked the start of the children's swimming season? My host was still his representative.

I responded to him as one would to a star of the films one saw in childhood—with a kind of wonder untarnished by time. The lords of the land had their own style of rule: the higher their station, the less they lorded. As if they were guided by some unstated principle that what they understood could not be clear to others. That the way they managed the world as their own domain would be sensed but not seen.

"My first posting was about May 1942 to Gaza, where I was assistant district commissioner under the very benevolent District Commissioner Ballard," he said, "and I was plunged straight away into the administrative side of the Gaza District, which included Beersheba, in a work that I hadn't done before and found extremely interesting and absorbing."

When I asked him for details, he said, "I have been looking at letters I wrote home at the time, giving my mother a description of the work. They might summarize it better than I can do now."

He looked through the letters he had prepared on the table and began to read from one of them: "In theory our powers are very considerable. In practice, very trivial. I combine in theory the function of prince and magistrate, consul, coroner, agriculturist, town-planning expert, director of tactical defense, settler of blood feuds, policeman, county councilor, and spy. In practice I spend a great deal of the time considering for instance whether to grant or refuse people permits to buy cartridges for the purpose of killing moles. The work is parochial, but it's not the worst of it. I have in fact one hundred thousand parishioners. What is chiefly irksome is bureaucracy."

A knock at the door interrupted the reading, and Julian left the room to talk to one of his employees. When we returned to the fireside I asked whether he would have entered service in the colonies had it not been for the war. "No," he said, "I don't think so. I was just at the end of my time in Oxford. I had vaguely thought of becoming a barrister, but had never thought of taking up work that would take me abroad. I was very fond of my home here."

He proceeded to tell me that he had become so attached to Palestine that he decided to stay there after the war, and left only at the end of the Mandate. He continued in colonial service in different places and ended up as governor of the Seychelles. "We were particularly lucky in what we did afterward, but nothing greally touched me like Palestine. I got completely caught up in the life, especially the Beersheba time. I was not quite as happy in the urban parts."

"Was it always the Arab population you were dealing with?" I asked, and he answered, "Mainly. Toward the end of my time in Gaza a first Jewish settlement was established near Beersheba, called Gevulot. And the man who established it and was the *mukhtar* visited me, quite a nice young guy. I remember our first visit there. It was with some misgivings that I viewed this settlement. It was right on the border. It could have posed a slight security problem."

And he stopped, but whether out of politeness or caution was not clear. It was obvious that he was keeping something to himself. I asked, "Wasn't it a strange phenomenon altogether, these kibbutzim?" "It was certainly strange," he agreed, a smile on his pleasant features—a face that inspired confidence. "It seemed to me, I must admit, not to belong to the country, to be something alien, and to our way of thinking it was creating a problem." He said the word *problem* in another voice, lower, which gave it greater emphasis, and added: "I didn't mind its creating an administrative problem. It seemed to me to be a political injustice."

I wanted to ask him a few questions, the principle one not related to the political injustice he had mentioned—I had already taken that into account, though it was strange and unsettling to hear him say it in his effortless manner. Mainly I wanted to ask him whether he had taken the trouble to find out what was going on at that new settlement. Hadn't the affection already reserved for the Arabs roused his curiosity? After all, it was an extraordinary phenomenon: a handful of young people springing up in the wilderness, surrounded by alien and hostile elements, beginning with next to nothing to make themselves a place in the desert. Perhaps he hadn't informed himself about their beliefs because they had come to transform the desert that he loved, and to disturb the Bedouin. Did he not at least sense the great adventure they had embarked on?

I did not ask him. Perhaps I was afraid of getting cautious answers, thoughtful of my sensitivities; Oxford was an exemplary host, practicing a kind of restraint that is oppressive in its own way. I said I believed he hadn't finished reading the letter. He rifled through the papers on the table and went on: "I am living at present at the district commissioner's, houses being scarce and expensive. My day begins at eight with breakfast—*laban*." And he explained, "Yogurt, I expect." I said, "We still call it *laban*," and Oxford smiled and said, "We call it *laban* here," and went on reading. "And coffee on the veranda overgrown with morning glory, and I read a little poetry with it out of your anthology. Then to the office, which is a newly built grim fortress, the type of many in Palestine. There are subjects of the district commissioner receiving deputations, remonstrating or cajoling, dealing as there may occur with problems of profiteering, drainage, air-raid disputes, education, fifth columnists, and quail netting."

He stopped to explain: "The Gaza Strip, the beach along Gaza, is where the quail landed, and they were netted as they flew in exhausted, and a sort of British sense of fair play dictated that nets should not be continuous along the coast, so the quails had some sporting chance of getting through. Each net had to be no more than seventy meters with broad spaces between them." "Did the Arabs keep to the rule?" I asked. "I don't think they did," he answered with a smile.

"I was transferred from Gaza to Beersheba, which I loved more," he continued. "And quite a lot of the work did involve a certain amount of tribal dispute, family dispute, sometimes blood-feud cases. They had to be judged and tried by the ordinary court, but this didn't get rid of the blood feud, and you had, after all, a powerful process of tradition for settling those disputes."

"Did you have to bargain?" I asked. "Oh, yes," he answered, amused. "There again one had to have the backing of an Arab district officer who knew the ropes, how to do it. One took part in it, I suppose, one had to convey a certain authority, but this was, as you say, full of bargaining. Initially the value of a man's life was 333 pounds, subject to all sorts of deductions and additions. But of course, the aggrieved party wouldn't admit that the life of any of their family was worth as little as 333 pounds. They would start with a much higher sum, a thousand, and then you said, 'But why? How much will you take off, and how much for God, for the Prophet—one hundred each—and how much for the high commissioner—fifty each—and how much for the lord?'" And I said, "You were the lord?" and he nodded. "I remember being very proud at one of those occasions having fifty pounds taken off for me, exactly the same as for the high commissioner."

And with a chuckle, as if recalling childhood pranks, he ended the story.

Anne, who had meanwhile come into the room, remembered Jerusalem as a cosmopolitan city, and talked about how good her days there had been. Julian, who also preferred Jerusalem to any other city in the Middle East, described Government House, where he had spent several months as secretary to the high commissioner. "It was very comfortable, lovely garden, an English garden, an English butler, a good cook. It was rather more paternal than Cairo. The tempo was slightly slower, too. Politically it was very difficult, but that didn't affect the place. It was like a little oasis. The news, the telegrams that were coming in, were very different, but the atmosphere was very calm in Government House itself."

Shortly afterward, when we went in to lunch, I wondered whether he felt, as I did, that we had been going round in circles without getting to the point, because he could not speak to me directly.

Perhaps Oxford also wondered about my silence. In any case, I certainly did: if I was not going to bring up some basic sense of decency less famed than that of the British, or a simple humanity less enlightened than theirs, why did I not at least mention in a few simple words the inherent solitude of the Jews in this world, and the fact that an English gentleman like himself was oblivious to it at the very moment when it was absolute?

"Anyway," he said after a while, "when all this was put into the melting pot, one began to take more conscious political stands, and equally, or soon after, one had to contemplate British withdrawal." And I, with a heavy feeling that I had missed my chance, remarked: "Interesting, the way you link the two." He quickly saw what the implications were: at first they felt no need to take a political stand, and when they were put to the test and required to fight, they began to think about withdrawing. He replied, honestly enough: "They were linked in time."

He described the last days in Palestine, beginning in a light enough tone: "Really, in the last months we were involved in packing up, as it were. We were besieged all the time by pathetic pleas for protection from outlying villages, Arabs. I think that the Jewish settlements were fairly confident of being able to protect themselves, but not outlying Arab villagers, who were uncertain. They used to come pleading for rifles to defend themselves, including a party of nuns who had a convent in the Galilee, whom I, quite surprised, saw coming to my house in Nazareth, the reverend mother saying, 'Could we have some rifles?' And of course in those cases one was absolutely powerless to do anything effective to protect them.

"It had become by the end very difficult to do anything, to the extent that our preparations for withdrawal were going on while all around the Arab states..." He stopped for a moment, looking for the right word, and I suggested "...were invading." "Yes, invading," he agreed politely, "or keeping order, another way to put it," and he gave a short laugh. "Or preserving the status quo. But anyway, filling the gap, the vacuum, and so causing a great deal of uncertainty."

That exchange—his insistence on changing the word *invading*, and that abrupt laugh—made it clear that there was no point in talking about a persecuted people and Holocaust refugees who were expelled; that was all discounted in favor of the integrity of the beloved land, Palestine, and its authentic inhabitants, the Arabs. Oxford was captivated by the Arabs, I realized. He was British, bearing the white man's burden, and wanted to benefit the natives he loved. And in love, after all, it is emotion that reigns, and all the rest—intellect, logic, education, British standards of restraint and fair play—are at its service.

If he wanted to protect all of those, therefore, he had to ignore the Jews in Palestine. He did not take them into account, not really, just as those Jews themselves had not taken the Arabs into account, in order to keep the purity of the faith that had brought them to the country. At that moment, as I tried to see the country through his eyes, I suddenly saw it in reverse, a negative of a familiar photo: what existed in reality was a blurred image, empty of the Zionist dream that came true. I realized then that I was not the only one upset; so was Oxford, who was being the perfect host, and who answered my questions honestly. "All that period was very sad," he noted, and here again distinguished between employees of the administration in Jerusalem and the young people like himself who were working in the field and had close ties with the natives, and therefore witnessed the disaster as it took place.

"I was wondering how one felt leaving all those places, folding up the empire, so to speak," I said, and Oxford replied: "It was often sad. And in practice, a lot of the places we served in got into difficulties if not civil wars after we had left. But Palestine was different. At the time of leaving we knew we were going to abandon it. There was nothing more one could do, and one was going home, and that was the worst, one was leaving it to chaos.

"We didn't see it at the beginning," he went on after a while. "Until quite late, 1946–47, we didn't think it likely that we would withdraw. But then the possibility began to appear to us. And then the political situation got so clouded—the higher echelon in Jerusalem was carrying out whatever was to be British policy, which was of course rather oscillating and fairly unpredictable—and the Americans became influential enough, and we, to some extent, lost our drive or our will, and one began to think a little bit more what our political duty was and what politically was right or wrong, and everything became complicated. But to begin with we had natural sympathy with the people we were working with and therefore wanted to see how much we could help them."

Anne Oxford poured the coffee. There was something withdrawn about her, as if she were silently hoping that we would set aside this matter, which apparently could not be set aside. I don't remember whether we exchanged small talk or sat in silence. For my part, I was thinking about the relationship between loss of will and a duty that has become political, and I had the feeling that Julian Oxford was still turning over in his own mind a matter that he had already examined from every angle. After all these years, someone from the other camp had appeared, and when he attempted, with good will, to tell her the story, he found himself speaking with a heavy heart about a place he had loved, about the people he and others like him had failed, about events that a man like himself would not call tragic but that in a certain sense turned out to be, for him as well.

"One of the things that struck me is that people are still very emotional about Palestine," I said to him when we were again seated near the fireplace. "Well," he said, "Zionism was always an emotional thing, you know, from the very beginning, and that rather set the scene. And inevitably the Arab national movement is equally emotional as a reaction against it, a kind of emotional feeling in that they would be dispossessed from their own home." "And the British?" I asked.

"I think that people who were working in Palestine really started to love it," he answered. "Most people who worked among the rural Arabs came to feel in many ways attached to them, whatever their defects, and their defects were obvious and not always totally unsympathetic."

"For the British it was very important to be impartial," I remarked, "and things reached a point where it was not easy to remain so." He thought for a moment and then said, "If one was merely administrating in the field, then I think it was not at all difficult to remain impartial. One had to, one was administrating according to the law quite impartially. Inevitably one felt bound to help people who needed help. The Jews could look after themselves, so inevitably a lot of one's work was administratively designed to help the less advanced Arabs. But making allowances for that, I think that the people administrating in the field did remain quite impartial until the end, in contrast to the central bureaucrats in the Secretariat, who did not have so much direct contact with the people." It was interesting, I thought, that whenever he said "the people" he meant the Arabs, and as far as he was concerned there was no contradiction in that. A kind of naïveté, a quality untouched by sophistication, allowed him to apply his concept of impartiality to them alone. "Did you have a feeling at the time that the British would leave soon?" I asked. "No," he protested, "not until quite near the end, when it seemed all decided." And when asked when that actually happened, Oxford paused to reflect while lighting his pipe. "I think that this dividing point came when we realized, those of us working among tine Arabs, that the latest declared policy—the White Paper—which we thought of as a sensible policy, and one that we should have stuck to, when that began to be called into question, first because of pressure and the demands of Jewish immigration and so on." Here he stopped: we were approaching dangerous ground, and he was considering what to tell me and how to put it. I was also silent, cautious.

From time to time my thoughts return to that silence. Why was it so fraught? Why had Oxford's restraint evoked such an extreme response in me? And if I'd had such intense feelings, why had I not expressed them? Was I afraid he would dispense with the matter in a few polite words that would hurt me even more? And perhaps I was overcome by a curiosity to hear for myself someone defending the White Paper as the right policy, the same White Paper that had brought my parents out in the streets for the first and last demonstration of their lives? It was strange to hear, years later, that that was the name for other regulations as well. To my parents, the White Paper had been nothing short of disaster from an unexpected quarter—the British whose job had been to prepare a national home for the Jews. And here was a respected representative of those same British, telling about it in his way, in a moderate tone, rationally, and in the same tone mentioning the demands for Jewish immigration, a euphemism for the desperate illegal immigration of those years.

He said: "When I was in Nazareth, we felt a need to make a last visit to places we really loved—Beersheba and Gaza and through Transjordan, because I had a certain number of ties in Transjordan over those tribal cases in Beersheba, as lots of the tribes and some of the disputes were arranged across the border.

My wife was just about to have our first baby, and the Lebanese doctor said, '*Ne sautez pas trop.*' So we did have that last journey around all those parts and said good-bye to our friends there. It was March 1948. My wife left in April. I stayed until the very end."

CHAPTER ELEVEN

"We lived very slowly"

The Israeli Arabs are those Arabs who were inhabitants of Palestine during the Mandate and stayed within the border of the state of Israel after the war of 1948. There were six hundred thousand Jews and more than a million Arabs in Palestine before the war of 1948, but after the exodus of 1948–49 the Arabs who stayed in Israel became a small minority. Most of the population of the large mixed cities left. In Haifa there were seventy thousand Arabs before the war, and after the conquest of the city by the Jews only fifteen thousand remained. In Jaffa there were eighty thousand, and about ten thousand stayed. The Arab minority in the new state was leaderless, isolated, and restricted in its movements because of the closed borders and the military rule imposed on them by the Israelis. Some laws passed by the Israeli Knesset in those days—the most notorious of which was the law of "Absentees' Property"—enabled the appropriation of land from Arabs who became refugees during the War of Independence or were absent from their domicile at the time.

Over the years, military rule was abolished and Israeli Arabs became a large and well-organized national minority, constituting twenty percent of Israeli population, most of them Muslims and the rest Christians. According to the basic principals of Israeli law, Israel's Arab citizens enjoy equal rights. But in fact there is social and economic discrimination against them. Israeli occupation of the West Bank and the Gaza Strip since 1967 brought about a nationalistic awakening, and the Israeli Arabs started calling themselves Palestinians. Though most of them see themselves as part of the Israeli population and have no intent to live outside its borders, difficult questions of identification with the Palestinians in the occupied territories and loyalty to the State of Israel have arisen.

It was only the huge bonfires that evening in Jaffa's Ajami quarter that reminded me I'd come to visit Yakub Hananiya, the head of the Orthodox Christian community, on Lag BaOmer, the Jewish holiday when they lit bonfires. I was with a companion, on foot, and we wound our way down the narrow streets without sidewalks, now and then crossing an empty lot, passing among the ruins of buildings in which middle-class Arabs lived before 1948. It wasn't a long walk, but totally unfamiliar. I had never been here before, except for the short sprint from the car to one of the restaurants in the area, and if anything had caught my eye then it was one of the beautiful homes that remained, or the sea, suddenly in view.

We were approaching the sea when there was a screech of brakes and a large American car pulled up beside us, packed with young men who exchanged a few words of Arabic with my companion. "Drugs," he said, when the car had sped off on worn treads, and he led me toward a large, open area. In the twilight it was hard to discern what was there, but judging from what remained around the periphery, it seemed to have been built up at one time. Children were flocking toward the lot, and they seemed to be busy building campfires, but I could hardly believe that the Arabs were celebrating Lag BaOmer.

We had meanwhile reached the house, also amid ruins. We entered the courtyard full of fruit trees and went into a kind of closed-in balcony, where the large family had gathered—children and grandchildren, some of whom lived in the house, some of whom had come for an evening visit. From there we passed into the main room of the house. The father of the family, Yakub Hananiya, a charcoal merchant, invited us to sit near windows facing the sea.

It was a spacious room, dimly lit and filled with heavy furniture that had been moved there from other rooms because household repairs were under way, my companion explained to me, while our host, a man of about seventy with a pleasant, reserved face, waited in silence. I asked Hananiya whether he preferred to speak English, and he said Hebrew was okay; his tone, familiar from earlier meetings with Israeli Arabs, conveyed that that's the way it is, an "okay" that is not so okay. Hananiya, like other Arabs who had grown up before 1948, remembered a country in which many of the Jews and British spoke Arabic, and he still wasn't taking for granted that Jews don't make more of an effort to learn the language now.

I began speaking in Hebrew, raising my voice because of the din around us—from the next room came the sounds of the family and the television, and from outside, the clamor of children—and Hananiya listened politely to my explanations but said nothing. I asked whether he had been in Jaffa in the Forties, and he replied, "Yes, I was in Jaffa in the Forties, and I am a native of Jaffa. My family has been here for a very long time. I don't know exactly how long, but more than two hundred years," and he fell silent.

I asked when he had finished his studies. "In '41," he said slowly, searching for the words in Hebrew. "I still had one year to go, but in 1941, my father, who was a citrus merchant, went bankrupt. At that time Italy entered the Second World War and it was hard to send oranges to Europe, and especially to England, and I was forced to go out and work." Here he went into detail about his various jobs, some with the English, and the more I listened, the more I sensed that there was not much point to this conversation—a feeling familiar from previous encounters with Israeli Arabs. It was familiar, in fact, from childhood, when neighbors and relatives who arrived after the Second World War talked about places and lives that were no longer, and what they had to say—and repeated often—aroused no curiosity. On the contrary, I used to feel that they were talking according to a formula, holding anything that had happened before the war in a favorable light. It was their right, after all they had been through, and no one commented on it. We weren't allowed to say or even think anything critical about them: let them correct as they would a past that had been sundered from the present.

I wanted to speak about this sundering of past from present with the Arabs who had remained in Israel, to hear in their own words about when it had occurred and the point at which they realized that what had been would be no more. Had it happened suddenly? It didn't look as if I would find out from Hananiya. He was proceeding politely with a rather mechanical description of his last job before 1948. "I was feeling good then. I was the manager of a firm that dealt in wheat and barley and tea and coffee. The owner was in partnership with the Arab Federation Company, and I managed it all for him." I asked whether he had known any Jews at the time, and he told me about a few he had been friendly with, noting that many Jews used to eat in Jaffa, and the Arabs used to go to cafés in Tel Aviv. "But we used to go to the Orthodox Club every day," he said, "every evening we would get together there. The club had 1,990 members, and that's besides women. Every month we brought in speakers from Egypt and Lebanon; there were always lectures on great books from the Arab world. Every week or two there were parties in the club. We had a ping-pong team, a billiards team, boxing, and basketball. There was a record library and a large library of Arabic and English books."

A moment later he said, "All my books are in crates." I said that must be because of the household repairs, and he said, "No, because of my eyes. I can't read." "And your children?" I asked. "They don't read Arabic," he replied. "They read Hebrew. All they can read in Arabic is a newspaper." And I thought then, what do I really know about them, and what do they know about us? They, in the given situation, constantly observe us, and we, in the same situation, never observe them.

Why had I come, I asked myself. Wasn't I asking the impossible of Yakub Hananiya? How could he tell me about the Arabs who had stayed, condemned to being the few, set apart quietly and without ado from the Jewish majority? How could he speak to me—a member of that majority—about the days when the Arabs had been the majority, and the period when our dream became a reality that turned their reality upside down? As long as he was reticent, he could protect what had been, but his very speaking of it and my listening to him—there in that room that was foreign but not entirely—diminished that past.

I decided to ask about marginal things—where the Orthodox Club had been, for instance. When he told me the club had been near the French Embassy, which was once the home of a big citrus merchant, I thought to ask about the citrus trade. "There were a few large-scale dealers," he said, "and there were some like my father who had maybe thirteen or twenty thousand crates of oranges and would market them through the major dealer, in England or somewhere." "Where did he get the oranges?" I asked, and he said, "Jaffa. Don't forget, Yazur, Salameh, all the villages from here to Tel Litwinsky to Ramla, the whole area was filled with citrus orchards. Beyond Jerusalem Boulevard it was all orchards. During the Mandate, just walking down Jerusalem Boulevard in the springtime, you'd smell the orange blossoms."

The tone of our conversation changed. It was still somewhat circular, but his manner grew lively as he talked about the Jaffa markets and the various buildings, some of them still standing, and about the sea so near, which was very calm that night: "We used to go to the sea very early in the morning. There was the Jaffa Club for the English, and nearby, our beach here in Ajami, and another one on the border of Bat Yam. We used to go at six, seven, seven-thirty, we'd swim and get out of the water. Not like today, when people go at noon. The girls used to go when it was dark, so they wouldn't be seen."

"The sea was beyond my dreams," said Suad Karaman, in English. A poet and teacher, she was a member of one of the wealthy families in Mandatory Haifa. "I never learned to swim. Sometimes in the evening, when it was cool, I would walk with my mother and sisters. Here we were very conservative. Even as a child, as a growing girl, I was always conscious of being a feminine figure walking among men through those crowded marketplaces, and I would feel shy, passing in front of those glaring eyes. Only twenty years later could I stop in the street and shake hands with a man and talk to him."

Karaman had met me this time at a café in a new shopping center above Yefe Nof Street in the Mount Carmel quarter, and not in the one home that remained in the family, in Ibten, near Kfar Hasidim. It was a large stone house that had been built in the Thirties and served as a country home until 1948. This was not the first time we had talked about "those days," but it was the first time she had described them as the days "before '48." I had the feeling it was easier for her to talk there—in the café that was a kind of balcony suspended above the sea, above Haifa Bay and the lower city at whose upper limit the Karaman house once stood, and above the Hadar HaCarmel quarter, at whose upper limit my parents lived before '48. This time we were meeting on neutral territory, which offered the vista but not the sense of place.

"All the customs, the Muslim traditions, were carried to the last details," she went on. "I was veiled when I was thirteen or fourteen, a black veil, chiffon, which I threw across my face. Then I was asked to get married to my own cousin. I didn't want to, and I was forced to leave school, and I waited for my older brother to come from Beirut University. I was hoping he would be on my side, but he really didn't help. He wouldn't come out against my marriage. My parents took me around to Damascus and Lebanon on a tour, you know, bribing me, putting me in a good mood. And my mother, whenever she heard of a newlywed bride, would take me there and let me see the trousseau and say, 'Shall we do this for you?' And I said, 'If you like it, do it for yourself.' But she really ordered the trousseau and fancy underwear. You had to have a set of nightgowns with a robe de chambre. It was a hostess gown and it had to be hand-embroidered in Beirut.

"When we came back to Beirut as refugees they were very different. We went there in April 1948. We were not beggars, but Palestinians were not having a nice time in Lebanon. A year or two before, when a Palestinian went there in the same way that an American tourist would come here—our Palestinian pound was very strong in comparison with the Lebanese pound—we met people who enjoyed life. Women were so vibrant with life, so joyful, bubbling with mirth, and very generous. Food was exquisite and people were very soft-spoken. They were very different from the people here. We are serious people, we are gloomy people, and suddenly, when we came back as refugees, we were mocked, and I don't know how bad it was in the refugee camps."

"When you went to Lebanon, what did you have in mind?" I asked cautiously. "Well," she said, "we thought we would be there for a few months, until the armies cleared up everything. And that's why my uncle and my father stayed here and my mother stayed with them. They looked after the farm and the cattle. 'We can't leave it,' they said." "Why did the Arab people, who were so attached to land, leave so easily?" I asked. "Not so easily," she answered, her low, beautifully modulated voice emphasizing every word.

"There were Jews and Arabs in Haifa who went from house to house, asking the Arabs not to leave," I said. "But you can't tell frightened people who are being bombarded by shells from up on Hadar HaCarmel not to go," she protested. "The position of

Haifa helped, too. If the Arabs had been on the mountain, maybe it would have been a different situation."

I didn't persist. What was the point of an exchange that sank deeper and deeper into the ruts of an argument Jews and Arabs had traced many times before, each according to his inclinations—but Karaman went on: "My uncle went to them and said, 'Don't leave, Haifa is going to be an open city.' But they couldn't believe him. Especially as the way to Lebanon and the sea was open to them. Everybody knows that the English helped the Arabs to leave the country. They opened the port. People locked everything and left, thinking they would go for a month or two and the neighbor would take care of everything.

"We left for Lebanon in the spring," she said. "Women, expectant mothers, children—and when summer came we took a house in Baabda, and later, in winter, we had to go back to Beirut because matters were not settled." "How did you communicate with your family when you were in Lebanon?" I asked. "There was no telephone, no post. Only through messengers," she said. "A man would come across the border. And on May 15—it was something we couldn't believe. I would look at *Time* magazine and see all the Arab countries around this little Israel—it was a real physical and mental shock to us. We couldn't really accept it, we couldn't believe it. We couldn't understand it. We saw that those who had the power didn't do what could easily have been done. We couldn't believe how this charade was acted. That was the most difficult part of it. It was a very severe blow not because the Jews took the land but because we let them take the land. When I think of it, it all comes back. It was sickening.

"My uncle tried hard to get us back. And when he got a permit we were allowed to come across the border. Not at Rosh HaNikra, but at Rumesh and Hurfesh, two Druze villages. Hurfesh is in the Galilee. Across the Lebanese border, in the valley, is Rumesh. We walked from one village to the other, and our luggage was put in sacks on donkeys. We crossed the border. There was a man from the Jewish Agency there with my uncle, and he had all the official papers with him, and we came back home. We were the first family to come back. It was summer 1949."

"What was it like?" "There was a sense of adventure when we woke up very early and we were transported by a big vehicle that took us all to the village. We said good-bye to our relatives there and then we crossed the border. It was still early morning when we came across the wadi and the valley and we saw our uncle waiting on the hilltop." "Did the country look different?" I asked. "No," she replied. "It looked very beautiful, and very sad. I don't know. Different emotions." And after a moment she added, "Here we are, back home after we had been refugees.

"Haifa was so gloomy, deprived. Nothing in the shops. Anybody who went to Haifa had to take a sandwich with him to be eaten on the street. And when my first child was born I got all her things from Beirut. My aunt came over from Beirut and she brought me a whole suitcase for the baby because here I could find only a little wool that I knitted for her." "How could your aunt come and go?" I asked. "There were ways, coming through Rosh HaNikra or through Amman," she explained. "Later, when my uncle died, all the family came from Jerusalem through Amman. That was 1952." And it occurred to me then that the closed borders were never altogether closed to Israeli Arabs. "Where was your uncle buried?" I asked her. "In Ibten," she replied. "It is the family cemetery. My father, my uncle, my mother, my brother, my two cousins, they are all here."

And because she had said, "They are all here," I noticed that her "here" was beyond the view from the café. Northeast of where we sat, in the heart of the fertile coastal plain, was the estate of the Karaman family, amid the cultivated farmlands through which roads had been paved, now surrounded by Jewish settlements and not far from a hill on which, after the establishment of the state, Galilee Bedouin had been settled: it was also called Ibten. Suad and Darwish Karaman today live in one wing of the second floor, in a few spacious rooms in which little has changed. Heavy, old furniture, mainly German. There are almost no Arab furnishings, but there's a profound silence, a certain gloom, and the emptiness of expanse. The central room serves as the dining room; the original dining room is closed for most of the year, opened only when the large family gathers from around the world.

On those occasions the dining-room table, which seats a hundred, is set; during the Mandate, representatives of the British government used to gather there, with Arab notables and sometimes a few Jews with whom they had ties of commerce and friendship. Karaman described those dinners: "My uncle would sit at the head of the table and he would just look at us, and we understood what he wanted. We had to look after the guests because this is our culture. You shouldn't eat, really. You should sit with the guests and let them enjoy the food. And with his eyes my uncle would maneuver all. In the Fifties, when [Haifa mayor] Abba Khoushy would have parties for big business deals connected with the Carmelit [underground funicular], and it was the time of the rationing, and many of those parties were done at the house, of course my uncle would not accept anything for that. He would say, 'We are not a hotel in Ibten.' " Since she did not go on, I tried to imagine how the head of the family, who died shortly thereafter, had greeted the new regime with a pride that exacted a heavy price—he had already lost a considerable part of his property—a pride that was in fact a refusal to accept the new reality in which he was called on to offer his hospitality.

"Was there a fear of the Jews before 1948?" I asked, and she answered, "At first nobody was afraid of the Jews. We thought of them as weaklings in a fight—that they were not brave but they were clever and hardworking." "Did you think there was something in them that was superior in any way?" "Not superior," she said, "but in Haifa, a new city, a mixed city, more organized, modern, they proved their ability. Haifa was a city of foreigners. Even the Arabs who came to Haifa came from other places. When the city was still growing, the Jews grew with it, gained a foothold in it.

"They were clever," she repeated. "They were very polite until they had their country. They had no choice. They had to be. They were submissive like somebody who creeps in the dark to take hold of something slowly and silently. We felt that an unknown element was taking its place in the country. When they became stronger—and I, in the back of my mind, can remember the parades in Hadar HaCarmel on the First of May. They were singing 'Emek, Emek' [about the Jezreel Valley] and they had torches. I still remember it though I don't know the words."

I don't know whether I was surprised, but it was certainly unpleasant to hear this description of the Jews in the neighborhood where I grew up. For a moment I considered whether to try to tell her who they were, then I thought there was no point. Even if she had not paid them any particular attention in those days they would always be, as far as she was concerned, neighbors hatching plots. Looking back, she saw them not only as dedicated to the achievement of their goal but also as systematically carrying out a predetermined program. As Walid Khalidi wrote in 1984, in the photographic essay called *Before Their Diaspora*:

> From the beginning of their colonization of Palestine the architects of the Zionist dream excluded from consideration its potential consequences for the Palestinians. The reality of Zionism as translated on the ground was rarely perceived as diverging from the dream which was (and still is) regarded as pristine: any divergence between reality and the dream was only a momentary aberration from the dream.

"In Haifa we saw Hadar HaCarmel built up little by little," said Karaman. "We all knew that the Jews were coming here to take part of our country. So we didn't like the idea at all, and we didn't believe it was going to happen." And after a moment she said: "Our street, which is on the border of Hadar HaCarmel, on the corner of Sirkin Street—there were many steps on this side of the mountain, and the house was at the top of the steps—and when I think of my childhood, I think of this house, of its rooms, its gardens. It had beautiful gardens. The gardener had worked in Abbas, the Baha'i gardens, and he brought all the ideas from there."

From the café the view of the sunset was complete, and the city seen in the light of the lowering sun was like a relief map—a look in keeping with Karaman's descriptions: she had the active role of guide, and I was in the passive role, a tourist hearing an explanation of what had once been here. Until she said:

"Only a few years ago my husband took me through our street, and it was the greatest trip. I felt such nausea when I saw how it turned out to be. The other houses are still there. Those are stone houses, specially built. Of course now they are not glorious anymore, but they are still there like old women. Like old women in their eighties." And after a short laugh she added, "And then I saw that the iron gate of our house had been torn down. I didn't actually see it torn down—I would have bought it—but suddenly I came to the corner and there was no gate. There was a supermarket there. And I went into the supermarket and I felt I was going into my house: which part of my house was this, where was that?"

And if it had been a family home that, over the years, turned into a supermarket in some city in some country that had not changed hands, I suddenly wondered: How would it have looked to her then? How would it have looked to me? How do we really see things, I asked myself; are they not in some kind of no-man's-land where we have a common interest in leaving them? She, because she is still not able to accept the circumstances in which her home became a supermarket, and I, because I will not undertake to say to her that this privilege, however painful, of bringing up the past without having that considered overindulgence, is dangerous. Had I said that, had the fabric of conversation been torn once, perhaps it would have been possible to see what was beyond it, in that no-man's-land.

"And Sirkin Street, which was at the corner, what was it for you?" I asked. "It was our Haifa inhabited by foreigners," she answered. "People who suddenly had an army, had soldiers, had power. Suddenly we would see a policewoman in the street, and my uncle would joke and say, 'Oh, you sweet little thing. I am taking orders from her.' And my other uncle, my mother's brother, when identity cards were given and they were in Hebrew—he wouldn't take his. He said to us, 'This is a souvenir. Keep it here and good-bye.' The same night he left for the border." "Did the identity cards have Arabic as well?" I asked. "Yes, of course," she answered. "And it had *'Falastin'* in Arabic. The first identity cards had 'Palestine' on them. I still have my mother's. It says 'Hakumat el-Israil, Falastin.' I should have shown it to Golda [Meir] when she said, 'Palestine—there is no such thing.'"

"Did it really sink in that this was a different place you had come back to?" "No. At the beginning, no. Though when we left, Haifa had fallen already. There were no more Arabs in Haifa. But we came back to a different name—it was no more Palestine—and a different situation, and I had to accept all that, and the fact that we were now ruled. Of course we had the British Mandate, but we used to feel that this was our country and the English were just helping us to manage it." And I realized then that the Mandate by its very nature administered no small measure of hope, not only to the Jews who were singing "Hatikvah" (Hope) but also to the Arabs, who had no need for such an anthem. And in that last period, when the government with its people and its equipment were being evacuated, even that measure was no longer administered in a regular manner. There was a period in which no one knew what would happen: not the English, who were dutifully carrying out a program of withdrawal that took only themselves into account; not the Jews, who were suddenly left in an emptying land;

not the Arabs, who wanted to believe that everything would be resolved in short order.

At the same time there was a sense of tense anticipation among the Jews, as Richard Graves, the last governor of Jerusalem, wrote: "At certain moments in history, dynamic movements occur, which cannot be checked by logic, convention, or even the ordinary process of law. They are usually conducted with such enthusiasm and such conviction that they succeed in snatching success against overwhelming odds. The Zionist urge to possess their own home and state in Palestine is such a movement."

Yigal Gera, whose family was also part of the old Yishuv, lives in a mixed neighborhood in Haifa; he had worked as a senior engineer with the Shell oil company in the Forties. "For us, the Arabs weren't just any old thing," he said. "We lived together. The company doctor, Dr. Khoury, was a good friend of mine. I visited him at home and knew his wife, and they used to visit us, and they were very nice people. Maybe in his heart he said to himself, 'I like Yigal and yet I don't like the idea that little by little they're wiping us out here.' No Arab ever made a secret of it—the arrival of the Jews and what that would lead to worried them. No doubt about it. Worried the intelligentsia, too, and also the people who benefited most from the Jews. They said it outright, it was all in the open. They were opposed to Zionism and to the Jews. They wanted to slaughter us, there should be no doubt about that. There were lots of them then, and they were just waiting for the right moment to wipe us out.

"We had Arab clerks," said Gera, "who were so surprised by the fact that a month had passed already and they hadn't yet returned home, they hadn't yet wiped us out, that one of them sent me a message through the company, via Cyprus, saying 'Do me a favor, Yigal, and stop by my house. I have a spigot at the back that's not too reliable. I think I didn't close it well.' All this when nothing remained of what had been in his house.

"When Haifa was taken and the Arabs fled," he said, "my mother came running in and said 'Go look for Selma.' She had worked in our house for seventeen years, brought up the three children. When I was little she used to hit me. That was her job. She loved us and we loved her, it was something special. And afterward, too, no one got married without getting the okay from her. The Arabs were rounded up in Wadi Nisnas, and I went down there. I did a search. Altogether there were three thousand Arabs. The area she lived in had been evacuated. There wasn't a soul there. So I came back to my mother and told her, 'I can't find her,' and my mother said, 'Go to her house,' and I said, 'Ma, the Hagana is there, there's no one left,' and my mother said, 'Go. She hasn't run away. She's very fat. She's not running anywhere. Go find her.' So I went back and she was the only one left in the neighborhood, sitting there on the balcony. I said to her, 'How did you manage to stay?' and she said, 'Just imagine, our heroes'—these are her words—'all ran away and your buddies came in,' and, you know, the Arabs have a custom of putting portraits of family and friends on the walls. They hang photographs. So one of the guys was walking around—to this day I don't know who it was—and he said, 'What do you have to do with the family of Yigal and Gershon Gera?' So she said, 'I brought them up, I'm Selma.' So he suddenly says, 'This family is staying. No one's being evacuated here.'"

❖

"Actually on the day in 1947 when the UN passed the partition plan, I was in Tel Aviv, but I didn't know anything about it," said Yakub Hananiya. It was quite late in the evening by then, after a long talk about Jaffa and its merchants and their houses and the newspapers that were once published there, and after one of the daughters had served us soft drinks and Turkish coffee, which used to signal the end of a visit. But Hananiya hadn't finished his story. "And then I see people and cars and taxis. Everyone shouting, pleased as punch. What was going on? And suddenly the road between Jaffa and Tel Aviv was blocked. I didn't know what to do. I saw a Jewish taxi driver and I said to him, 'Take me to Jaffa.' 'I can't,' he said, and he took me as far as the corner of Herzl and Salameh, and I fled to Abu Kabir and never went back to Tel Aviv. They cut off the Arab-Jewish bus line. The Jews attacked, the Arabs attacked. All night long you heard shooting, and sometimes there were attacks within the city. Until we reached the point where the English fled. But you know what—the Jews had Ben-Gurion and the Hagana and the Etzel. And us in Jaffa, we had an emergency committee."

"What did the emergency committee do?" "They raised money, collected arms, and everyone with his own gun was afraid of the others. There were no police, there was no one to take charge; it was every man for himself." "And what did a paramilitary Arab organization like the Najada do?" "They had some place that they used to go and guard—Najada and Kutuba (paramilitary organizations) were divided into groups. There were groups in Manshiyeh, in KarmehTut, in Jabalia. Each one was its own boss. There was no connection between them all, and there wasn't anybody to make the connection, each one had its own interests. The Iraqi army, which was in the Triangle [a group of Arab villages to the northeast], sent some big officer to Jaffa, and he saw the situation, all the groups and the people who had no idea what war was, and he went to that committee they had turned into an emergency committee and he said to them, 'You have to mobilize your young people and we'll help you make a kind of army in Jaffa.' The committee opposed it. They said, 'We don't want to have a mess in Jaffa.' Yes, that's true, they didn't want their sons to go off to war, and he said, 'If you don't want to defend your city, the Iraqis will not protect you.'"

"And what did you, the young people, think?" I asked. "We thought, you know, everyone has to defend his city," Hananiya replied. "So why didn't you organize?" I asked. "Who would organize us?" he asked, and I: "What did you think was going to happen?" He answered slowly: "There were some people who knew the city was going to get it. They fled. Simple people said the British had left with helmets and would return with kaffiyehs, that they wouldn't really leave, so these people went off thinking they would spend a week or so in Lebanon and then return to their homes. And there were people who stayed put. They were the smallest number."

"What did you think would happen?" "I didn't know. I stayed because I didn't know what would happen. I said to my boss, 'Stay. I'm staying. You stay, too. Don't leave the house. I'll bring you whatever you want.' He said to me, 'Okay, I'm staying.' I went back to my place. I went to his place the next day, and found he had left the keys for me with someone and gone in the middle of the night. I thought I'd take care of the house for him, and then I moved here. Our whole street left, except for my family and my mother's family. My mother, may she rest in peace, wanted to go. I told her, 'With the money we have we can spend a month in a nice hotel, we'll eat and drink the money and afterward'—I have four sisters—'what am I going to do with them, sleep in the street? Let the Jews kill me, kill the whole family, I'm staying.' And I stayed."

"Why didn't other people think that way?" "There were people who were scared. They thought the Jews would come and kill everybody. There were people who wanted to have a good time, people who knew, and took their money and went, those were our rich people—the committee was theirs—and they left the city without a leader. They left earlier. When people saw how that committee fled, they started running, too. They said there was no way out, only the Arab armies could save us. My ninety-year-old uncle was there, he and his family were in the port, waiting for some ship to come and take them to Egypt or to Lebanon. I said to him: 'Uncle, why are you so afraid for your life? I'm staying here. Are you any better than me? Come back home with the family.' He said to me, 'No, I want to go.' " And after a moment he said, "Maybe he wanted to have a good time there, too," and all of us—my companion and Hananiya and I—burst out laughing.

"Look," Hananiya said, when the laughter had died down, "every day people were waiting for ships in Jaffa Port. They started two months before May 1948, wanting to run. They didn't all leave in one day. There were one hundred thousand in the city. On May 15, there were about five thousand left in the Jaffa area. Maybe three thousand of them from Jaffa itself. There were some who left in small boats for Gaza. They went to Lebanon in larger motorboats. The rich people left in cars. We'd spend the whole day watching people leave. All of a sudden you see your neighbor. 'Where are you going?' 'I'm getting out. I'm going to Amman.' "

"And what happened after they'd gone?" I asked him. "It was quiet," he said. "The Jews were waiting for the day the Mandate would end." "And you were waiting too?" I asked. "They actually came in on May 14," he said. "I was with two friends near the English Hospital, and I see two guys hiding. I said to my friends, 'I think the Jews are coming, let's go back.' They called to us, 'Stand still.' We stood. The Jews came up to us and said, 'Turn toward the wall, put your hands like this.' I turned, I did what they said. One of them came over to me with his Sten, and I was sure he was going to kill us. I got a beating, but he didn't kill us." And with a smile he added, "I got a beating and I went home, and, thank God, the Jews came in and nothing happened. We lived, we worked. I've been head of the Orthodox community since 1950. We're about thirty-five hundred. We have a club, and an association, and a church. We have our property that we released from the [government] Guardian of Abandoned Property, and we rent it out to people and get money for it and that's what keeps us going. We have lectures sometimes. We have a football team, a basketball team."

And then I noticed huge bonfires through the window and asked, "What is this, do you celebrate Lag BaOmer too?" And my companion, who was also from the neighborhood, said, as if it were obvious, "We always do it before the Jews." "Since when have you celebrated Lag BaOmer here?" I asked, and Hananiya said: "Before 1948, on our feast of the Exaltation of the Cross, we used to make huge bonfires, the way the Jews do on Lag BaOmer. That was in September, and we'd spend a month beforehand collecting wood, getting the pails of water ready. Exactly like the Jews." "And how long have you been doing it on Lag BaOmer?" I asked. "Many years," said my companion. "I used to do it too when I was a kid.

And the Arabs dress up for Purim before the Jews do, too. We even celebrate it in school." Hananiya said, "The Jews don't really make bonfires. The Arabs do. In the early years I remember seeing the sky red and the fire brigades rushing all over." And when I protested and said the Jews do make bonfires, my companion said, "Yes, but the Arabs do it for days at a time." "Strange," I murmured, and he smiled merrily and said, "In Jaffa everything is strange."

Hananiya said, "We need a great writer to tell about the things that happened in those days." "What would you tell about?" I asked, and he repeated, "What would I tell about? What I remember now. But whoever was around then—his feelings are greater than his thoughts." After a silence he added, "For about a month nobody was here. Everyone had left and the Jews hadn't come yet. There was nobody in our street. Sometimes you'd walk down the street and see some friend you thought had left. We'd sit in a cafe, smoke a few cigarettes, smoke a narghile. During that month a sack of flour cost half a pound. Everyone bought ten sacks. Corned beef was half a pound, you'd buy two crates. The stores were open in Jaffa, all of them open. You'd go into a store, pick what you needed, take it home. We had all our food and we ate. Alcohol was free. Some people stole from the stores. Guys would come over to visit, sit and eat, drink. You'd go to a café, smoke a cigarette. No cigarettes? There was tobacco for the narghile. The port was open and whatever you wanted you could get there. They'd sell tobacco in big chunks."

"Doesn't sound bad at all," I remarked, and again we all laughed. Then I remembered one of the last chapters in Ze'ev Jabotinsky's novel *Samson*, called "Samson's Last Words." Samson had issued two orders to his people, and only later did he add a third. Perhaps he had needed some period alone before he could summon his man and tell him, " 'I have reconsidered and think it would be wise for you to tell them in my name not two but three things: to gather iron, to choose themselves a king, and to learn to laugh.' " Samson wasn't referring to our kind of laughter, there in the light of the big bonfires, but that is what we had together—laughter that was more shadow than light, but hearty nevertheless, even a little wild—and I had the feeling that the exchange I had had with this pleasant man was not all that flawed. I felt that we had gone a bit beyond our limited coexistence—each with his own habits, each with his own blind spots.

Hananiya said, "Actually it was a time when, how to put it, we weren't working at anything, we ate and slept and listened to the radio. We'd hear Jordan, we'd hear Egypt, we'd hear the Jews. It was an easy life. We lived very slowly."

CHAPTER TWELVE

"We simply vanished"

After Great Britain gave up India, the biggest and most important of the Crown colonies in 1947, it became clear that the empire was coming to an end. The next in line was Palestine. The British Mandate for Palestine should have been a glorious last chapter in the empire's annals, but in practice it was full of problems, and the British failure in its rule became more and more apparent. Both the Jews and the Arabs thought that the British had betrayed them. The Arabs demanded full independence in all of Palestine, while the Jews, who at first were in favor of a national home, now openly fought for the establishment of a Jewish state and were in revolt against the Mandate authorities. It was a time of terror and resistance movements. Armored vehicles and army units controlled the roads. General curfews were declared. British Army zones were encircled by barbed wire, mainly in Jerusalem, where a wing of the King David Hotel that served the administration was blown up by the Etzel, killing about a hundred Arabs, Jews, and Englishmen. British rule, which tried to be impartial and benevolent, slowly turned into an administration checking rival forces and finally defending only itself.

In the beginning of 1947, Britain declared the Mandate unworkable and referred the matter to the UN. UNSCOP proposed a plan for the partition of Palestine west of the Jordan into a Jewish state and an Arab state. *The proposal was accepted by the General Assembly in November 1947. The Jews accepted it wholeheartedly. The Arabs rejected it vehemently. The British refused to take upon themselves its implementation, and declared the Mandate ended in 1948, efficiently withdrawing from the country and leaving behind them a no-man's-land where armed hostilities between Arabs and Jews escalated. On May 15, 1948, the British high commissioner left Palestine, and the Yishuv declared the establishment of the State of Israel. Arab armies from neighboring countries invaded and joined the local Arab forces. A full-scale war raged until the signing of armistice agreements in 1949. This chapter is about some of the last Englishmen in Palestine and their diaries written in those days, when Great Britain gave up for the first time its imperial responsibilities.*

There was a fairly late party on the city walls of Jerusalem. How we all got there, I don't know, but that was very close to the end of the Mandate. That was the occasion when Henry Gurney, the chief secretary, and I escaped from the party, really, and went for a walk along the city walls, and we asked ourselves what we would do next if we didn't have ties, obligations, and so on, where would we love to be, assuming we survived Palestine, and he at once said to me, 'I think what I would love best is to leave all administration and go and teach in Africa. Administration is a second-class business.' "

Sir Bernard de Bunsen, the last director of the Education Department under the Mandatory government, told this story casually, and I thought about the walks such Englishmen tend to take, whether in an English park or along some dusty path at the other end of the earth. I imagined these two, not particularly drawn to a party on the walls. One of them was sitting opposite me, some forty years later, in his favorite armchair. A man of eighty, his long legs crossed, his thick glasses flashing back the light of an autumn sun, a large snow-white handkerchief of fine cotton, perfectly pressed, tucked into the pocket of his old tweed jacket. And the other one, how had the other one looked, the chief secretary, in charge of administration, declaring it, in a moment of honesty, a second-class business?

De Bunsen lived on a quiet side street in Hampstead. We sat in a room whose southern windows let in a soft light. It was late autumn, some bright leaves still on the large tree, and beyond it, at a suitable distance across the lawn, houses that were neighboring but not too near; nothing violated the special silence of this enclave in the big city.

Earlier on I had heard of the diaries Sir Henry Gurney had kept, but I had not bothered to track them down. I assumed that they were the type habitually kept by Englishmen of his class—daily entries that might be useful someday in writing his memoirs. But I wondered whether the chief secretary had really been eager to go teach in Africa, or was simply sick of administering—by then, administering the termination, not the transfer, of rule. What would he have written in his diaries, this man who had been charged with the practical aspects of ending the Mandate, what would he have said about an operation that became increasingly fraught? The further he progressed in his orderly evacuation, the faster civil war erupted in his wake.

How does it happen, how does one carry out such a plan from day to day and at any cost, I wanted to ask de Bunsen, but I didn't know how to broach the matter. Ostensibly, the shape of those days was plain enough—a gradual contraction of the Mandatory government—but in fact, amid this methodical withdrawal, everything happened quite unmethodically. Facts were being created right and left; was he aware of that when, for instance, he read the evacuation instructions of the Mandatory government, twelve basic instructions that were leaked to the American press in March 1948? Among them:

1. All files are to be destroyed.
2. All revenue and postage stamps and stamping machines are to be destroyed.
11. Criminal lunatics—first redistribute so that when released they are in the midst of their own population: Arabs among Arabs and Jews among Jews.
12. All plans and field records to be shipped in thirty steel cabinets to the United Kingdom pending transfer to successor.

That, too, was taken into account: steel cabinets bearing all the documents related to proper government would be launched at sea. They would not be transferred to anyone. As if the British had a plan for releasing reality from all control. This time they would yield to some other force, more natural—which the Jews of the Yishuv would call stygian and the Arabs fate, and the British would call ... what? What name would de Bunsen give it?

When I made an oblique attempt to bring up the subject, he laughed somewhat awkwardly and said, "I think I did find Jerusalem an intensely interesting place, I think the most gripping place I have been to notwithstanding the sound of guns. Of course I knew from the beginning that our tenure was very short. I can't say I ever had any glowing certainties at all." And he mumbled, in his manner of stylized obfuscation, a few things about the political state of affairs, which was a dead end until I realized he was not inclined to abstract discussion. It would be better to pose specific questions, not too many, and let him take them where he would.

"In the last twelve months we were so much living from hand to mouth that there was not an awful lot of time to think, just trying to hold on to things, keep schools running, pay the teachers. As the Mandate drew to a close, it was rather a desperate effort to enter the coffers of the government and to give everybody one year's salary, and we were asked to attend Barclays Bank, where the money in cash would be handed over to us, huge bags of money. This was in Allenby Square. Arabs were standing in groups, whistling, with arms, and we couldn't get in; the doors were closed, as it was too full. Eventually, after trying every possible way, we more or less forced an entry. And then, almost at once, there was a terrific din of shooting directed toward the bank. We were all bidden to go down under the counters, and then quite a junior member of Barclays Bank walked around and looked at his watch and said, 'It's all right, it's only three minutes to go.' He turned out to be right. And when I asked him later—he was working in Nairobi later—'How did you invent the figures?' he said, 'Well, you had to say something.'"

With a few bleats of laughter, he came to the end of a story he had told with ease, in that conservative English that has a certain muted elegance, and with a distance that is not just the distance of time, but the distance a person keeps from himself.

When de Bunsen arrived in Palestine in the spring of 1946, he was a new kind of Mandate employee. He was not from the

Colonial Office but from the British educational system. An intellectual, one could say, but I doubt he would have been pleased with the description, nor would he have called himself a scholar; perhaps he would prefer no definition. Even the title "Sir" unnecessarily emphasized the class aspect of a member of an old Norman family whose ancestor was a signatory to the Magna Carta. He never mentioned that, but talked about the liberal tradition of the late nineteenth and early twentieth centuries in which he had been raised: "I think that in my case I was brought up by Mother, you know, who had traveled in those parts, in those very early days, and regarded her Palestine days as a great event." He sounded a bit amused, as if to say, "There's a sort of madness in all that."

But when he spoke of the English liberal tradition, it was with gravity and respect. It was a tradition open to new experiments with the mind and soul, and he had some radical ideas for the conservative Arab schools:

"There was an amazing system, I discovered, and I was about halfway toward abolishing it by the time I left. Teachers were selected according to the institutions they had their education in. The [previous] directors of education felt there was nothing like Oxford and nothing worse than Cairo." Why had he insisted on such substantial changes, I wondered; as a professional he must have known that revolutions in education are rare, that everything moves slowly and investments are always long-term. Had this been a way of ignoring the end to which he was undeniably a partner? After all, he too followed the instructions, and he too had to curtail activities more and more so that on the appointed day he would walk out without transferring the department to anyone.

"When did you actually stop working?" I asked. "I didn't visit many schools," he replied, "but I do remember going to Ramallah in about the last week."

And after telling me how he had refused an army escort to the school, he went on: "The schools most remarkably, I think, both Jewish and Arab, kept on, and when I was asked back in England by people at Whitehall what horrors we were living, and I said the worst horror was a strike in an Arab school in Acre, they said, 'Oh, yes, everybody is so politicized out there,' and I said, 'Not a bit, they were striking against their medical officer to have their hair cut.'"
Again he concluded his story with a few bleats of laughter, which conveyed without explanation and without high-flown phrases that the approaching end of an activity does not necessarily render it meaningless.

Whether or not the end was near, they tried to go on with the normal order of business, to govern well, faithful to the spirit of the Mandate. With terrorism on the increase and the political situation growing more complicated, the administration applied emergency regulations, used a huge army to get the rebellious Yishuv under control, and brought in people from England who would be capable of functioning in a situation that was unfamiliar and in constant flux. De Bunsen, who was one of them, told about some of the others, more enlightened representatives of colonial rule, less rigid than their predecessors, more suited to meet the new, complex demands, and perhaps because of these very qualities, heralding the end of that rule:

"There were some good people on the whole, I would say, intellectually abler than district commissioners or people anywhere in Africa, but caught up in a situation in which they had really nothing to say." And after a moment he added: "I was very much impressed, really, with Henry Gurney, although he didn't look impressive at all. Some didn't like him very much. I think he had something constructive within him. Of course he was there briefly, and he was not everybody's cup of tea by any means." Here he stopped. I had already noticed that notwithstanding the responses he always gave willingly, and his muttering, his speech had a rhythm of its own. He wasn't fond of orderly conversation or of direct answers, but favored a kind of meander punctuated with silences, and I simply had to wait for him to resume talking, which he eventually did:

"I think the civil service of course as a whole, they would have regarded their job rather as my brother did in Sudan—at best as one was looking after the underdog. And for them who had been many years in Palestine, the underdog was the Arab. And they had not experienced the Central European situation, even in the war they were not very touched by it. I came through Europe, and my family were all involved in trying to help refugees, you know." And after a pause, he added: "It looked as if we hadn't anything constructive to say about the future." I asked him whether it had been possible to foresee a future for the place without taking sides. He acknowledged that it had been very difficult, and when he had returned to his own thoughts, it occurred to me that in England he wouldn't have seen any difficulty at all. There, among equals, it was permitted to take stands. In England there was fair play, and throughout the empire one was "fair" to the local subjects; de Bunsen, who had apparently been considering the matter, said:

"I arrived just before the King David Hotel was blown. I remember having a long talk with the chief secretary at the time— I think it was then Shaw, Sir John Shaw—who had his arm in a sling and his leg in plaster. It was back in the office, and he said, 'Now, you are new to the country. If you feel you are getting bitter about one side or the other, do for heaven's sake realize that there is the rest of the world to go to. I am going.'"

And they did have places to go—elsewhere in the empire and to England itself—if they didn't want to turn bitter or hate the natives. And that too was a very colonial kind of privilege; the policemen, soldiers, and clerks had nowhere to run from the hatred and the bitterness—and neither did the local people. Moreover, a system that allows someone to leave brings someone else in his place, and that someone else was Sir Henry Gurney, the last chief secretary; at that point I mentioned his diaries. "It would be interesting to know what was in them," I remarked. And de Bunsen, who didn't know of their existence, responded with a polite murmur which meant, "Let's leave that aside." Again I had come up against that code within his easygoing evasions. He added: "He longed to teach in Africa and found himself in this impossible job, and then went to another impossible job as high commissioner in Malaya and got murdered."

If that's the case, then only the diaries remain, I said to myself, and again I wondered what had been recorded every day by the man who kept things going until May 15, 1948, undoubtedly carrying out with exemplary precision and order a task that left increasing disorder on its completion. De Bunsen went on: "I found him both congenial and wise, but more and more of course he got sucked into this military operation while realizing it was no solution at all, that the end was inevitable, but there he was."

"How did one cope with anarchy at the time?" I asked. "From day to day, really," he said. "Anarchy of course is never quite as bad, moment to moment, as it sounds. Life does persist even when the Jerusalem water and electricity supplies began to fail." His tone was jocular. Had life then become an orderly passage from moment to moment, anticipating the moment when they would disappear in an orderly fashion? There was something fascinating in the prospect of civilized people, dedicated to enlightened government and public order, who were in fact charged with dismantling that order.

I asked de Bunsen whether he had kept a journal during that period. "Perhaps I did, yes," he said, and after a moment explained that it was not really a diary but brief notes. I asked whether I could see them, or some of them, and he said that he would look for them, that he had no idea where he had stuck them away. Then he added: "Probably it had a depressive effect on people. I can remember some new colleagues being appointed to the education center who seemed, despite the King David blow-up, to assume that they were there for life. No, there is a depressive effect on people; if not their nerves, they lose their appetite because there is no future, really. I think there would be limits to how long the human brain can carry total uncertainty, except that there would be an end and it would involve us all."

In the notes, which he did in fact find and pass on to me, it seems that he himself had reached that impossible limit he had spoken of. This is what he wrote on February 2, 1948: "Increasing feeling of futility from a job which is withering away, in which you can get nothing done, no safeguards against chaos ahead. A long afternoon and the evening with nowhere outside to walk to. Arab liberation army now more or less in Jerusalem. Behaving so far but embarrassing to the army and government. But is there a remedy, and don't we intend to let things slide? Demoralization is increasing pretty rapidly. Unless you believe in God there is now no reason left why we shouldn't accept it all and just sit about waiting for another two and a half months for May the 15th, listening to the shots."

For ninety days he made notes, not in notebooks but on lined sheets. Occasionally he comes out with a confession or some protest against what is happening. Sometimes he only reports, but in those notes there is none of his distance and irony. Only near the end, perhaps because it seems only an end, does the familiar tone return:

"Wednesday, March 23... Spent the morning planning to get the examination papers for Palestine Matric [final high school exams] from Bloom's [Jewish colleague in the Education Department] house in Rehavia to the zone for distribution to the Arab centers. Eventually I met him at the Gaza Road barbed wire at the exit of Zone B, for which he has no pass, and we transferred them through the barbed wire from his to my car, to the amusement of the soldiers."

And a few days before he was to leave, on April 25, 1948, he notes with irony: "The wireless system seems to have collapsed, and we will live in a land of rumors."

De Bunsen gave me the notes several weeks after our meeting. But before that he put me in touch with Richard Stubbs, who had headed the Information Office in Jerusalem until May 14, 1948, and who asked me when we spoke on the phone whether I wasn't writing this book for the Jewish Agency or some other agency of the State of Israel. He went on to say that he had recently seen a television program about Ben-Gurion that had been embarrassingly pro-Israel, in his opinion, and he assumed it had been financed by one of those organizations. When I had explained to him that I was writing on behalf of no one, he set up a meeting with me in London at the bar of a large hotel near Liverpool Street railway station in the City. He brought with him a great deal of written material—a very large, thick bound notebook—and from time to time consulted it to check himself. But after a while Stubbs forgot the notebook and got caught up in amusing stories about the days of terror and the days of battle and the watercolors of Palestine landscapes that he insisted on painting under all circumstances and how he had gone out one pleasant April day to the balcony of his office to paint the Judaean Hills. He sat there for two hours until someone opened heavy fire on him.

After describing how he had run inside and another employee had gone out to the balcony to rescue the watercolor before it was perforated with bullets, he said: "I was violently anti-anti-Semitic. I didn't believe in Zionism, but I was very fervently pro-Jewish, and certainly they all knew that I was very sympathetic to the Jewish situation." The large bar was already full of travelers and young people who worked in the City and had stopped in for a drink or a bit of pub fare. Stubbs went on telling me about the last days. When he was about to get on his train, I asked him whether the large notebook he had brought with him was the diary he kept at the time, and he explained that immediately after returning to England at the end of the Mandate he had shut himself up in the country for a few weeks and written his account of the recent period in Palestine.

At our second meeting, in his beautiful home, a Georgian rectory in the heart of the Suffolk countryside, he read me selections from the notebook about the bar of the Information Office, which in the last months was the haunt of foreign journalists as well as the Arabs and Jews who came to pass on information, and about the funeral of one of the Jewish employees of the office, when everyone—the rabbi, the family, and all the other mourners—fell flat over the open grave, ducking gunfire. From time to time what he read brought up other memories, and he would elaborate or tell how, for instance, it was discovered that all the phones in the office were disappearing one by one, and he, Richard Stubbs, negotiated with the employees an agreement for dividing up the office furnishings—rugs, chairs, equipment—on condition that they remain in place until May 15, 1948.

He read to me for hours on end, even after he had grown hoarse, and it was almost time for the train to London. It was cold. Through the French windows you could no longer see the hillside, a patch of land in the muted green of winter, nor could you see the walls of the house, in that pink hue typical of the area. Stubbs said he would send me the remaining chapters, but the part about the night of May 13 he wanted to read before I left:

"I went back to the office at 9:30 p.m. to issue the final broadcast speech of the high commissioner, and I walked up to my office on the third floor and I was waiting for the telephone call to tell me that the broadcast had been made, as my old wireless had already been looted. My thoughts were disturbed by movements in the outer office. Through the half-open door I saw to my astonishment a man on his hands and knees unscrewing the remaining telephone receiver. Without thinking I took up the ancient revolver which was the only item of the safe which we had not disposed of, and which I had been warned long ago would mean sudden death to anyone using it, and for safety had no ammunition, kicked open the door following roughly a pattern I had learnt from the films, leveled the revolver at the man's back and shouted 'Hands up.' He leapt to his feet and I demanded to know what he was doing. He said he was just removing the telephone. 'I can see that,' I said. 'But why?' 'For safety,' he replied. Obviously he was just completing the telephone loot. I was so depressed that if I had not wanted that receiver to get my message from Government House, I think I might have let him take it."

Closing the notebook, he added, "I arranged with the chief secretary that when the speech begins he would ring me up and tell me if there were any changes from the original." I asked him whether he had heard of the diaries of Sir Henry Gurney, and he said he hadn't, but he didn't think I would find them very interesting, since the man was very formal and very British, and here he told me how he had brought him to a press conference in Tel Aviv. It was summer and the Jewish journalists were wearing open-collared shirts; the chief secretary said he had no intention of speaking before people who had not bothered to put on a tie, and stalked out of the hall.

I continued to try to track down the journals of Gurney; eventually I discovered that they were at Oxford, in the Middle East Centre of St Antony's College, and I wrote a letter of inquiry. While I was waiting for an answer, which was slow in coming because of the Christmas holiday, de Bunsen called me and said he had found the notes he had made in the last months of the Mandate. He also had remembered another person who was with him in Jerusalem during that period, named Donald Baron.

We arranged a visit, and a few afternoons later Baron arrived at the flat where I was staying in London. He was an Oxford graduate in history, who in the Forties had been in the Royal Air Force in Egypt, and was sent to Palestine in 1946 to replace a minor official killed in the King David bombing. He was much younger than de Bunsen, without the British formality of the previous generation. He saw himself as a representative of the Commonwealth, offering a new kind of service to the colonies: "Not in a paternal kind of way. Not in a sense that one was asked to help to administer a group of people who were in some way inferior." And when I tried to understand the nature of this service—whether it was a kind of aid, whether he saw himself as a foreign expert—he replied: "Though it may sound a curiously trite and unimportant point, I think it was an important point for everybody who did it; they felt they had something to offer. It is certainly part of this curious public school system. It now exists for people who go abroad under various voluntary organizations like Oxfam, people who do the same sort of things we wanted to do, but they haven't got quite the same opportunity."

"What exactly did you mean by 'the same opportunity'?" I asked. Baron, who understood that I was hinting that the pattern had remained imperialistic, the pattern of do-gooders throughout the world, smiled faintly and asked whether he could read here and there from the notebooks he had brought with him. These were diaries he'd kept regularly, he explained, glancing at the tape recorder to check whether it was on. He read sections about his training as an employee of the administration, a prolonged training that continued throughout 1947 and included extensive trips throughout the country and Arabic studies—he was just ready to begin work when the English decided to "give up" the Mandate—and

I asked whether the timing didn't seem to him preposterous or at least strange. To my surprise he said that only two months before the end did he realize the Mandate was coming to a close, and when I pointed out that the English had announced they were leaving and had set a date, he replied: "I suppose nobody believed them, really, and I suppose we never believed them." "What did you think would happen?" I asked, and his answer was, "I suppose we had been brought up on the idea that the British had managed to win a war, and this was an aftermath of the war, and somehow it would be brought to a conclusion. I don't think we ever believed the British would walk out the way they did, leaving chaos in the country, because it never happened anywhere else."

Here he began to compare Israel with other places—mainly in Africa—where he had been and participated in the handing over of government. Then he showed me some photos, one of them of a cocktail party on the balcony of the Mandatory building in the main airport of Palestine near the Arab town Lydda. Among the men and women in rather formal summer clothes was one who resembled him a bit, a good-looking young man with a thin mustache, wearing a summer suit, and Baron said, "Yes, that's me," and added: "People whom I have met since would ask me, 'Why on earth did you want to go to Palestine? We would want to go to Nigeria, which was the largest British colony, or to Ceylon.'"

Baron was a pleasant man not inclined to profound discussion. We talked about concerts in London and the fog that was descending and about the fact that he had never been to Tel Aviv. I offered him sherry. It was already six and he mentioned that he had to go. As he gathered his notebooks, he asked whether I had taped his reading. I walked him outside. The street ahead was invisible in the fog. It was an evening when planes are grounded. He walked off in the direction of the tube.

Donald Baron died a month later of leukemia, but I found out only some time afterward. At about that time I received permission to come and inspect the diaries of Sir Henry Gurney. I stepped onto the express train for Oxford one morning, and by noon I was sitting at a table in the Middle East Centre of St Antony's with a brown cardboard box in front of me containing a thick sheaf of typed pages. The first page was an introduction by one of the deputies, mainly describing Gurney's total equanimity:

"When it fell to me to report to him out of office hours on some further 'bloody' incident, his reaction was always the same. After a courteous word of thanks for being kept informed, he enquired whether there was anything useful he could do. If there was not (and usually there was not) he would say in his quiet way, 'Well, I might as well go and play the round of golf I had planned.'

"I well remember, many years later, discussing Gurney with Mrs. Golda Meir... and the question of his imperturbability cropped up. 'Yes,' she said, 'that was why we hated him. No one in that position had any right to be unruffled. He ought to have been pacing his room day and night, trying to find a solution to the Jewish problem. It was our objective to "ruffle" people, but we could not make any impression on him.' "

The following pages were an introduction by the chief secretary himself, and there he explained that the notes—which he did not consider a diary—had been written in a rush, half an hour here and half an hour there, during the last sixty days of the British Mandate in Palestine, and this is how he defined the activity of those days:

"During the last two months therefore one of the administration's tasks was to cut off the branch on which it was sitting. The branch must hold until May 15th, but must fall exactly on that day.

"Palestine Postscript—A short record of the last days of the Mandate," he wrote after the introduction. Here and there were handwritten corrections, in ink, and I wondered whether Gurney had made them himself. Heavy snow began falling in the yard of the Middle East Centre, which is in an unattached building. I was the only person in the room, and the director of the archives, who would tiptoe in from time to time, told me they were expecting a blizzard and the rails were freezing. I hurriedly photocopied the diary pages and rushed to the station. That evening in London, in a flat made even quieter by the heavy snow still falling outside, I began to read the notes.

I spent days reading them, and compared them with those of de Bunsen, with the last segments Stubbs had sent me, and with portions of Baron's reading that I had recorded. Suddenly I had pages upon pages of diaries and notes; they had told me more in writing than in speech. The English, in Palestine so briefly, had felt an urge to record events during the last days of the Mandate. Most felt an urge, that is, but the chief secretary had had an absolute need to keep notes. Perhaps because he presented to the world such a tranquil, unperturbed face, he had sought an outlet in these closely written sheets. They conveyed a kind of immediacy—whether he was assessing the situation or describing the garden flowers, everything was charged with that necessity of putting what was happening into words. Sixty days, more than a hundred pages, and this entry—these are only selected portions—opens the record:

MARCH 15

"On this wet and cheerless day in Jerusalem—it was snowing this morning—all is quiet, because in this weather both sides prefer to remain indoors. But the nightly battle begins regularly about 8 o'clock and continues sporadically till dawn.... The sky on these occasions is crisscrossed with tracers, yellow for the Arabs, red for the Jews."

MARCH 17

"I thought today: 'If Palestine has to be written on my heart, must it be in Arabic and Hebrew?'"

As if the Arabs and the Jews are the true reason for this awkward situation. But perhaps that is the only way the man in charge of the withdrawal and the anarchy that comes in its wake can respond. He is certainly aware of the details, and the details speak for themselves:

"Some of the stations are now guarded by Arabs and others by Jews, and I understand the engine crew change their hats according to the station they are running into. What keeps the Railway running? The answer is (almost) a lemon, as it won't run at all after the citrus crop for the British children's orange juice has all gone out in three weeks' time."

MARCH 20

"Last night there was really a good battle when fifty Jews attacked Beit Safafa.... But today has been our first glorious spring day; the air itself almost coruscating in the brilliant sunlight in which every stone and tree becomes a jewel—*urbs Sion aurea*.

Jerusalem the golden; or, as Josephus put it, a golden bowl full of scorpions."

Did he also see the English in this golden bowl? It seems he did not. Was the increasing disgust also a last defense of that government? But he always has time to notice the landscape, and to describe precisely:

"Palestine light is of incredible clarity. It is brittle rather than glaring; translucent like cold spring water. In March and April among the hills of Samaria, Galilee and TransJordan, the wild flowers sprinkle the rocky and pale green landscape with red, yellow and blue. Sometimes the red anemones cover a whole hillside, and the blue lupins shine for miles and miles like great splashes of ultramarine paint spilt among the young grass."

MARCH 26
"Good Friday. How quickly the days pass and how much the same they all seem."

MARCH 27
"I was looking today at a full-page advertisement for the United Jewish Appeal in the *New York Times*.... The art and the publicity technique are first class; but they are used only to deceive. The Zionists know well the decent instincts of the Gentile, particularly the British and the Americans, that he can exploit to his own ends. In doing so he creates anti-Semitism, and he knows it, but he takes the line that this is his nature and he cannot help it. It is part of the suicidal make-up, a seed of his own destruction, which he knows he carries, and this makes him desperate, ruthless, and utterly self-centered.

"The Arab feels as strongly about the freedom of his country as an American would if a Jewish State were proclaimed in New York.... He is easy-going to the point of indolence, disposed to cruelty and capable of only about one idea at a time. The idea is formed on emotion rather than from any rational thought; it is nursed and chewed over on innumerable occasions in coffee houses and in the press, until it is firmly stuck and nothing on earth will shift it."

He turns his severe and penetrating glance to the locals—mainly the Jews—and never to the British. They are not subject to inspection. That's where he stops seeing. But he is always aware of the direction things are taking, and of their significance, however grave.

APRIL 2
"A lovely afternoon in which, after a game of tennis, we got down to working out the actual run-down of civil staff, leaving only fifty British officers (outside the Railway and Customs at Haifa and Police and prisons) in Palestine after the 28th of April. Gradually the superficial problems are beginning to sort themselves out. The fundamental ones remain untouched."

APRIL 7
"It seems already clear that the UN can produce nothing effective in a month's time, and it is a disheartening job going downhill day after day towards the precipice. This Gadarene tendency seems to appeal to many people in Palestine; but to those British officers who have given all they had to the good of the country it is sheer disaster."

A disaster for the British who are leaving, and what about those who are staying? Meanwhile:

"A large cocktail in the Officers' Club next to the King David this evening. This Club was only finished two months ago, and it always amused us that work was going ahead on it all the time the Information Office across the road was trying to make people believe the British were going in May, whatever happened."

Absurdity is a given, and so he writes the next day:

APRIL 8
"This morning the Arabs recaptured Castel.... We can no longer intervene in these battles. Neither side wants us to. Like Tweedledum and Tweedledee, they have agreed to fight a battle."

APRIL 11
"The Arabs have been guilty of many horrible barbarities and are selling picture postcards of some of them. No doubt we shall have a competition in atrocity stories before long."

APRIL 15
"The Belgian Consul-General's milk donkey is still lying outside his door, and no one can move it for Jewish snipers.... The Palestine donkeys have the most patient and pleasant expressions of any of the living occupants of this country."

And on April 16, as battles raged and no one knew whether the Mandatory government would be able to stay until May 15, he writes: "If someone were to put the Security Council on the Greek stage, it would go something like this . . .

> Chorus of British delegates:
> STROPHE: We are going on May 15th.
> ANTISTROPHE: On May 15th we are going.
> JAMAL HUSSEINI FOR THE ARAB HIGHER COMMITTEE: We are prepared to agree to anything that does not include partition, Jewish immigration, and a Jewish State.
> MOSHE SHERTOK: We are prepared to agree to anything provided it includes partition, immigration, and a Jewish State.
> SENATOR AUSTIN: All I suggest is something that commits nobody to anything at all.
> PRESIDENT TRUMAN (OFF): I am still backing a partition."

Thus, over several pages, he put words into the mouths of those over whom he had no control, amused himself at the expense of the people responsible for the despicable situation, the people who were forcing him into actions that had nothing to recommend them.

APRIL 19
"It is wise to put this withdrawal, which seems of such importance to us, in its proper historical perspective. Those who were responsible for the Balfour Declaration knew all too little of the long story of this country; if they had studied it they could never have involved Britain in a sixth Crusade, though I well remember

thinking in 1918 that there was something creditable in the declaration and in the association of British arms with the return of the Jews to Palestine."

From the heights of the Sixth Crusade, he plunges again to the level of daily infuriating evils; whatever one makes of them, that is what they remain:

APRIL 20
"Last night we spent some time on one of the difficult small problems in an effort to be just at the expense of our own interests. The Enab Police Station near the Arab village Abu Gosh on the Jerusalem-Latrun road had now to be evacuated. If no warning is given to the Arabs, the Jews will occupy it. On the other hand, it is in an Arab village and if the Arabs have it and can hold it, they can effectively block the road which we are trying to keep open. These 'Tegart' Police Stations are built like fortresses and would be difficult to capture against determined resistance, or even to blow up, if properly watched. We decided that the Arabs must be warned.

"The garden is now at its best, and I picked a large bunch of sweet peas yesterday. These are flowering among wallflowers, irises, cyclamen, stock and violets—all at the same time. By June they will be dried up and gone."

And down the hill they go, approaching the nadir, the end. If there is a direction, it is unavoidable—and perhaps there is only acceleration.

APRIL 21

"The military view of the future became clearer today. The situation is full of paradoxes. First, we are staying on merely to get out, and by staying on make getting out more difficult. Secondly, whereas until recently we were staying on to help the Army to get out, now the Army is staying on because for political reasons we are not allowed to go, although the Army wants us to. It is quite clear that the situation in Jerusalem is not appreciated in London. We have now no petrol and no kerosene; enough heavy oil to keep the electricity supply going for another ten days; and about a week's diesel oil for water supply, which has to be pumped up two thousand feet and may be blown up at any time. It has been twice already."

APRIL 27

"A convoy (the penultimate civilian convoy) leaves early tomorrow for Lydda, where we hope the planes to fetch them will be able to land. After that there will be only twenty of us left, and very few Palestinian officers."

APRIL 28

"Got up at 5.45 and went to see the convoy off the King David at 6.30. About one hundred British, including many heads of departments. It was quite a bit of history, though it didn't look like it. Air passengers in old makintoshes are not a stirring sight. But this party represented the main body of the Government leaving Jerusalem, the Holy City, in the early light of a grey morning: policemen in blue in their green armoured cars, the parting of many friends and the finish, in some cases, of a life's work.

The press and the photographers missed it, and it all went off soberly and quietly, with handshakes and some rather studiously casual waves, hiding all kinds of thoughts and emotions. None of us would have it otherwise; every sign of sentiment had been magnificently dulled."

APRIL 29

"It is a fact that the Government of Palestine cannot do very much. The Courts have stopped and so has the Post Office.... The prisons are not functioning either.

"We came into our prison, the King David, last night—Gibson, Dorman and I. Hamburger, the Manager, went to great trouble to furnish rooms for us and provide a dinner according to King David standards, which are as high as anywhere in the world. We sat down to a seven-course dinner, beautifully cooked and served. This afternoon, driving through the German Colony [an Arab neighborhood], we saw lorry after lorry loaded with household effects, people and baggage on the way out of Jerusalem. Others have gone into the Old City for refuge.

"Many of the rich have suddenly discovered that they have pressing assignment in Cairo or Beirut. This is Arab fickleness at its worst, with black market and throwing of the blame on somebody other than themselves, i.e. the British."

During the next few days he had almost no time. Yet he was increasingly devoted to his notes, it seems. There was some point to the writing, he apparently felt—which there was not to any of his other activities.

MAY 7

"After lunch I set off for Jericho with the High Commissioner for a meeting with Azzam Pasha which we have been trying to arrange for some days, to discuss the truce for Jerusalem. We reached Jericho at 3.00 and Azzam and his party arrived a few minutes later. Nine of us sat down in a small and very stuffy room in the Police Station on very hard wooden chairs and talked across a small table with a dirty pink tablecloth and one ashtray. Nothing else. It contrasted sadly with the panoply and appurtenances of the United Nations, but the very simplicity of the room emphasized the air of reality we all felt."

And on May 15, after landing in England, Gurney—whose photo I never sought, as if intending him to remain imageless, only typewritten words—recorded:

"We had thought out and planned this last day so often, that its historical importance had long given way in our minds to details of timing and transport. Nothing was left to Chance. This bare and naked narrative leaves untouched the mountains of paper and telegrams that had been devoted to it. In the end, like all well-organized operations, it all looked very simple."

Did he too feel that there was something incomprehensible in all this? Explicit instructions, clear details. Results as well— parts, but no whole. "No one makes history, no one sees it, just as no one sees the grass growing," wrote Boris Pasternak. And what would the chief secretary have said to that—a realistic man, expert in the details of the reality darkening before his eyes? A man of middle age, presumably, whose featureless figure I imagine not on the last day of the Mandate but on the morning of April 28, bidding farewell to a hundred employees of the Mandate standing on the large pink stones in front of the half-destroyed King David—senior officials and young people, all of the same class—raised in Imperial Britain, put through public school, trained for colonial service: human beings of a different order.

A large, undoubtedly quiet group of well-bred people, a good number with diaries stashed in their baggage; one didn't show feelings, one wrote them down—but not feelings alone. De Bunsen, who was among them, kept his papers in his pocket. The last director of education in Mandatory Jerusalem, he made some notes while on the plane; he wrote regularly and up to the last moment, as if undertaking to document the anarchy that reigned in contravention of all English tradition, up to the moment when he ceased bearing witness. That in itself was important to him, a part of the tradition that was no longer equal to reality, but to which he was still devoted.

When I went to see him for the last time, to return the notes, and remarked that the flight must have been bumpy when he wrote the last entry, as I had been unable to read his handwriting, de Bunsen apologized for the great inconvenience reading the diaries must have caused me and for the boredom that must have overcome me, and listened to my vigorous protests with some embarrassment, and in the midst of this embarrassment, when I tried to make the leap from the pages to the man who had written them, he told me in brief about the death of Donald Baron. Outside it was a midwinter day, the sky low and drizzly; I asked what had happened that morning after they left Jerusalem.

"I probably left with the last exodus from Lydda," he began hesitantly. "We went down in a convoy guarded in front and behind us because of sniping that was going on on the road, reached Lydda airport, and found it totally deserted, I remember, and we sat there without any information at all as to what might happen or what they were trying to do with us. Various planes just went overhead, and like people on a desert island, we waved to them indicating our presence, to no avail at all. Lydda airport had been absolutely ransacked. The perimeters were still under control of the British Army, but nothing within. However, in the end a plane did come and we piled in somehow, as best we could with our luggage, and when the engines were going we noticed that the Union Jack was still flying over Lydda airport. And since it was wholly unlikely to be out there of all places, we thought we had better remove it, so we sent the youngest member, a young district officer, back across the tarmac to pick it up." He laughed a bit, as if shaking off the incident and the special fluency with which he related it, starting shyly and ending up speaking in stories. In the silence that descended again his lips moved slightly as if he were muttering to himself, and I imagined that spring night and the flowering citrus orchards whose scent must have reached the deserted airport.

"Do you remember any leave-taking from people in Jerusalem?" I asked him. "I am sure we said farewell," he replied. "Well, I think, I think we simply vanished, really. I must have said good-bye to some of the Arab colleagues remaining—some had already fled to Beirut or Damascus—and the Jewish ones. It did become difficult to reach the Jewish ones. No, I think we just sort of vanished off the face of the earth, really."

We talked some more, about Africa, where he had spent so many years, and about the riots there that had seemed to him quite innocuous after Jerusalem, and a short time later, when I got up to leave, we realized that the morning's drizzle had turned into pounding rain, and de Bunsen began a minor tirade against the weather and said he would give me an umbrella. There was a whole collection there that people had left, he said, and took one out of a wooden box near the front door. I was almost at the bottom of the stairs when he said, "Farewell," and I thought it was good that I was far enough away not to have to respond to such a formal good-bye.

I walked through the streets of Hampstead, rain washing over the old umbrella, and I thought about the way people use that expression aside from "farewell party" and whether de Bunsen would have addressed me the same way years ago, when he was a young man with new ideas about England and the world. Or was this a manner of speech that he had adopted in the course of time, given the tremendous changes in England itself?

Had de Bunsen chosen to be one of those who never gave up doing things on a grand scale, a practice that had been possible in the empire, among the illusions it offered, but had developed in England itself? Did he prefer being an Englishman of the previous generation, unashamed that on that green and rainswept island there was still some form of innocence and old-fashioned honor, things from a different, premodern world, and on their behalf might he perhaps have said in a few simple words that there had been no ceremonies and no farewells because the English had not committed themselves to an end or to a beginning, and in those days, days with no horizon, they could leave that place only thus, by vanishing into thin air?

About a hundred people on park benches crammed into the plane, and the old York bore them through the sky along with order and privilege and good intentions—not devoid of colonial condescension—but also with the potential for another kind of life, one not made of merciless hopes and timeworn local materials, as was the lot of those who stayed on. I had no memory of their leaving. Was it obvious, or had I simply grown tired of hearing about it? There were other things to think about. The older children were bringing around their finds from the abandoned Arab houses. That was new—the things themselves and the delight in having them. No one talked about the English. They were gone.

Epilogue

"Of course it was beautiful. At that distance incredibly beautiful. Nostalgia has a magic impact on memory," said Hisham Sharabi when we met in Washington.

He was talking about Acre—actually about a photograph of it hanging on his office wall at Georgetown University, where he was a professor of European intellectual history. He was slight of build, wearing a light summer shirt. His face had an olive-tinged pallor to it, and in his large, dark, expressive eyes there was a calm of the acquired sort.

We talked about Jaffa, where Sharabi had been born and lived, about Acre, where he used to spend his summers, and about Tel Aviv. We talked about the last days of the Mandate and about the days that followed; we hardly spoke of the uprising in the occupied territories that had begun a year and a half earlier. Even without our mentioning it, the subject was never shunted into a corner. It was part of the new reality, and because of it we had a certain freedom of speech. We no longer had to resort to formulas of explanation or apology or caution, to phrases about guilt and conqueror and conquered. It was because of the uprising, in fact, that we could discuss what I had wanted to: shifts in memory after forty years, the last years of the Mandate as a time of transition, and recollection itself.

"You know," he said, "the older one gets, the closer the earlier memories come to one, and at my age, now that I have just entered my sixties, little things come out with total clarity and bring back a world that has long since disappeared. For some reason, Acre seems to have a hold on me." After a moment he added, "If you want to see this picture on the wall—this is where I used to swim as a little boy."

Remaining seated as I got up to look, he explained that the uppermost photo was of Rosh HaNikra and the bottom one of the walls of Acre's old city, where his grandfather's house had been. The middle photo—the seashore—had been taken from a spot by that wall, and it showed the stretch of beach that could be seen from the windows of the house. The office wall with the photographs was opposite his desk. When he sat at his desk, he could see books, Tunisian rugs, a swath of campus through the window, and the three pictures. I remarked that, judging by the lumps of tar along the shoreline, the photo had been taken not long ago. Sharabi said, "That beach used to be completely wild. Nothing on it."

He talked about how he had continued going to Acre every summer, even when he was sent to boarding school, even when he was a university student in Beirut. Immersed in the Christian, Western education that enlightened families gave their sons, he would return to spend the summer with his grandfather and grandmother, who asked him to go to the mosque and to read from the Koran, and he did those things for them, without any great faith and without thinking much about it. Everything was taken in stride—young people captivated by the West and their more traditional elders accepted each other with tolerance. The world was still stable, comprising change without adapting to it and without resisting it. And within this tranquil world there were also Jews—distant, almost invisible.

"My memories of the Jews were a series of fleeting impressions," said Sharabi, and after describing some of them, mainly the Jewish bathhouse near his home in Manshiyeh, Jaffa, which was set on fire in the riots of 1936 and burned all night—the burning building still figures in his dreams—he added: "I remember buying the Everyman edition of *Crime and Punishment* one afternoon in a Jewish bookstore in Tel Aviv, but I never went into a Jewish home, and Jewish life and the Jewish community were as distant from where I stood as England was."

He went on in his understated manner, handling the words as if they were fragile objects: "They were very foreign to us and very strange. I was not aware of their existence in Palestine. Amazing, isn't it? To think that every summer I would go from Jaffa through the entire region where you had so many settlements, but what I saw on that road from Jaffa to Haifa to Acre were the Arab towns. Now and then, if we saw Jews, I didn't notice them.

"I remember in 1947. It was before we left. I was nineteen, I mean, fully aware, and I remember saying to a friend of mine when the troubles started, 'The poor Jews, I wonder what is going to happen to them.' I was sure that if this continued they would be crushed. The last thing in my imagination was that we were about to be displaced, that we were about to be overcome by a force that was far better than anything that Arab or Palestinian society represented."

"Did you ever think about the future of the country?" I asked. "Belonging to a Muslim family, middle-class, professional background," answered Sharabi, "we represented the most secure kind of consciousness, of sensibility. I had no worries about the future, neither personal nor national. I thought that the world was extremely well organized and that everything was in place, and that things would only become better as one grew older."

"Things were happening quite quickly after the Second World War," I said. "Jewish terrorism, clashes with the British—did you think about Zionism at all?" And he shook his head. "The curious thing is, when I look back, maybe it was not too curious. We had no inkling whatsoever about what had happened in Europe. We are talking about 1947. I search my memory and I find not a single inkling of Jewish suffering, of anything that would lead us to think, 'This is happening because that happened'—to make a linkage, and the surprising thing is that it is not only me." "You did not feel threatened in any way?" I asked. "None whatsoever at that time," he replied. "Things changed after I had left. I was going to study at the University of Chicago and come back—things changed after that.

"I got the story of what was happening in 1948 daily from the *New York Times*. It used to arrive in Chicago at eleven o'clock in the morning, and I would go to the bookstore for it. Then I would sit on a bench and read it all by myself. It was the most shattering experience, those months, when the whole thing was like a nightmare that came in installments day after day—Palestine being overrun and the whole thing collapsing. Then I learned about my family—they made it to Beirut and they were safe, but then it was reduced to that: my family was safe. Everything else had collapsed."

"You never felt an urge to go back?" "Of course I did," he replied, "and this was suggested to me many times, especially after 1967, but the occasion never arose, and I didn't see much point in it, to tell you the truth; I mean, who wants to go to Acre? I mean, it would break my heart. The things that I was told that have happened there since. I mean, even without the devastation, the seashore of childhood happiness will never be the same."

After a moment he added: "The friend I used to swim and fish with—he and his brothers in Acre—died a few years ago. I have never felt such a loss. With him I feel that I have suddenly lost part of my past. It's a very strange thing. In my memory I used to think of him and of his brother and other friends of ours, but now that he is gone his death is also in my past: that little boy died."

"Do you think that the fact that one doesn't go though one could is really because one wants to keep it as it was?" "In your own memory? I suppose that this is an unconscious thing that mainly prevents me from wanting to go. This is one way of preserving the past." He was speaking in that same voice that at first seemed to me understated and that I now realized was deliberately restrained, as if he had undertaken to be matter-of-fact.

"As a young person at the time one did not care for one's surroundings. The world is the field of one's action. It is only much later that you realized what happened. The immediate effect of 1948, sitting in Chicago reading the paper, absorbing the events, is one of total confusion, nightmare, but not understanding at all. It is much later that the loss comes to you. And paradoxically, it is only when this loss is felt that you realize what you had. Having is really losing in this sense. You have something only when you lose it. So home is the most beautiful thing, the most beautiful object.

No matter how ugly objectively it is, it has the most privileged place and it is discovered at a much later age, particularly when it has been lost. And then the longing for it becomes overpowering. I think that many immigrants who always talk about home in Lebanon don't talk about home the way I do about Palestine because they haven't lost it even though they haven't seen it in forty years."

"I feel I can ask you this," I said. "How does one avoid being sentimental about it, nostalgic?" "One starts by being sentimental," he answered with a smile, "and when you meet Palestinians talking about home they always exaggerate, sentimentalize experience. But as one matures, so to speak, as one grows older, as one becomes more serious about it, one does not want to make an issue of it, to influence people. I don't care how people feel about it, about my cause, whether they are with me or for me. I don't, and I don't care about making a good impression on them, and this is when you reach the threshold of honesty, being able to talk truly without an effort to appear truthful, you know. I don't have to make the effort. I either talk or not talk, and I chose to talk to you, but when I do talk now I can do it with total honesty." "Was there a time when you couldn't do it?" I asked. "Oh, yes," he hastened to admit. "And even now I wouldn't talk like this every day to anybody. I mean, there is a reason why I am doing it. You are writing a book."

"Do you think there is a sense of freedom that one has because of all that?" I asked. "Absolutely," said Sharabi, "It is a kind of liberation." "Liberation from what?" "Liberation from everything that has in the past blocked one's feeling, one's capacity to see things openly, to relate to others in ways that are open, liberation from—and this is very important—from the constant tendency to misrepresent things to yourself, which I think is almost automatic."

After a pause he said slowly: "As the future recedes, the past becomes more prominent, but at the same time bitterness becomes less. There is a sense of reconciliation with destiny, I suppose; this is one's fate, so your attitude toward it is not so much of anger, of regret, so much as it is an attempt to understand it, to relive it, and almost involuntarily incidents, faces, relations, come back to one with startling vividness and it becomes less politicized, which on the political level curiously enough makes one willing to be reconciled. I suppose before I die I want to settle this problem."

In the plane, on my way back from Washington, I thought about Sharabi's summer trips to his grandfather's house, about the Arab towns he saw on his way from Jaffa to Haifa to Acre, about the Jewish settlements he never even noticed. And the words of Yitzhak Ben-Aharon came to mind: "We grew up too soon, and that's what kept us from turning into an eternal youth movement running only itself according to some anarchic or archaic idealism removed from real life. Very early we were forced to combine our youthful experience with some historic undertaking that pulled us out of the situation as it was, and actually made more acute for us what was so classic in a youth movement—utopia—a utopia somewhere over the next hill. Palestine appeared to us an empty wasteland, and here we were, advancing on it, young as we were, in order to establish a utopia. We were on the verge of a revolutionary clash and we knew that failure meant annihilation. We could not afford to lose."

Participants

LULIE AB'UL-HUDDA. Born in Cairo. Spent her childhood in Jordan and Jerusalem; her father was Jordanian prime minister. Graduate of Oxford in history. During World War II launched a society to fight illiteracy among Arabs, under the auspices of the Arab Office. Art historian, specialist in Pissarro. Lives in London.

TAQUI ALTOUNIAN-STEPHENS. Born in Aleppo, Syria, to an Armenian-English family. Her father, a physician, was a close friend of T. E. Lawrence's. When World War II broke out, the family moved to Jerusalem and she worked in the Mandatory Administration's Information Office. Married Robert Stephens of the *Observer*, who was also working in the Information Office during that period. Left in 1947. Author of the autobiographical *In Aleppo Once*.

SHIMON AVIDAN. Born in Germany, went to Palestine in 1934. Served in defense and security positions in the Thirties. In World War II headed the German squad of the Palmach, and was later responsible for the other special squads—Arab, paratroopers, etc. Commanded the Givati Brigade during the War of Independence and concluded his army service as head of military operations. Served in various posts within the left-wing Kibbutz Artzi movement, including secretary-general. A member of Kibbutz Ein HaShofet.

JOHN "BILL" BAILEY. Born in England. Mobilized in 1940, served in the glider platoon in World War II, seeing action in France and Germany. In Palestine from 1945 to 1948, he was a company sergeant major in the 6th Airborne Division. Assigned to camps on the Sharon plain, in Jerusalem, and in the Gaza Strip. After long service in the career army throughout the Commonwealth, returned to England. Worked as administrative director for law firm in London.

DONALD BARON. Born in England, graduated from Oxford in history. During World War II served in the Royal Air Force in Cairo. In 1946, sent to Jerusalem at his own request. After extensive training as a minor official in the administration, worked as district officer in Jerusalem until the end of April 1948. Served in various locations throughout the Commonwealth; last position was as United Kingdom representative to the International Sugar Organization.

SIR HAROLD BEELEY. Born in England. Graduate of Oxford, where he later served as lecturer in modern history and did research on the Middle East for Chatham House. During World War II worked in the Research Department (Middle East Division) of the Foreign Ministry. Appointed adviser on the Middle East to Foreign Secretary Ernest Bevin and served as secretary of the Anglo-American Committee. Later filled other senior positions at the Foreign Ministry, including ambassador to Egypt, to the Soviet Union, and again to Egypt.

YITZHAK BEN-AHARON. Born in Bukovina. Went to Palestine in 1928 as a member of the Hashomer Hatzair socialist movement. Among the founders of Kibbutz Givat Haim in 1932. Was serving as Tel Aviv Workers' Council secretary in 1940, when he volunteered for the British Army's Royal Pioneer Corps. Taken prisoner after the surrender of British forces in Greece, he spent most of the war years in a POW camp for officers in Germany, where he did intelligence work for the British underground. In 1946, still a second lieutenant in the army, he returned to his kibbutz, Givat Haim, and was immediately arrested and imprisoned as a leader of the organized Yishuv. After the establishment of the state, served as secretary-general of the Histadrut labor federation, member of Knesset, and government minister. Among the leaders and intellectuals of the labor movement.

SIR ISAIAH BERLIN. Born in Latvia, educated in England. Philosopher and professor of the history of ideas at Oxford. Close friend of Chaim Weizmann's and visited Mandatory Palestine many times. Lives in Oxford and London. Among his books: *The Hedgehog and the Fox, Four Essays on Liberty, The Crooked Timber of Humanity.*

AVRAHAM BIRAN. Born in Rosh Pinna. After archaeology studies in the U.S., he served in the Mandatory Administration as district officer for the Jezreel Valley and, later, Jerusalem until 1948. With the establishment of the state he was appointed governor of the Jerusalem district and a member of the Armistice Commission. Headed the Archaeology Department at Hebrew Union College in Jerusalem.

SIR BERNARD DE BUNSEN. Born in England, graduate of Oxford. Headmaster and supervisor in the English school system before he was appointed director of the Education Department in the Mandatory Administration in 1946–48. With the end of the Mandate he was sent to Kenya, where he worked for many years in education. Concluded his service in the Commonwealth as vice chancellor of the University of East Africa.

HENRY CATTAN. Born to an Orthodox Christian family in the Old City of Jerusalem. M.A. in law in France and in England. Well-known criminal lawyer in Palestine during the Thirties and Forties, lecturer in law in Jerusalem, follower of the mufti. Representative of the Arab Higher Committee at the UN. In 1948 moved to Beirut, and from there to Paris. Author of political works on the problem of Palestine.

BARON MARTIN CHARTERIS OF AMISFIELD. Born in England, educated at Sandhurst. During World War II served in Palestine in intelligence, headed British Military Intelligence from 1945 to 1946 with the rank of lieutenant colonel. Worked in the War Office, then served as secretary to Queen Elizabeth from 1952 to 1972. Was the provost of Eton College and chairman of the trustees of the National Heritage Memorial Fund.

HUGH CLARK. Born in England. Enlisted in 1944, serving in the 6th Airborne Division in Europe and then in Palestine, from 1945 to 1948. Assigned to camps on the Sharon plain and in Jerusalem; demobilized with the rank of captain. Works in management of a construction firm. Lives in Surrey, near London.

GAVRIEL COHEN. Born in Jerusalem. Joined the Palmach in 1946 and fought the War of Independence in the Eastern Galilee, the central region, and the south. Professor of the history of Palestine at Tel Aviv University, dealing with the Mandate period, among others. Among his books: *Churchill and Palestine, The British Cabinet and the Question of Palestine*.

AUNI DAJANI. Born in Jerusalem, graduate of Oxford and Cambridge in law. In the Thirties and Forties worked as an advocate in Jerusalem and Jaffa and lectured at a law school in Jerusalem. In 1948, left the country and went into business. Immigrated to London.

SELMA DAJANI. Born in Jaffa. Her father, Dr. Fuad Dajani, founded the hospital there that bears his name. Studied law in Jerusalem, married Auni Dajani, left Palestine in 1948.

HIRAM DANIN. Born in Jaffa. In the Thirties worked for the Mandatory government on land settlements. In the Forties undertook land purchases for a settlement-development company. In the Eighties served as a member of the Israeli government committee that registers land in the West Bank.

KHALIL DAOUDI. Born in Jerusalem in the Dajani ancestral home on Mount Zion. Worked for the Mandatory Administration in Jerusalem. In 1948 left his home in the city's Baq'a quarter and moved to Brighton, England.

MEIR DREZDNER. Born in Romania, educated in Haifa. Joined the Palmach in 1944. Served in various command positions and fought on a number of fronts, including as Palmach commander at Mount Canaan.

concluded his service as deputy regiment commander. After the War of Independence, studied civil engineering, specializing in hydraulics.

MIRIAM DREZDNER, NÉE MEDZINI. Born in Jerusalem. A medic in the Palmach, serving during the War of Independence at Mount Canaan. High school biology teacher, married to Meir Drezdner.

MENASHE ELIASHAR. Born in Jerusalem. Carried on the family businesses, including cigarette import and land purchase. In the Thirties founded the Kedma Mizraha ("Facing East") society, whose goal was to increase understanding between Jews and Arabs. Headed the Jerusalem Chamber of Commerce for many years.

RACHEL ELIASHAR, NÉE KOKIA. Born in the Old City of Jerusalem. Married to Menashe Eliashar. Lives in Jerusalem.

LOTTE GEIGER. Born in Germany, went to Palestine in 1933. During the war worked for the censor in the Mandatory Administration, and later as assistant to the head of the Public Works Department. After the establishment of the state, held a senior management position for Rogozin Industries in Ashdod.

YIGAL GERA. Born in Haifa. Worked in the Forties as an oil-equipment engineer for Shell. Later held senior positions in Israeli oil companies.

STANLEY GOLDFOOT. Born in South Africa. Arrived in Jerusalem during World War II as a foreign correspondent, mainly for South Africa. A member of Lehi. Used his position as treasurer of the Middle East Society to carry out espionage. Became a member of the Temple Mount Faithful.

SIR HENRY GURNEY. Born in England. Served as chief secretary of the Mandatory Administration from 1946 until May 14, 1948. Later appointed high commissioner in Malaysia and was murdered there in the early Fifties.

YAKUB HANANIYA. Born in Jaffa. Worked in the Forties at British Army camps, and in the last years of the Mandate ran a store in Jaffa. After the establishment of the state he was appointed head of the Greek Orthodox community in Jaffa. Charcoal merchant.

WOLFGANG HILDESHEIMER. Born in Germany, went to Palestine in 1933, and after art studies in London returned to Palestine with the start of World War II. Worked at the Information Office in Haifa and Jerusalem and returned to England in 1947, then moved back to Germany, where he served as an interpreter at the Nuremberg Trials. Painter, writer, playwright. Moved to Switzerland. Among his books: *Mozart: A Biography*; *Marbot: A Fictional Biography*.

SIR MICHAEL HOGAN. Born in Ireland. Went to Palestine in 1936 as junior advocate. Served as prosecutor and judge and ended his Palestine service in 1948 as Crown councilor. Remained in Haifa for several months after the Mandate ended, as legal adviser to the police and armed forces in the British enclave. Served in senior positions in Africa and Asia and ended his colonial service as Supreme Court justice in Hong Kong.

CHRISTOPHER HOLME. Born in England, graduate of Oxford. In the Thirties he was a Reuters correspondent in Europe, including in Germany and in Spain during the Civil War. Director of the Information Office during World War II. Headed the BBC's Drama Department.

EDWARD HORNE. Born in England, served in the CID in Palestine from 1941 to 1947. For several years was in charge of the intelligence offices he set up in Jenin and Netanya. Worked for the London police. After retiring wrote a book about the Palestine Police, *A Job Well Done*, and was appointed editor of the Palestine Police quarterly.

ALBERT HOURANI. Born in Manchester to a Lebanese family. Graduate of Oxford. During World War II served as assistant for Arab affairs to the resident British minister in Cairo. Worked for Musa Alami at the Arab Office in Jerusalem. Fellow of St Antony's College, Oxford, where he has lectured for many years on the history of the Middle East. Among his books: *Arabic Thought in the Liberal Age*, *Syria and Lebanon*, *A History of the Arab Peoples*.

SUAD KARAMAN. Born in Haifa. Married her cousin Darwish Karaman. In April 1948 went with the women of the family to Lebanon, returning in 1949 to the family home in Ibten. Poet. Taught English in the local Arab school. Worked as a presenter for many years on radio and TV.

JAMES LIVINGSTONE. Born in Scotland to a socialist family. Served on the British Council in Cairo during World War II and was sent to Palestine for several months to promote English-language studies on kibbutzim. Deputy to the head of the British Council in Jerusalem from 1946 to 1948. Later represented the council in a number of other countries, including Iran.

FAITH LLOYD-PHILLIPS. Born in Australia. In Palestine from the late Thirties to 1948. During the war worked for the Red Cross in Jerusalem. Widow of Ivan Lloyd-Phillips, who held various positions in the Mandatory Administration in Tiberias, Haifa, and Jerusalem and finally served as district commissioner in England.

LEILA MANTOURA. Born in Jerusalem. Daughter of Tawfiq Canaan, well-known Jerusalem physician and folklorist. Moved to Beirut at the end of the Mandate and, in the Seventies, from there to England. Owned a gallery for Oriental art objects in London.

NASER AL-DIN AL-NASHASHIBI. Born in Jerusalem. Graduate of Beirut University in political science. Worked in the Arab Office in Jerusalem during the last years of the Mandate. In the Fifties and Sixties edited the Cairo newspaper *Al-Gomhuria* and later moved to Europe. Writer and journalist. Among his books: *Return Ticket* and a biography of Musa Alami.

NAHUM NIMRI. Born in Poland, educated in Haifa. Studied architecture at the Technion. Intelligence officer in the British Army, serving in Lebanon, Syria, and Iraq. Prepared a handbook on the Bedouin of the Fertile Crescent for army intelligence. With his release from the army, during World War II, did public relations work for a potash company in Jerusalem. Intelligence officer for Lehi and for that purpose founded the Middle East Society of Jerusalem. After the murder of Count Bernadotte, the UN mediator, left the country and went into business in Geneva.

NUZHAT EL-NUSSEIBEH, NÉE EL-GHUSSEIN. Born in Wadi Hanin, near Ness Ziona, in the family castle. Married Anwar el-Nusseibeh in the Forties and lived in Jerusalem and Ramieh. At the end of the Mandate returned with her family to East Jerusalem.

LADY ANNE OXFORD, NÉE PALIERET. Born in England. During World War II served in the British Army in an intelligence unit in Jerusalem. Married Lord Oxford in Palestine.

EARL JULIAN OF OXFORD AND ASQUITH. Born in England, graduate of Oxford. Served in the British Army in Syria and Palestine in 1941–42, and joined the Mandatory Administration in 1942. Served as assistant to the district officer for Gaza and the Negev, as secretary to the high commissioner, General Cunningham, and ended his Palestine service in 1948 as deputy commissioner of the northern district. Various postings throughout the empire, his last as governor and commander of the Seychelles Islands.

YEHOSHUA PALMON. Born in Tel Aviv. From the Twenties, served in the Hagana intelligence. Later active in land purchase. Commanded the Arab squad of the Palmach, which engaged mainly in sabotage. After the state was established, served as Arab-affairs adviser in the prime minister's office.

SIR IVO RIGBY. Born in England. Held various positions in the legal system of Palestine, 1938–48, concluding his service as Crown councillor. Last position in the imperial service was as Supreme Court justice in Hong Kong.

TERRY SHAND. Born in England. Served in the Palestine Police from 1944 to 1948. Bodyguard to the chief secretary and the commander of the army. Publisher of books on education and religion. Chairman of the organization of Palestine Police.

YA'AKOV SHIMSHON SHAPIRA. Born in Russia, went to Palestine in 1924. Worked as an advocate during the Thirties and Forties, appointed by the leaders of the Yishuv to defend illegal-immigration cases in the courts. After the establishment of the state, served as attorney general and justice minister.

HISHAM SHARABI. Born in Jaffa. After studies at the University of Beirut went to the University of Chicago in 1947. Professor of European intellectual history at Georgetown University. Among his books: *Neopatriarchy: A Theory of Distorted Change in Arab Society*; *Embers and Ashes*; *Arab Intellectuals and the West*.

FUAD SHEHADEH. Born in Jerusalem. Studied at the law school in Jerusalem during the last years of the Mandate. After 1948, settled in Ramallah and practiced law.

RICHARD STUBBS. Born in England. During World War II worked in the British propaganda office in Cairo. Served as head of the Mandatory Information Office from 1946 to 1948. Later worked in public relations. Took up painting.

JOHN TILLETT. Born in England, joined the career army in 1938. Served as commander of the glider platoon in World War II, and as company commander with the 6th Airborne Division in Palestine in 1945–47, with the rank of major. He spent time on the Sharon plain, in Jerusalem, and in Gaza, and took part in actions against the Yishuv. Headed the army of independent Uganda and later served at NATO headquarters. Retired with the rank of colonel.

VICTORIA VALERO, NÉE HACHMISHVILI. Born in Jerusalem. Widow of Dr. Gavriel Valero, Jerusalem physician. Lives in Tel Aviv.

GABRIEL ZIFRONI. Born in Tel Aviv. Correspondent for the London *Daily Telegraph* during the Forties, close to Revisionists, with friends among the Arabs and English. At the end of the Mandate, continued as foreign correspondent and as editor of the Hebrew daily *Haboker*.

MICHAL ZMORA-COHEN. Born in Jerusalem. Daughter of Moshe Zmora, a prominent Jerusalem advocate who was involved in both Zionist circles and British legal circles and served as president of the Israeli Supreme Court. Musicologist. Headed the Music Department of Israel Radio.

Chronology

NOVEMBER 2, 1917. Balfour Declaration.

DECEMBER 9, 1917. General Allenby enters Jerusalem.

JULY 2, 1920. Civil administration replaces British military government. Sir Herbert Samuel, the first high commissioner, serves until the summer of 1925.

JULY 3, 1922. The British government publishes its policy guidelines for Palestine in a White Paper (Command Paper No. 1700), stating that Jewish immigration will be determined each year by Palestine's economic capacity and that Transjordan is to become a political entity separate from Palestine.

JULY 22, 1922. The Council of the League of Nations approves the British Mandate for Palestine.

AUGUST 25, 1925. The second high commissioner, Lord Plummer, arrives in Palestine and serves until the summer of 1928.

JULY 5, 1928. The third high commissioner, Sir John Robert Chancellor, takes over, serving until 1931.

AUGUST 24, 1929. Arabs attack Jews in Jerusalem, and the riots spread throughout Palestine (Hebron, Tel Aviv, Be'er Tuvia, Kibbutz Hulda, Safed, etc.).

NOVEMBER 20, 1931. The fourth high commissioner, Sir Arthur Waucope, arrives and serves until March 1938.

APRIL 19, 1936. Arab attacks on Jews in Jaffa. Beginning of the Arab Revolt, 1936–39.

APRIL 22, 1936. Palestine Arabs declare a general strike, demanding a ban on Jewish immigration and the sale of land to Jews; they also demand independence in Palestine. The strike continues until October 12.

APRIL 25, 1936. The Arab Higher Committee is established, with the grand mufti of Jerusalem, Haj Amin el-Husseini, elected chairman.

DECEMBER 10, 1936. Tel Amal, the first Jewish tower-and-stockade settlement, is established in the Beit She'an Valley.

JULY 7, 1937. Publication of the Peel Commission report. The main recommendation: division of Palestine into a Jewish state, an Arab state, and a British enclave.

MARCH 3, 1938. The fifth high commissioner, Harold MacMichael, arrives. Serves until the summer of 1944.

SEPTEMBER 30, 1938. The Munich Agreement.

OCTOBER 14, 1938. Conclusions of the Woodhead Commission: retreat from the Peel Commission conclusions.

JANUARY 14, 1939. Assessment by the military chiefs of staff; war breaks out in Europe: the support of the Arab countries will be vital to Britain.

FEBRUARY 7–MARCH 17, 1939. The St. James Conference, in which the British, Arabs, and Jews participate. Adjourns in deadlock.

MAY 23, 1939. The British House of Commons approves by a vote of 266–179 a White Paper (Command Paper No. 6019) that would give independence to Palestine in five years, with an Arab majority guaranteed; drastically reduce Jewish immigration; limit the right of Jews to purchase Arab land.

SEPTEMBER 3, 1939. England and France declare war on Germany after the invasion of Poland.

JUNE 10, 1940. Italy joins the war on the German side.

JANUARY 22, 1941. Haj Amin el-Husseini offers his cooperation to Hitler.

MAY 1941. German forces reach Syria and Lebanon to assist the Vichy forces.

MAY 15, 1941. The Hagana command decides to set up the Palmach commando units, within the cooperation agreement between the Jewish Agency's Political Department and the Special Activities Department of the British government.

MAY 20, 1941. David Raziel, commander of the Etzel, in Iraq on a British military mission, is killed in the Rashid Ali revolt.

JUNE 7, 1941. Allies invade Syria and Lebanon, with the participation for the first time of several Palmach scouts.

JUNE 20, 1941. German and Italian forces under Rommel penetrate Egypt.

JUNE 22, 1941. Germany invades the Soviet Union.

DECEMBER 7, 1941. Japan attacks Pearl Harbor. Germany and Italy join Japan and declare war on the United States.

JANUARY 20, 1942. Avraham Stern ("Yair"), commander of Lehi, is uncovered by a British intelligence officer and shot to death.

FEBRUARY 24, 1942. The *Struma*, with 750 Romanian immigrants aboard, sinks in the Black Sea.

MAY 5, 1942. Zionist conference in New York publishes decisions that become known as the Biltmore Program: transfer of authority for immigration and development from the Mandatory Administration to the Jewish Agency and establishment of a Jewish commonwealth in Palestine. The plan is approved by the reduced Zionist Executive in Jerusalem in November 1942.

JULY 1942. Days of El Alamein. The British Army retreats from the Western Desert to El Alamein. German forces invade Egypt; danger of German-Italian invasion of Palestine from the south and from the sea.

SEPTEMBER 1942. First news of the scope of the Holocaust reaches Palestine.

NOVEMBER 4, 1942. The Eighth Army destroys the German army at El Alamein.

DECEMBER 17, 1942. The radio stations of England, the U.S., and the Soviet Union broadcast special announcements regarding the extermination of Jews by the Nazis.

APRIL 19, 1943. Beginning of the Warsaw Ghetto uprising.

OCTOBER 1, 1943. First Jewish paratroopers from Palestine and in Romania, part of the "cooperation" with the British Special Operations Executive.

NOVEMBER 16, 1943. British search for Palmach members at Ramat HaKovesh, starting a series of actions against the organized Yishuv, including arrest and trial of Hagana members for possession of arms.

FEBRUARY 1, 1944. Menachem Begin, appointed commander of the Etzel, declares a revolt against British rule in Palestine.

FEBRUARY 12, 1944. First Etzel actions: bombs in the immigration offices of Jerusalem, Haifa, and Tel Aviv.

JULY 19, 1944. Lord Gort named high commissioner, serves until autumn 1945.

AUGUST 3, 1944. Lehi attempts to assassinate High Commissioner MacMichael, a few days before he is to complete his service.

OCTOBER 21, 1944. Arrest of 251 Etzel and Lehi members and their expulsion to Eritrea.

NOVEMBER 6, 1944. Lord Moyne, a member of the British War Cabinet and resident minister in Cairo, is murdered by Lehi members.

DECEMBER 11–15, 1944. The British Labour Party convention in Bournemouth approves the postwar party policy, including recognition of the Zionists' right to a country in all of Palestine.

MAY 8, 1945. Germany surrenders.

MAY 10, 1945. The Arab League is established in Cairo.

AUGUST 29, 1945. Illegal immigration resumes with the arrival of the *Dalin*, with thirty-five people aboard.

AUGUST 31, 1945. President Truman recommends to the British government that it allot one hundred thousand immigration certificates to displaced Jewish Holocaust survivors.

OCTOBER 10, 1945. The Palmach springs 208 illegal immigrants from detention camp at Atlit. Large army and police forces lay siege to Kibbutzim Beit Oren and Yagur, demanding that the immigrants be turned over.

OCTOBER 31, 1945. First actions of the Jewish rebellion: the Palmach sinks three British boats and sabotages the railways at fifty points throughout the country. The Etzel attacks the railway station at Lydda, and Lehi the oil refineries in Haifa Port.

NOVEMBER 8, 1945. General Alan Cunningham, the last high commissioner, arrives to replace Lord Gort.

NOVEMBER 13, 1945. The British foreign secretary, Ernest Bevin, announces in Parliament the establishment of the Anglo-American Committee of Inquiry into the Problems of European Jewry and Palestine.

NOVEMBER 25, 1945. Following the seizure of the immigrant ship *Berl Katznelson* on the coast at Kibbutz Shefayim, the Palmach attacks police stations at Sidna Ali and Givat Olga. The British Army responds on November 26 and 27 with searches and a curfew on agricultural settlements.

JANUARY 1946. The Arab League begins a boycott of all Jewish goods made in Palestine. The British government declares independence for Transjordan.

JANUARY 28, 1946. The British government allots fifteen hundred certificates a month to refugees, pending a political alternative to the White Paper of 1939.

APRIL 25, 1946. Lehi members kill eight British soldiers in a Tel Aviv parking lot.

MAY 1, 1946. Publication of the Anglo-American Committee report. Among its recommendations: permit the immigration of one hundred thousand Jews within three years. The British prime minister makes its implementation conditional on the dismantling of the Hagana.

JUNE 17, 1946. The "Night of the Bridges": Palmach units bomb all bridges connecting Palestine with its neighbors. Lehi members attack the Haifa railway station.

JUNE 29, 1946. Black Saturday ("Operation Agatha"), when political leaders and Hagana and Palmach commanders are arrested. Kibbutzim throughout the country are searched for weapons, and members are imprisoned.

JULY 22, 1946. Etzel members blow up a wing of the King David Hotel, headquarters for the Mandatory Administration and the British Army. About one hundred killed: Jews, Arabs, and English.

AUGUST 5, 1946. The British cabinet sets new policy on illegal immigration: expulsion of immigrants to camps in Cyprus. Implementation begins a week later, on August 12.

FEBRUARY 22, 1947. The British government announces its decision to hand the Palestine question over to the United Nations, following the failure of the St. James Conference.

APRIL 16, 1947. Four Etzel members are hanged in Acre Prison.

APRIL 29, 1947. Special UN General Assembly session on the Palestine question. Soviet foreign minister Gromyko delivers a surprisingly pro-Zionist declaration. The assembly decides to set up a committee of inquiry, the United Nations Special Committee on Palestine (UNSCOP).

JULY 18, 1947. The *Exodus* reaches Haifa Port with forty-five hundred illegal immigrants aboard. They are put aboard British warships, expelled to southern France and from there to Germany, reaching Hamburg on September 9,

JULY 31, 1947. The Etzel responds to the hanging in Acre Prison by hanging British sergeants near Netanya.

SEPTEMBER 1, 1947. Publication of the UNSCOP report, which recommends the partition of Palestine.

SEPTEMBER 25, 1947. Eleven new settlements established in the Negev.

SEPTEMBER 26, 1947. The British government declares its intention to give up the Mandate for Palestine.

NOVEMBER 29, 1947. UN General Assembly approves the proposal for the partition of Palestine by a two-thirds majority.

NOVEMBER 30, 1947. Arab attacks on the Jerusalem commercial district and Jewish buses on the way from Netanya and Hadera to Jerusalem. Beginning of the War of Independence.

DECEMBER 15, 1947. The British administration withdraws from Tel Aviv.

DECEMBER 29, 1947. Arab workers kill dozens of Jewish workers at Haifa oil refineries.

JANUARY 9, 1948. Arab attack from Syria on Upper Galilee kibbutzim.

JANUARY 14, 1948. Attack by about one thousand members of the Arab Liberation Army on Gush Etzion, the settlements south of Jerusalem.

JANUARY 16, 1948. A company of thirty-five Palmach members leaves Jerusalem to reinforce Gush Etzion. All killed in battle with hundreds of Arabs.

FEBRUARY 14, 1948. Lamed Hei Operation: Palmach forces raid Kafr Saba in the Galilee. Bombing of the Sheikh Hussein bridge and the water pipeline on the northern border road.

FEBRUARY 16, 1948. Attack by the Arab Liberation Army on Kibbutz Tirat Zvi, in the Beit She'an Valley.

MARCH 19, 1948. The U.S. withdraws its support for the UN General Assembly decision on partition and suggests instead a trusteeship.

MARCH 25–29, 1948. A number of Arab successes in the war for control of the roads brings the Jewish strategy to a point of crisis. March 25–27: Battle for Nebi Daniel with a convoy returning from Gush Etzion. March 26: Attack on a convoy to Kibbutz Yehiam in the Western Galilee. March 29: Attack on a convoy to Hulda.

APRIL 1, 1948. UN Security Council summons the General Assembly to reconsider the partition plan.

APRIL 4, 1948. Beginning of Operation Nachshon, to open the road to Jerusalem. For the first time, the Hagana adopts a strategy of taking over Arab villages and maintaining outposts to secure the roads.

APRIL 8, 1948. In the Battle for the Castel, the commander of Arab forces in the Jerusalem area, Abd el-Qadir el-Husseini, is killed.

APRIL 4–17, 1948. Kibbutz Mishmar HaEmek is attacked by infantry, artillery, and tanks of the Arab Liberation Army under Fawzi al-Qawuqji. The Hagana launches a counterstrike, defeating Qawuqji and thus controlling the area between Mishmar HaEmek and Megiddo (Jezreel Valley).

APRIL 9, 1948. Etzel and Lehi units attack the village of Deir Yassin, near Jerusalem, killing about two hundred residents.

APRIL 15, 1948. The final stage of the British withdrawal. The offices of the civil administration and army units gradually evacuate rural areas and mixed cities. Beginning of the evacuation of the Eastern Galilee. The British Army withdraws from its positions in Safed, Rosh Pina, and Nebi Yosha, leaving Nebi Yosha and key positions in Safed to the Arabs, and the Rosh Pina police and army bases to the Jews.

APRIL 18, 1948. The Hagana takes Tiberias. British Army commanders offer the Arabs of the city help in evacuation.

APRIL 21–23, 1948. The Hagana attacks the Arab areas of Haifa. The British commander offers his arbitration in the negotiations for Arab surrender. The Arab leaders reject the terms, and most of the population flees.

APRIL 23, 1948. The Hagana launches Operation Jebusite in an attempt to take Jerusalem. The British commanders force the Palmach to give up control of the Sheikh Jarrah quarter but allow it to take the Katamon quarter.

MAY 1, 1948. Beginning of Operation Yiftach to take control of the Eastern Galilee. By May 11, Safed is in Jewish hands.

MAY 12–14, 1948. The four settlements of Gush Etzion fall, after attacks by the Arab Legion.

MAY 13, 1948. Jaffa surrenders to the Hagana.

MAY 14, 1948. High Commissioner Sir Alan Cunningham leaves Palestine. A few hours after the termination of the Mandate, the State of Israel is established. Arab armies invade Israel.

Acknowledgments

I would like to thank the following people for the conversations that were essential to the writing of this book: Lulie Ab'ul-Hudda, Vera Adamson, Taqui Altounian-Stephens, Samih Arbid, Shimon Avidan, Yochanan Bader, John Bailey, Beryl Barnham, Donald Baron, Harold Beeley, Yitzhak Ben-Aharon, Isaiah Berlin, Avraham Biran, Joy Bourdellion, Bernard de Bunsen, Henry Cattan, Martin Charteris, Hugh Clark, Clothilde Chayat, Stan Collinge, Yusuf Copti, Bert Craft, Max Crichman, Elizabeth Cunnigton, Geula Dagan, Auni Dajani, Salma Dajani, Hiram Danin, Khalil Daoudi, Robin Davis, Meir Drezdner, Miriam Drezdner, Menashe Eliashar, Rachel Eliashar, Fredric Fletcher, Mary Frangi, Shalhevet Freier, Lotte Geiger, Yigal Gera, Stanley Goldfut, Ora Goyten, Emil Habibi, Yakub Hananiya, Patricia Hay-Will, Wolfgang Hildesheimer, Michael Hogan, Anthea Holme, Christopher Holme, Edward Horne, Makram Huri-Mahul, Ishaq Musa el-Husseini, Arthur Ingram, Sidney Johnson, Nehamam Jacobs, Suad Karaman, Shemuel Katz, James Livingstone, Faith Lloyd-Phillips, Mary Mansfield, Leila Mantoura, John Mckindrow, Lola Messer, John Morrison, Jalib Nashashibi, Naser al-Din al-Nashashibi, Thomas Newman, Nahum Nimri, J. L. Niven, Anwar el-Nusseibeh, Nuzhat el-Nusseibeh, Bert Ogdan, Anne Oxford,

Julian Oxford, Jack Padua, Yehoshua Palmon, Yochanan Pelz, Ivo Rigby, Mustafa Saif, Victor Sair, Ruth Sandleson, Fanya Shalom, Terry Shand, Ya'akov Shimshon Shapira, Hisham Sharabi, Fuad Shehadeh, John Sherringham, Obry Sivan, Yesma Steering, Robert Stephens, Richard Stubbs, Fred Taylor, John Tillett, Victoria Valero, Patrick White, Hugh Willatt, Gabriel Zifroni, and Michal Zmora-Cohen.

To Gillian Grant from the Middle East Center at St Antony College, Oxford; the British Council in Tel Aviv and Helen Weisbrod of the British Council in London; William Squire, former British ambassador to Israel; and David Samuel for their great help.

To Amos Elon, Albert Hourani, Gavriel Cohen, and Amos Oz for their invaluable advice and comments.